Football's Twelve Apostles

DESERT ISLAND FOOTBALL HISTORIES

	ISBN
Aberdeen: A Centenary History 1903-2003	978-1-874287-57-5
Aberdeen: Champions of Scotland 1954-55	978-1-874287-65-0
Aberdeen: The European Era	978-1-905328-32-1
Bristol City: The Modern Era – A Complete Record	978-1-905328-27-7
Bristol City: From War to War 1915-1946	978-1-905328-43-7
Bristol City: The Early Years 1894-1915	978-1-905328-51-2
Bristol Rovers: The Bert Tann Era	978-1-905328-37-6
Cambridge United: The League Era – A Complete Record	978-1-905328-06-2
Cambridge United: 101 Golden Greats	978-1-874287-58-2
Carlisle United: A Season in the Sun 1974-75	978-1-905328-21-5
The Story of the Celtic 1888-1938	978-1-874287-15-5
Chelsea: Champions of England 1954-55	978-1-874287-94-0
Colchester United: Graham to Whitton – A Complete Record	978-1-905328-35-2
Colchester United: From Conference to Championship	978-1-905328-28-4
Coventry City at Highfield Road 1899-2005	978-1-905328-53-6
Coventry City: The Elite Era – A Complete Record	978-1-874287-83-4
Coventry City: An Illustrated History	978-1-874287-59-9
Coventry City: The Seven-Year Itch	978-1-905328-44-4
Derby County: Champions of England 1971-72, 1974-75	978-1-874287-98-8
Dundee: Champions of Scotland 1961-62	978-1-874287-86-5
Dundee United: Champions of Scotland 1982-83	978-1-874287-99-5
History of the Everton Football Club 1878-1928	978-1-874287-14-8
Halifax Town: From Ball to Lillis – A Complete Record	978-1-874287-26-1
Hereford United: The League Era – A Complete Record	978-1-874287-91-9
Hereford United: The Wilderness Years & More 1997-2008	978-1-905328-50-5
Huddersfield Town: Champions of England 1923-1926	978-1-874287-88-9
Ipswich Town: The Modern Era – A Complete Record	978-1-905328-24-6
Ipswich Town: Champions of England 1961-62	978-1-874287-63-6
The Old Farm: Ipswich Town v Norwich City	978-1-905328-12-3
Kilmarnock: Champions of Scotland 1964-65	978-1-874287-87-2
Leyton Orient: A Season in the Sun 1962-63	978-1-905328-05-5
Luton Town at Kenilworth Road: A Century of Memories	978-1-905328-10-9
Luton Town: The Modern Era – A Complete Record	978-1-874287-90-2
Luton Town: An Illustrated History	978-1-874287-79-7
Luton Town: Staring into the Abyss	978-1-905328-46-8
Manchester United's Golden Age 1903-1914: Dick Duckworth	978-1-874287-92-6
The Matt Busby Chronicles: Manchester United 1946-69	978-1-874287-96-4
Motherwell: Champions of Scotland 1931-32	978-1-905328-54-3
Northampton Town: A Season in the Sun 1965-66	978-1-905328-01-7
Norwich City: The Modern Era – A Complete Record	978-1-874287-67-4
Peterborough United: The Modern Era – A Complete Record	978-1-874287-33-9
Peterborough United: Who's Who?	978-1-874287-48-3
Plymouth Argyle: The Modern Era – A Complete Record	978-1-874287-62-9
Plymouth Argyle: 101 Golden Greats	978-1-874287-64-3
Plymouth Argyle: Snakes & Ladders – Promotions & Relegations	978-1-905328-34-5
Portsmouth: The Modern Era	978-1-905328-08-7
Portsmouth: From Tindall to Ball – A Complete Record	978-1-874287-25-4
Portsmouth: Champions of England – 1948-49 & 1949-50	978-1-874287-50-6
The Story of the Rangers 1873-1923	978-1-874287-95-7
The Romance of the Wednesday 1867-1926	978-1-805328-56-7
Seventeen Miles from Paradise: Southampton v Portsmouth	978-1-905328-41-3
The Southend United Chronicles 1906-2006	978-1-905328-18-5
Stoke City: The Modern Era – A Complete Record	978-1-905328-47-5
Stoke City: 101 Golden Greats	978-1-874287-55-1
Potters at War: Stoke City 1939-47	978-1-874287-78-0
Swansea City: Seasons in the Sun	978-1-905328-02-4
Third Lanark: Champions of Scotland 1903-04	978-1-905328-03-1
Tottenham Hotspur: Champions of England 1950-51, 1960-61	978-1-874287-93-3
West Bromwich Albion: Champions of England 1919-1920	978-1-905328-04-8
West Ham: From Greenwood to Redknapp	978-1-874287-19-3
West Ham: The Elite Era – A Complete Record	978-1-905328-33-8
West Ham: 101 Beautiful Games	978-1-905328-48-2
Hammers Through the Looking Glass	978-1-905328-23-9
Wimbledon: From Southern League to Premiership	978-1-874287-09-4
Wimbledon: From Wembley to Selhurst	978-1-874287-20-9
Wimbledon: The Premiership Years	978-1-874287-40-7
Wrexham: The European Era – A Complete Record	978-1-905328-49-9
Wrexham: Through the Trap Door – The Road to Hell 1998-2008	978-1-905328-49-9
England's Quest for the World Cup – A Complete Record	978-1-905328-16-1
Scotland: The Quest for the World Cup – A Complete Record	978-1-897850-50-3
Ireland: The Quest for the World Cup – A Complete Record	978-1-897850-80-0
Billy Walker: Once, Twice, Three Times a Winner	978-1-905328-42-0
Blinded by the Lights: A History of Night Football in England	978-1-905328-13-0
Red Dragons in Europe – A Complete Record	978-1-874287-01-8
The Book of Football: A History to 1905-06	978-1-905328-00-0
Football's Twelve Apostles: The Making of the League 1886-1889	978-1-905328-57-4
Football's War & Peace: The Tumultuous Season of 1946-47	978-1-874287-70-4

Football's Twelve Apostles
The Making of The League
1886-1889

Series Editor: Clive Leatherdale

Thomas Taw

DESERT ISLAND BOOKS

First paperback edition 2009
First hardback edition 2006
by
DESERT ISLAND BOOKS LIMITED
7 Clarence Road, Southend-on-Sea, Essex SS1 1AN
United Kingdom
www.desertislandbooks.com

British Library Cataloguing-in-Publication Data
A catalogue record for this book is available from the British Library

ISBN 978-1-905328-57-4

Printed in Great Britain
by
4Edge, Ltd, Hockley, Essex

Contents

Introduction

The first season of the League is both a very long time ago, and still with us. In the structure of its competition, only one thing has changed – now a win gains three points, instead of two. Nothing else.

Otherwise there are a lot of differences. This story of the making of the League relies on its telling at the time. Some differences are explained. The dominant contexts of this story are fixtures and football as work. The meaning and practice of fixtures 'before the League' can be puzzling: they challenge our taken-for-granted assumptions. Cup-ties we can understand – they are still with us.

But the rest ... We tend to take refuge in two myths: that the League rescued professional football from imminent ruin; and that these other matches were friendlies. The early chapters tackle these myths. Pre-League fixture-making had its problems, and the League helped solve these, to some extent in unexpected ways. But these fixtures did not lack competitiveness, and they had a structure, albeit somewhat opaque. The reader will find little difference in the passion of reports of League and pre-League matches.

Football as work was a major challenge for the 1880s. The ideology of sport had become dominated by the values of 'muscular christianity', and the personal attributes that middle and upper-class participants could acquire through sport. The rise of professionalism, and the consequent dominance of working-class players, recalled another tradition – of betting, of prize fights, of patrons and trainers, of partisanship. The League cemented the triumph of professionalism.

Some things never change. Refereeing decisions enraged players and onlookers alike, especially offsides. As goal nets were not introduced until 1891 their absence 'was a constant excuse for claiming goals'; but no penalties, not even for 'handball' to prevent a goal. And without penalties, there was no penalty area, and in fact the interior of the playing-pitch was unmarked until 1892.

Otherwise, modern readers will find strange some aspects of the accounts of matches. Particularly struggles around the goal.

Goalkeeping was different. It always is. Goalkeepers are heroes and villains, saving or being blamed for goals. In the 1880s they were often both saviour and martyr. The goalkeeper creates a problem for football's rules. He can handle the ball. That is a major advantage. In modern rules this advantage is constrained – quite severely, because deliberate transgression leads to sending off – by the penalty area. In the 1880s, without a penalty area, goalkeepers were constrained by physical challenge. They had to be ready for anything. So, like their 21st-century counterparts, 1880s goalkeepers played a lot with their feet and might only rarely handle a ball.

Definitions of what a goalkeeper could do or what could be done to a goalkeeper relied a lot on football's common ancestry with rugby. When he caught the ball he was fair game. If he was charged over the goal-line, a goal would result. If he dropped the ball a scrimmage might develop, in which players hacked at the ball or were on top of it or each other, until the ball emerged one way or the other.

A goalkeeper could catch the ball and throw away or kick from hands if he had time, but more often he had to dodge attackers (before or after catching the ball) and kick, fist and throw away, sometimes under severe pressure. Judgment was all. Sometimes he might wisely just step over the line and concede a corner. These rules meant physical challenge was at its greatest near goal and, as in later times, strategy addressed not only the rules but custom and practice. The attacking team aimed to land centres and corners into the centre of the goal, where good attacking strategy required forwards get to the goalkeeper before the ball did.

One guide on how to play the game, for the estimated 10,000 players in 1887, advised goalkeepers and backs on defensive tactics: 'always try, when fisting out a ball, to strike an opposing forward on the nose; it is good fun – for you; if, when saving a shot, an opponent tries to rush you through, throw the ball to the leeward side, and receive the rusher on the sole of your boot; this causes you more fun. When a high shot is coming into goal, both backs should stand with their feet well apart, and trip all the forwards who try to get past. If two pass at the same time, trip one, hold the other, and then claim a foul, there is nothing like being the first to claim ... if he falls to the ground, you had better lie down, too; it looks sympathetic.'

Goals of course were the thing, and yet goalscorers were not celebrated. The number of goals scored by a forward was not reported, only team goals. His past goals were not reflected on or enumerated. There were many statistics reported in both the League and pre-League seasons, but individual goalscorers were not among them.

Instead the team was key. Players were judged individually, often fiercely, but crucially as contributors to the team effort. Team formation was important, and had recently been settled as goalkeeper, two backs, three half-backs, and five forwards, organised spatially as right, centre and left. The most recent change had been to reduce the number of forwards from six, with the loss of a second centre-forward. The discipline of individual positions was firmly established, although players frequently changed positions during matches.

The biggest star of the late 1880s was a back, Nicholas John Ross, sometimes known as 'Old Nick' but usually as Jack Ross, and that is how he appears here. Ross's fame derived from his captaincy of the dominant team, Preston North End, and his personal leadership in taking the club from obscurity in 1883 to invincibility, a reputation they justified and extended over the five years before the League began in September 1888. The Father of the League, William McGregor, later paid tribute to Jack Ross as a 'moral force [with] a spice of devil ... animated by a stern sense of duty to his side'. Before the famous Preston v Villa Cup-tie in January 1888 (see pp.55-59), that encouraged McGregor to initiate the League, Ross's conviction was total: 'your Villa men have no chance: if our forwards let you touch it at all, I shall soon get it off you.'

Other backs were the stars of their sides. They were the outfield players on whom most responsibility fell: to save the goal, judge situations, to make brave tackles and big clearances.

Ross shared responsibility for North End's rise with William Sudell. Sudell had no title of manager, no one did. The vocabulary of management was more muted in football than America's pre-eminent professional sport, baseball [Goldstein, 1989, p.112-19]. Sudell was chairman of the committee, although he had the reputation for being autocratic. But in Victorian society each committee was different. Each had its own dynamic, its own politics. Although Sudell styled himself a gentleman, he was, like many committeemen, a salaried manager, in a cotton mill.

Others were shopkeepers, like Aston Villa's William McGregor, or had small businesses on the side, like Bolton's Jack Bentley. Club secretaries like Bentley and Villa's George Ramsay had accepted roles in player recruitment, but selection was a committee process, a club matter. North End, by comparison, had two secretaries, an honorary secretary – perhaps a way of paying and retaining England international forward Fred Dewhurst – and match secretary Nuttall. Neither of them seems to have had a role in team decision-making. Each club managed its affairs differently.

It will seem strange to modern eyes that McGregor, Bentley and Sudell all acted as umpire in games involving their clubs. They had to balance representing their club with the integrity of making the right decision. Contemporaries knew this was a tough ask. Tom Watson, later championship manager of Liverpool and Sunderland, asked: 'Do you know any young man who is tired of life and contemplates suicide?' 'Why?' 'I want an umpire for the season.' This 'twelfth man' appealed a decision as in cricket. Only if the opposing umpires disagreed was the referee required to decide. Umpires and referees are the anti-heroes of this story, as in this apocryphal exchange: 'Well Frankie, what shall I have to do if I umpire?' 'Oh you'll have to back up your side.' 'How?' 'Why, if the other lot say it isn't a goal you'll just have to say it is.' 'I see, and how if I referee?' 'Well, you'll get punched.'

Referee Sam Ormerod, who weighed 226 pounds, was in no hurry to rush around making unnecessary decisions. His favourite game was one in which the important points were resolved by the umpires. He did not give one decision but got the credit. So Ormerod was not in favour of neutral umpires. They exposed the referee: neutral umpires 'do not claim sufficiently, and the referee comes in for all the row'. Referees became the sole authority in 1891, and have remained exposed ever since. The role of appeals to provoke refereeing decisions ended in 1894.

Professional football, and the League, was only possible because the advances made in railway travel during the Victorian Age. But it was never easy, and the logistics, accomplishments and effects of journeys were important contexts of this story. Ormerod, for instance, handed his card to the reporter after his interview: SAM ORMEROD, PROFESSIONAL FOOTBALL REFEREE, ACCRINGTON. He reminisced about his 'roughest match', an 1886 drawn Cup-tie between Lincoln City and Gainsborough Trinity that Ormerod declined to take into extra time: 'I couldn't stand it.' He had left his Accrington home at 7am for a cross-country journey. His return was halted overnight at Retford, from 8pm Saturday evening to 3.30 Sunday morning, where 'it fairly snowed'. Home again at noon.

This is also a tale of two countries. England and Scotland found they needed one another early in football's development, but it was an awkward co-operation. One effect of the League was to supersede matches between English and Scottish sides. In the 1880s the Scots tended to refer to the English as Saxons and the English talked of Scotch, particularly in relation to the pejorative Scotch 'amateur'. I have retained this usage, restricting the use of Scottish to Scottish Cup, Association, international.

It is a tale of fierce local rivalries. In Lancashire between Preston, Bolton, Blackburn, Accrington and Burnley. And Lincolnshire between Grimsby, Lincoln and Gainsborough. Within each of these towns and within other footballing centres – Newcastle, Sunderland, Nottingham, Birmingham, Liverpool and Derby – sudden, strong attachment had developed to different clubs, and much of the passion lay in opposition to the other.

These derbies were the most dangerous of matches, and initially most were excluded from the League. It tamed local rivalries by imposing external moderating factors, creating more to worry about – League positions and League points. These rivalries became less intense because they became part of something bigger, something not local.

The story is told through the medium of contemporary newspapers. The Victorian Age saw a vast explosion in the volume and importance of local, national and specialist journals, yet the commonplace view is that its football writing is dull, lacking emotion and imagination. This book demonstrates otherwise, that it is as much concerned as later journalism with: the drama and passion of matches; judging players, clubs and authorities; and behind-the-scenes interviews, revelations and gossip.

Football was already big in Victorian society, something that could take over its capital, something that was part of the celebration of empire in 1887, at the Glasgow Exhibition or the Queen's Jubilee in London, before the Prince of Wales. The club chosen to represent professional football before royalty was Preston North End, appropriately because they had rightly earned their reputation as Invincibles, and because they had given football a 'scientific form', emphasising co-operation, predictability, teamwork.

Preston North End are central to the making of the League. In the three years between the regulation of professionalism in July 1885 and the establishment of the League in September 1888 North End scored nearly a thousand goals. Their main scorers – Jamie Ross, John Goodall and Sam Thomson – each obtained hundreds. Fortunately for following this story, and apart from their goalkeepers, North End hardly changed over 1885 to 1889, so references to the following players will recur during the text:

Goalkeepers: Billy Rose, James Trainer, Arthur Wharton, Bob Mills-Roberts. Full-backs: Bob Howarth, Jack Ross, Bob Holmes. Half-backs: John Graham, Davie Russell, Alexander Sanders 'Sandy' Robertson. Forwards: Jack Gordon, Jamie Ross, John Goodall, Fred Dewhurst, Geordie Drummond, Sam Thomson. Others appeared, but their only 'wandering star', sometimes with North End, sometimes with many other clubs, was John Goodall's brother Archie, a half-back or forward.

An Irish visitor attended a League match in Preston in November 1888. 'A small poster, in size about 24 x 18 inches, is sufficient to attract a crowd of 7000 persons.' The 'small sum of 3d' admitted to three sides whose 'benches were thronged with intelligent and enthusiastic artisans, whose pointed and witty comments on the play were scarcely less interesting than the game itself'. Their star forwards were pin-up Jamie Ross and speedy Jack Gordon: '[Gordon] is undoubtedly "deer" of the team, whilst Jamie Ross is the "dear".' North End's 'back-bone' was their half-backs: 'Russell, Robertson and Graham feed the forwards, feed the backs, and feed each other with mathematical precision.' Defensively, they anticipated a future beyond crude charging: '[they] obstruct his further progress by getting in front of him, and sending the ball to … a [nearby] companion … This seems very simple, but one needs to see the Preston North End play to appreciate the beauty.'

North End created a standard that had to be matched. That was not easy because William Sudell kept his team together. His Invincibles did not join other clubs. Opponents only learned their lessons by playing them. Yet the structure of formalised competition between 1883 and 1887 meant that North End had won nothing. This discrepancy between recognised champions and tangible championship caused a problem. It was personalised through Sudell and his team but it also created a wider unease. Football's morality was in the crucible. As long as North End failed to win the main prize, the hope of another kind of football – purer, less commercial, more local – might prevail. The Association's Challenge Cup was that main prize, and for one reason or another North End did not win it. North End epitomised professionalism – not its worst aspects, but its essence – and their lack of success in authorised competition was to some extent a judgment on that professionalism.

Somehow the League cut through. Almost by stealth, its regularity and the visibility of its competition took the heat out of the morality plays.

DEDICATION

To Stephen and Susannah – admiration from their father for their respective graduations.

Chapter One

The High Rip Gang

Saturday morning, September 8th, 1888, and the London papers were full of breaking news. A desecration of the body politique. The grotesquely mutilated bodies of two women were found in the alleys of Smithfield. Murder was already good news for the developing mass journalism of late Victorian England. These murders were a godsend. They were quickly linked to previous similar crimes and a running story took off, lasting until Christmas at least. A monster was afoot. Could he be found?

Except that at first more prosaic solutions were sought. The victims were prostitutes and, apart from their terribly gratuitous injuries, their deaths might be the results of over-zealous gangland discipline. The High Rip Gang became the first suspects. The East End of London was foreign and dangerous in so many ways. It was a rumbling threat to the authority of respectable West End. In both the previous years, in 1886 and 1887, East End-spawned violence had reached the very edges of the West End, in Trafalgar Square. The poor, the mob, promised to spill over and overwhelm their rich near-neighbours. The East End was literally foreign, the home of so many immigrants and refugees from Eastern Europe. And with the poverty, the immorality and the foreignness, gang rule offered a further distillation of dangerousness. The murders of Smithfield symbolised so many changes and threats. That's why the legend took such a hold and lasted so long. Not in its initial form. A High Rip Gang was too amorphous to do service for a monster, too unwieldy for newspapers, police and a vicarious public to pursue. The gang needed to get personal. And did, in the form of Jack the Ripper.

Saturday afternoon, September 8th, 1888, in the North and Midlands, the results of another gang's efforts took stage. The London press had been agog with the East End murders, and little else. The provincial papers dutifully followed the capital's lead and reported the night's maniacal deeds in dread tones. The Smithfield murders were a national interest, but it did not last as long. Birmingham and Nottingham, and Liverpool and the sooty football towns of Lancashire had their own murders.

And something new as well. These towns and cities were also the centres of football interest and football too got into the papers. Football changed on September 8th, 1888. No one at the time was quite sure how or how much. A league of clubs. At first, the reports of League matches were barely distinguishable from the other ordinary matches, both Association Football and Rugby. The Association and its London headquarters was what had mattered in football. The dates of the Association's Cup rounds, the draws for those Cups, the dates of internationals and inter-County Association fixtures: these were what gave the season its structure and authority. In comparison, the matches themselves seem to be ephemeral, of relevance to today and little more.

The League's High Rip Gang changed all that. They did not invade the consciousness and territory of football's West End from the East, but from the Midlands – William McGregor and George Ramsay of Aston Villa – and the North – William Sudell of Preston North End; Bolton's Jack Bentley and 'King' John Houlding of Everton. These were the gang who would rip the heart of football from the patrician Association and make it the People's Game. The League was their weapon.

As in other aspects of Victorian life, appearances were deceptive. This gang were not good sports. 'Rob Roy' McGregor looked the classic teetotal paterfamilias, but he was also a shopkeeper who gangsters steered clear of, and was something of a card sharp and an early spin doctor. Ramsay, possibly the real founder of the League, stayed in the background, loading the gun. Jack Bentley, everybody's friend, was always pretending to be someone else, but he was the one who took the professional League into the Association's committee rooms and strong-armed them into change. William Sudell made football a full-time profession adopting scientific methods of teamwork and proclaiming his innovation with missionary fervour.

This gang had little money. They had to work within the politics of their clubs and within the limits on their time. McGregor was a draper, constantly worrying that football would bankrupt him. Bentley was into many pies, including accountancy, and his stewardship of football clubs was marked by creative accountancy. And Sudell, who had a family of eight children, almost single-handedly ran a £60,000 cotton mill business, and a £3,000 football club business. He did not always scruple to keep their finances apart.

'King' John Houlding showed what capital could do in football. The rest of the gang never let the moneyman take over, but they knew he had to be assuaged.

Football's High Rip Gang were not to know the impact they would make. It had not been their intention or expectation. As soon as it was created, the League became something outside of itself, beyond its creators and beyond its direct participants. It became transfigured and tangible, and so belonged to onlookers too. The press could help that happen. The meaning and feeling of one match succeeding another in a reassuring but remorseless progression to a visible ending, each match connected to a whole in time and community, connected participants and onlookers alike. It made sense, and captured the imagination.

Chapter Two

The Riddle of the Invincibles

We in Lancashire are like you Scotch people, we love football, and we have been taught to love it through Scotchmen.

THE RIDDLE

Christmas 1886 promised a 'phenomenal' event in football history – 'the three best teams in the country' were playing each other in quick succession. The champions would surely emerge. On Saturday, December 25th a thousand Boltonians gobbled down their Christmas dinner to catch the 1pm special train to join 11,000 in Preston. The towns were in 'extreme rivalry'. The supporters would have to pay double, but had reason for hope. Wanderers were the only English team to have beaten North End since Easter 1886 – 3-2, in front of an overwhelming 16,000 Pike's Lane crowd a month earlier.

But the subsequent headlines were indigestible: 'Christmas at Deepdale. The Wanderers slaughtered.' Despite featuring 23-year-old James Trainer, the country's best goalkeeper, Bolton were completely outclassed. North End's definitive performance – 12-1. There was one consolation. Everyone agreed that they had seen a fresh vision. In fact, 'they had never seen football played before.'

So Preston were in the best of spirits when, two days later, they travelled to West Bromwich. Their party, including 'Mr Sudell, Jolly Sir John, Lord of the Treasury, and Mr Secretary Dewhurst', were 'bent on enjoying themselves' in the five compartments they occupied in a third-class carriage. They proved a mite too frisky: 'at Warrington Bob Howarth trusted to the assurance … that the train would stop a few minutes, and we made the rest of the journey without him.' Footballers will be footballers – North End could casually abandon their England back, and still face with confidence the only other team who had any pretensions to challenge them. And there were still some prepared to bet a hundred pounds that North End would beat Albion by six clear goals, on Albion's own ground.

Arthur Wharton never played for England and was only fleetingly a member of the world's best football team and club. A team that changed how football was played and a club that changed how football was organised. Yet in 2004 Wharton became the only 19th-century footballer to be inducted into Football's Hall of Fame. Suitably, at Preston. His achievement, as a black sportsman in an imperialist Victorian society, was to hit the heights of both sprinting (AAA hundred yards champion and record holder) and football (North End's goalkeeper), and then stick it out as a journeyman professional runner, pro footballer and league cricketer throughout the 1890s [Vasili, P 1998]. And do it with attitude. At their next train stop, 'the dark custodian' was asserting his identity, ostentatiously 'announcing himself as North End: Wharton strutted up and down the platform with some of Sir John Woods' "North End" posters placed in his hat in the form generally adopted by the "fly catching profession".' Here at Crewe, North End exchanged pleasantries with the Halliwell team (Bolton's other club, very happy at Wanderers' humiliation), *en route* to play Wolves. Preston also 'made shift with an enthusiastic member who wanted to back North End to beat Albion by six goals. Sir John wanted to take him up in a cool hundred – this is his minimum bet – but the enthusiast fought shy.'

Preston hurried across Birmingham in trains 'pretty well packed with spectators of the big match'. The crush was surely too big for West Bromwich's Stoney Lane: 'it is terraced round, and spectators were packed like sardines in a box.' Tom Smith, Albion's 'genial secretary, was quite on the job … there was plenty of room, for they had had four thousand more than there was on that day. I didn't know where they put 'em.' He took pity on top football commentator 'The Rambler', who was grateful to be 'chucked over the side of the stand, and found myself perched in the corner of the press box', with water falling on his 'writing utensils' and trickling down his neck.

North End had been unlucky on three visits to West Bromwich: fog the first time; a gale the second; and now five inches of snow with more falling. Preston felt lucky, having inflicted one of only two Albion defeats all season – 7-0 on December 4th, 1886. Not one Throstle predicted a win. North End began in 'cool style' until 'good goods' arrived for Albion – Arthur Wharton 'knocked the ball through his own posts instead of letting it go'. Then a second. 'Albion had all the luck,' with their Bob Roberts a 'gem of a goalkeeper'. When Wharton was 'floored twice … the gods behind received the darkie's downfall with exclamations of delight'. North End kept on passing when they could feasibly have just run the ball through several times. Even a 'prolonged scrimmage in front of Albion's goal' was frustrated – 'without exaggeration, I should say the ball was sent in goal and returned twenty times before it was finally cleared. It was headed out, kicked out, rebounded out, fisted out.' Not North End's day. They lost, and 'naturally downcast', 'left by an early train for merry Brum, there to drown their sorrows,' 'sadder but wiser men, realising the difference between a victory of 12 to 1, and a defeat of 5 to 1.'

Albion felt 'champions of the champions', and suggestions that Bolton had any chance of 'pulling the match off' next day were greeted with astonishment. Wanderers had to walk from well-named Snow Hill station, all the while braving taunts of '12-1' from the locals. Both teams ploughed through slush, but Bolton's star winger, Kenny Davenport, 'sped up the wing like a deer.' Albion tried to knock him off his stride, but he 'bounced about like a piece of India rubber'. Kenny and his opponent 'went for each other like two bantam cocks'. It was 1-1 until Wanderers' Welsh half-back (Bob Roberts) beat Albion's England goalkeeper (Bob Roberts) with a header. Game over.

'The Rambler' returned replete, but puzzled: 'verily football is a curiosity … It will be a long time before I witness the three best teams in the country defeat each other on three consecutive days.' A fellow scribbler essayed a poetic moral:

There were three champion football clubs –
Three champions were they;
They vowed they never could be licked.
And all felt blithe and gay …
For Preston beat the Wanderers
Then fell an easy prey,
To th' Midland crew, who claimed the crown,
But the Wand'rers said 'Nay!' …
Then riddle me this riddle out,
Oh, assure it, I pray!
What is now the Champion club,
This, or that, or they.

THE INVINCIBLES: AUTUMN 1883 TO SPRING 1886

In fact, this was poetic licence: Preston North End were universally acclaimed as the champions – and had been since the 1883-84 season, when they signed Jack Ross and others like Jack Gordon and Geordie Drummond, Davie Russell, Sandy Robertson. The success of this wholesale 'Scotch importation' led a jealous Blackburn correspondent to use 'invincible' as a sneer in 1883 [Hunt, 2000 p.51], perhaps echoing the Irish terrorist group that notoriously assassinated Queen Victoria's minister in Ireland, Lord Cavendish, in May 1882 [Schama, 2002, p.374]. From sneer, North End became the 'beau ideal of football skill and chivalry'. But the poet could pose his riddle because there was nothing tangible to say so. Preston were key to the establishment of the League. They had set the terms: by their innovative style; by their overwhelming results; by their internationalism; and by their failure – Preston had not yet won the National Cup, the only existing yardstick of success.

The road from 1885's acceptance of professionalism to the 1888 League was largely on North End's back, and we can best appreciate that journey over the next two chapters by following them and surveying the places, personalities and issues.

A major change during this period was a retreat in nationality, from the Britishness of 1886-87 to the English League of 1888-89. In July 1885 the Association yielded to the power of the Lancashire clubs, led by North End's William Sudell, into recognising professionalism. With strings. The Scots had no truck with that. Their clubs ignored the 1885-86 National Cup, although their champions Queen's Park had been unlucky finalists in 1884 and 1885, and no English clubs toured Scotland. Some Scottish Association councillors were willing to play really hardball: unless the English promised to exclude professionals, 'The International' would not happen. The International had been played between England and Scotland since 1872, and was a touchstone of football's progress.

Others saw that way madness lay. Everyone knew Scotland was better at football and beating the auld enemy was the way to revel in it. The English pros held no real fears: everyone knew that their best professional players were Scotch. And besides, the Scotch clubs – officially amateurs all – were being driven to bankruptcy for want of English visitors.

The Scottish Association blinked first, and hot on the heels of The International in Glasgow on March 31st, 1886, came The Grand Football Match on April 3rd between their respective champions. Queen's Park represented Scotland although their pre-eminence was under threat from the coming teams of Dumbartonshire – Vale of Leven, Renton and Dumbarton. For England, there was no choice. Not the three times Cup winners of 1884/86, Blackburn Rovers. Not Bolton Wanderers who won three cups in 1885-86 and beat Blackburn three times. Only one team could welcome back the 'good old days' to Scotch football – Preston North End, still unbeaten for 1885-86.

Because of professionalism in one form or another, only Rovers of these top teams had competed in 1885-86's National Cup. No wonder they were regarded as the 'luckiest club in football'. North End's visit was the real thing: a massive 11,000 attended Hampden Park. But the Scotch clubs and authorities maintained a schizophrenic attitude towards professionalism for another half-dozen years, so that when the English stumbled across the future paradigm of commercial football, league competition, the Scots were in no position to join. The League became English when it might have been British.

THE SCOTCH GOSPEL

1886-87 was the first season in which all Associations, however reluctantly, accepted the existence of professionalism. In that sense, the first modern season. Top football was a British affair. Scotch 'professors' had shown the 'toilers' in the factories and mills 'the unfolding intricacies and beauties of the game'. When Accrington players saw the original Scotch pro, Fergy Suter, play for Darwen he 'taught us a lesson that day. We had never seen the likes of him before. His play was really beautiful.' Suter was the first prophet. Then came Jack Ross of North End.

But the summer of 1886 had also been the first in seven years when there had been no Scotch importation. Although over half of North End, Accrington, Burnley and Halliwell's players were Scots, the message was that Lancashire football, the home of open professionalism, had achieved maturity: 'we do not require them.'

Champions North End were thought unlikely to eclipse 1885-86's great achievements, when they lost only two of 64 matches, scoring 318 goals and conceding 60. They beat English Cup holders Blackburn Rovers four times, Lancashire Cup holders Bolton Wanderers three times, and amateur standard-bearers Corinthians twice. But in 1886-87 North End would contend the Cups themselves. The two-years residential qualification had so far straitjacketed them, but now only forward John Goodall and England international goalkeeper Billy Rose were still excluded (hence Rose's frequent replacement by Arthur Wharton).

The Scots were impressed by North End when they toured in August 1886 – 'mi' eye, did za sa that ... Never see'd naught licht it' – Dundee (Thursday, won 8-3), Arbroath (Friday, 6-2), until Glasgow (Saturday), where Third Lanark Royal Volunteers achieved 'the greatest victory we have ever registered', 4-2. 'Mr Sudell's best managed' club was 'one of a very few worthy of unlimited confidence'. Meaning, when you advertise a match on the strength of the opposition's reputation, 'the North End never travel weak.' But they could complain. Dundee Strathmore's Athletic Grounds was in a big hole, with no grass and you strip under an arch of the new Tay Bridge. Arbroath made other preparations. They put a canvas tarpaulin over the wall to limit free views and had two or three balls for emergencies: i.e. if one went into the sea, gardens etc. Not that North End put it there, or put it about. Narrow and bad grounds, rough and tough opponents, William Sudell imposed a principled commitment to scientific football: 'you know we cannot play rough, but these fellows went for us; I will never go yonder again.' A year later North End's August tour was to Dundee, Arbroath and Glasgow …

Preston hit their autumn stride by re-asserting superiority over their leading English rivals: Blackburn three times, 6-1, 6-1 and 7-1, Halliwell (10-1), Notts County (14-0), Wolves (5-0) and Albion (fielding their Cup runners-up eleven) 7-0.

Only Bolton hung tough. Their first match was won by North End through a was-the-ball-over-the-line dispute. Surveying referee Fitzroy Norris took ages to decide, surrounded by spectators and players – 'one lot claiming for, and of course, the rest stoutly objecting.' Umpire Sudell and Wanderers' goalkeeper Trainer wrestled over the 'measuring stick' to indicate where the ball reached, from which Norris took a line of direction with the 'uprights and allowed for half circumference of the ball and decided it was ten inches over'. Wanderers won the return, 3-2, before a gate second only to the 25,000 (£463 taken) at the legendary Notts Cup-tie in 1884. Beating North End was really something. These were all 'ordinary club fixtures' (redefined as 'friendlies' by the League), but in 1891, reflecting after three years of League competition, Wanderers' half-back Bob Roberts rated this November 1886 victory as his best ever.

On successive September Saturdays, North End defeated both the English (Blackburn Rovers) and Scottish (Queen's Park) Cup holders 6-1 on their own grounds: 'North End are playing a better game than I have ever seen any club play.'

The recent history of North End and Queen's Park captured something of the relationship between history and future, amateurism and professionalism, nationality, and the rhetoric and reality of football finance and violence. The threat to the Scotch amateur status quo was represented as much by North End's personnel as style. Preston's regular team had eight Scots, but few had been famous when they left Scotland and only two were brief internationals. The threat was that any English club could take good but not great Scotch footballers and, through professionalism, make them world-beaters.

An ordinary club win was one thing: 1-6 had been Queen's Park's heaviest ever loss, but just another win on the road for North End. When the clubs were drawn in the National Cup a month later it was something else: winning the Cup was Preston's obsession, Queen's Park's pride. It was not then the English Cup. This was bigger, and seven Scottish champions had entered. But the timing of a Cup fixture was a delicate matter involving a third party. Sudell's rivalry with the Blackburn-dominated county Association always simmered, but now he needed them and a deal was done: 'the bitch between the Lancashire Association and North End has been smoothed over.' Sudell unusually agreed to release his players for an inter-county Lancashire eleven, whilst the Association persuaded Queen's Park to delay the National Cup-tie until North End felt ready.

The build-up to the October Cup-tie was unprecedented, as Queen's Park made desperate efforts to strengthen a team beaten so humiliatingly by North End's 'as active as cats' side only weeks before. Thousands overwhelmed the police to get a free view from Mount Florida. The official paid crowd was 15,200, and the addition of interlopers, members and those in the stands produced a consensus that the crowd inside Hampden was 20,000. £380 was the largest-ever sixpenny gate.

Preston impressed: 'trig and neat in their white shirts and dark blue knickers.' The chief source of attention was Arthur Wharton 'the 100 yards amateur champion … a wiry smooth-looking specimen of the half-caste'. The atmosphere was unpleasant. One famous ex-international/Corinthian stood in front of the grandstand insulting the professionals throughout. A Queen's Park forward cursed umpire Sudell when he insisted on the correct way (i.e. English, it had been a matter of dispute) of throwing in. North End held control throughout, and twenty-year-old Jamie Ross scored the third and final goal. 'Ross junior' had proved 'fairly on the dot' many times this season. In deference to his elder brother Jack 'Old Nick' Ross, the new star was known as the Little Demon. Now his minor devilry provoked a major riot. Minutes from time, Ross junior made a back and tough Scottish international Bill Harrower somersaulted over: 'the most frightful fall we ever witnessed in the football field, and, as he hung in the air for a second, our blood ran cold. How he escaped a broken neck is marvellous.'

The multitude were enraged, and Harrower's father had to be stopped from attacking Ross. The recent humiliation with its sense of outrage lay partly behind the response, as three to four thousand 'howling savages' leapt the barriers: 'if one's blood ran cold before, our very heart stood still now! Was the man to be murdered before our eyes!' Some eminent Queen's Parkers – Don Gow, Wattie Arnott and David Allan – rescued Ross, albeit at the cost of being hit themselves. The teams in the pavilion became the 'prisoners of an infuriated mob', howling and shouting. The president of this amateur establishment lamented: 'if this was to be the usual thing he would bang up the whole concern, and sell it off.'

The Invincibles split up. Bob Howarth got as far as the goalposts where he was surrounded, rough-handled and driven back. Arthur Wharton 'would not play again in Glasgow for a great deal'. John 'Safety Valve' Graham 'was set upon immediately he got outside the ground'. A policeman told him he was on his own. 'He got into a cab which was smashed, and was again set upon … he fought his way to a tramcar.' Having been seen wielding his fists, Graham was 'immediately hauled out by a policeman and marched through the streets in his football "togs" to the Strathbungo police station'.

Nicholas 'Pa' Jackson, leader of the Corinthians, was always on hand at a football occasion. Now he acted the Spartan, assuring the 'menacing' crowd that Ross would be punished. One respondent replied 'he wouldn't leave the ground until he saw the little d**** hanging in shreds from the flag-pole'. The Scotch patriarch Charles Campbell, recently retired after thirteen internationals in thirteen years, also went Greek, appealing 'Demosthenes-like' to the unpacified.

Meanwhile Jamie Ross found a volunteer to impersonate him. An Edinburgh friend ran for it as Queen's Parkers made a convincing show of hiding someone in their midst, before revealing they had no little d****. 'The bird had flown.' How? That evening an intrepid Scotch reporter was ushered by Old Nick into the presence of the Little Demon, and found him at about 5ft 7in and around 9st a surprisingly undevilish figure. Also, reassuringly, Ross junior was receiving solace from a lady friend, 'tenderly interested in his welfare.' Jamie told of his Dr Seuse-like flight. Ross, escorted by Queen's Park's international Allan Stewart, went out through back windows, climbed over railings, across fields, around a brickfield, pursuit still audible, into Palmodie St, where he collapsed: 'I lay down exhausted, and felt done up, that had they come on me at that moment, I would have let them kill me.'

FIXTURES, WHAT FIXTURES?

To Queen's Park's 'indelible disgrace', caused by 'riotous conduct', was soon added a different level of football dishonour. The aftermath revealed the complexities of pre-League fixture arrangements. Their secretaries negotiated as if the riot had never taken place. The Cup-tie had been a matter for the Association. But their earlier September fixture was an autonomous contract between the clubs, and the return a matter of obligation. As North End had come to Glasgow, Queen's Park were honour-bound to visit Preston on Christmas Day. But they welched. North End were not used to being messed about. Fixture problems might be complicated, but North End made it a simple test of honour, and publicised Queen's Park's breach. Queen's Park's secretary pleaded for the privacy of their correspondence, and explained they had no choice. Christmas Day or not, their Association required Queen's Park to play in the Scottish Cup. North End's match secretary Nuttall was having none of it:

'What I do know is, that I put it plainly to you – foreseeing something of this – that we should prefer to cancel the match of 25th September unless you should give us a distinct assurance to play here on the 25th December. You gave us what ordinary mortals would consider such an assurance, and then "wriggle" out of your engagement. I shall publish.'

At the same time as Queen's Park disappointed North End, the new Scottish power, Renton, let down an equally indignant Bolton (who threatened legal recourse). The Lancastrians made the best of it. North End and Wanderers played each other, and to avoid a repetition of the dangerous crush of the previous Christmas, put prices up – the 12-1 game that began this chapter.

Arranging fixtures was an extremely time-consuming and complicated business. It was partly a matter of class relations. Queen's Park and North End were pretty equal, and both were superior to most others, but this superiority was at stake in every match. Each result changed these relations, either subtly or significantly, both between the two competitors and others in the football community. An important concept was aggregated scores between clubs over a season: if Club A beat Club B 6-0, and then lost 0-2 and 0-3, Club A might still be ahead 6-5 on their season's contests. 'Co-relational trials' were equally important: if North End beat Blackburn Rovers 7-1, then neighbours Blackburn Olympic would aim to do better, or less bad – a 1-5 defeat would be a 'co-relational' success.

Already some fixtures were traditional, and the expectation of the respective communities that there would be matches influenced these clubs to make these fixtures. These expectations might be disturbed by arguments and offences – North End had fallen out with Aston Villa and Accrington before 1886-87 so there were no matches until new marketing opportunities prompted reconciliation. Just as 'honour' in some way or other might disturb fixtures, once renewed it carried a new power – for a return match.

The other major determinants were money – sharing gates or 'guarantees', originally a protection for visitors, but quickly an incentive – and logistics, particularly when a tour was put together. Reporter 'The Rambler', a former club secretary, emphasised that fixture-making 'means everything' and had to 'pay'. Pro clubs had expenses of £20 a week, so home-and-away fixtures with the many lower-class clubs issuing challenges meant certain loss. On the other hand, Monday fixtures meant 'clear gain, as he gets two matches for one week's wages'. 'Rambler' calculated that four-fifths of 'broken engagements' were due to cups.

With Queen's Park defeated, the Cup moved on to another Scoto-Saxon showdown. Blackburn Rovers, having a poor season, had been 'rolled over most unmercifully' by Renton. After three seasons, there would be new National Cup champions. Probably the winners of Renton's next tie, for they drew Preston.

Preston warmed up for Renton during a freezing winter holiday with matches autonomously arranged between clubs. Christmas saw a plethora of touring Scotch teams. Preston faced Third Lanark Rifle Volunteers on New Year's Day 1887. It was icy throughout the country. Elsewhere, the Corinthians' goalkeeper broke the ice in his goalmouth with a hatchet, and the miners of Shankhouse Black Watch with pickaxes. However cold, everyone tried harder against the champions, especially as the Volunteers still bathed in the warmth of beating Preston in August 1886. Subsequent losses to other English clubs mattered little: these matches were not 'in the same hemisphere with the North End match'. Odds were 10 to 1 against another Volunteers win but Preston left it to the last kick. Third Lanark protested furiously. Offside! Or time's up! To no avail. These were not friendlies. The respective team bosses Sudell and Crerar 'argued the toss' for another 24 hours, a dispute 'conducted in half-a-dozen different hotels'. One win each. Sudell suggested a decider on neutral territory. Moneyman 'Sir John' as usual upped the ante: what about further matches on each other's ground, the winner taking the proceeds. Whichever, it was up to them. No one told them who to play.

Glasgow Rangers visited Preston on holiday Monday, January 3rd. Rangers were so weak, and goalkeeping in these conditions so 'bitterly cold', that Wharton persuaded captain Jack Ross to swap places, so Wharton could go full-back. The Scots were offended by the implied insult, exacerbated by its racial overtones: 'Wharton should give over that too ostentatious parade of conscious superiority which he is only too inclined to deploy to his applauding admirers.' Arthur proved somewhat clumsy in the outfield, prompting judgment that he would not 'pass muster' for North End's second string. When his own-goal provided Rangers' sole consolation in a 1-8 loss, Ross had had enough and consigned Wharton back to goal. The Scotch judgment of Rangers was harsher: 'the light blues had never made such a mess of themselves before.'

The weather was still terrible on January 8th. At Bolton's Pike's Lane that day, some bright spark had an idea for trampling down the six or seven inches of snow: they threw out a ball and youngsters ran after it for twenty minutes. The Wanderers and their opponents, Birmingham's St George's, were less inclined to leave their nests, 'apparently after a severe struggle as to whether the game was worth a candle.' It was colder at Blackburn, where North End played, but not against Rovers. Blackburn Olympic was a club in decline since being the first Northern, workingmen team to win the National Cup in 1883, symbolically beating the Old Etonians. Now, after four successive years of winning the Cup, both Blackburn clubs were out and there were fears the town was falling out of love with football. The atmosphere recalled the ruins of the Coliseum and Pompeii. At a Rovers game, a player complained to youngsters playing behind the goal, receiving the response – 'we're having a game to ourselves: yours isn't worth watching'. The Olympians were receiving 'offensive remarks' from many, who 'when the Olympic won the cup, were ready to toady to them at every turn'. They needed an attractive fixture to boost club coffers: liabilities £370, assets £120, creditors restless.

As a benefit for the victims of football economics, it failed. The snow and a bleak Arctic wind made the 'fastnesses' of Olympic's picturesque ground at Hole i' th' Wall resemble a 'polar region'. Reporter 'The Grumbler' thought himself a 'poor, shrivelled victim'. He listed innumerable Victorian diseases, then said (ironically) 'the only infallible cure to a suffering world – Become a Football Reporter'. His pleadings with his editor cut no ice: 'you had better face it. There's no better match in the county. Go and have a look at the North End.' Having 'scaled the snow-glad heights' beforehand, and then tripped on the ice and rolled down the hill afterwards, 'Grumbler' resented reporting the play: 'Why didn't you sit on the palatial stand and inhale a ton or so of east wind.' Unsurprisingly, but sadly for Olympic, only 1,500 paying customers turned up.

Jimmy Costley proudly wore his 1883 National Cup medal on his watchguard when he attended the 1928 Cup final. An Everton player in the first League season, Costley reminisced about Blackburn's Olympic-Rovers rivalry: before one cup-tie with Oswaldthistle, 'the Olympic team were kept hidden for two hours at the bottom of a coal pit ... they thought they were going to be 'shown something'. Really they were hiding me from Rovers' spies'. Rovers eventually got their man, and now Olympic's younger stars Edgar Chadwick, Bill Townley and Jack Southworth were about to 'go over to the enemy' (Rovers), and eventually represent England. This cold day Southworth preferred the warmth of a Saturday matinee performance in Mrs Duval's Theatre Royal band; whilst Townley's no-show was simply that of a 'wandering star of late'. The match was anti-climax: North End won 6-0 when freezing fog ended the show early. Blackburn Olympic would never recover.

And so back to Scotland. If North End could beat their new champions, Renton, surely they would win the National Cup. Preston had now knocked out Queen's Park, and Renton had defeated the 1884/85/86 winners Blackburn Rovers. Showdown.

The tie was obviously the match of the season, although only the locals thought Renton could win. The fixture negotiations were a match in themselves. Rumours abounded. It was said the unprincipled English Association were 'arbitrarily depriving Renton of the choice of ground', the big advantage given by the draw. North End's influence was apparently limiting Renton to a choice between their own village ground or Edinburgh, where most of the Scotch North Enders originated. Renton preferred the obvious alternative of a big Glasgow crowd. But North End recalled how Jamie Ross barely escaped alive from their last trip.

The dangers of English clubs playing at Hampden Park resurfaced when a pitiless rainstorm caused the abandonment of Queen's Park's Christmas match at half-time, with Aston Villa leading 5-1. Queen's Park, once themselves invincible, had now been beaten by three English teams this season. 'Come out you cowards,' yelled the crowd. Villa were no cowards. They had scored twenty goals in three matches in four days, and against Hibernian their centre-half Fred Dawson reacted against his umpire, William McGregor, being attacked. Unfortunately, he mistook *The Scotsman*'s reporter Ogilvie as the assailant (Football Reporter as Dangerous as well as Uncomfortable Occupation): 'he struck his unoffending opponent while in the act of jumping over the fence in front of the grand stand, and a second time while on the point of rising, with blood streaming from his face.' The 'impulsive and pugilistic Dawson' hesitated to compensate the victim: 'the smashed hat, the blood stained overcoat and vest cost money.' Who should replace them but 'the individual who rendered them useless?' The Edinburgh police urged a complaint but Ogilvie was 'more humane'. At Hampden, when the crowd got neither Villa and Queen's Park, nor their money back, they 'smashed the [reporters'] tables' and benches, the remnants of which they threw at the few police, then 'leveled the goalposts', then 'get the payboxes'. Finally, the flag over the members' stand was 'ruthlessly hurled down, trampled upon and torn'.

The Renton v North End National Cup-tie threatened more of the same. The English took precautions against 'the disgraceful scenes which you Scotsmen seem to be getting so fond of … North End will play in cast-iron suits to protect themselves from the "madding" crowd'. Bereft of a big city setting, the 'wee kindra' club' erected three grandstands at their Tontine Park, and charged high prices – a shilling to enter the ground (two to four times as much as the League prices twenty months later); an extra shilling to the stands, two shillings for the reserve stand. The press worried that Tontine's telegraphy infrastructure was 'indifferent': a single instrument, operated by a young man especially brought from Edinburgh. If it failed, the news would have to be taken by horseman to Dumbarton, miles away, or the Saturday evening Lancashire establishments – dining rooms, smoking rooms, billiards rooms – would be sorely disappointed.

Four hundred supporters saw North End off to Glasgow on a dismal, Friday evening. Strangely, despite the cold, an accompanying reporter likened Preston station's 'yellow, impenetrable fog' to the 'Black Hole of Calcutta'. The players shivered until their saloon carriage was fitted to the 'smoking and puffing' monster. On board, Ross junior warmed himself playing cricket (a roll of paper as ball) with Fred Dewhurst (and Arthur Wharton at short leg). Ross senior got off at Motherwell to ask a porter for the prospects of playing. Too cold, but if you play I hope you beat 'Rantin's swaggering lot'. There was nothing to do in piercing Glasgow at 11pm, so Davie 'Sweeney Todd' Russell shaved John 'Ineligible' Goodall with a table knife. As Saturday morning was colder, they visited Hampden Park to confirm play was impossible. AAA champion Wharton and Corinthian Dewhurst took off into the thick fog on an impromptu race, and returned impressively quickly. The Hampden fixture (a Scottish Cup semi-final between Hibs and Vale of Leven which soon had an unexpected significance, see below p.32) was postponed, but no news came from Renton. The team set off, all the time more supporters joining the train, but all the while passing fields full of 'icy forebodings'.

They found nervous Renton officials. Despite members sweeping the pitch throughout the night, their 'surface [was] as hard and unyielding as macadam', yet the crowd was being admitted. Trains were coming from all over. Things were getting out of control. The higher the prices, the greater the need to deliver. But what was the product? A 'great fite', or a game of football, or one between acknowledged champions of two nations, or a decisive knockout tie for the National Cup?

North End's backers took no chances. The previous week, North End won 6-0 'floundering about a bit on the snow'. So Preston's twenty-strong party included their shoemaker. They had footwear with strips of India-rubber affixed for grip on the hard ground, as well as another set with the 'regulation flushed leather spikes'. Renton put their faith in a nail between the spikes, but needed a club member with a handy pair of pincers to extract a nail that went into the sole.

Old Harrovian referee Morton Betts quickly decided Tontine Park was 'quite unfit for play'. The Scots demurred, but 'North End sheltered themselves under the referee's decision, and declined to play the cup tie'. It gave them an out. In London, the Association's Cup was looking untidy: too many protests, too many overlapping rounds, perhaps too many Scots. The North End tie started six weeks after the other third round matches, in which Villa and Wolves played four times. Their epic tie brought a tremendous reward – an aggregate £553 – but complicated any understanding of the Cup's progress. Association secretary Charles Alcock, desperately trying to simplify the competition, 'wired North End at Renton that they must finish the tie that day.'

North End would only play an ordinary match on the 'unplayable' ground. They had to do something. Betts cautioned the players against charging on the 'cruel-looking surface'. Despite their later alibis, Preston were confident: one player 'when stepping on the field generously offered the writer a pair of the best town-made gloves if North End did not score six goals'. Others were spreading other bets: 'the Renton folk did not relish the presence of English bookies in their ground … They'll be better watched next time.'

On arrival, Arthur 'Othello' Wharton had taken the eye with his 'turban, and the jaunty style in which it graced his figure had caused youngsters to grin from ear to ear'. But he gave the real game away. North End defended Renton's early rush without conviction and 'Wharton let the ball pass him'. His indifference said, no cup-tie. The crowd shouted 'Play the Tie', led either by 'ragged urchins' who got in free, or those in the stands who were the 'biggest losers'. Twenty police were helpless when 'hundreds of spectators invaded the ground in a threatening attitude, and there was nothing for it but to play a cup tie'. Or at least, Renton officials said so, 'simply to delude the crowd,' who otherwise wanted their money back. But who was fooling who? The club had spent on building stands, and as the poem had it:

A child might understand,
The Club had biz in hand.

More climbed over the railings or pushed through the gates. The official crowd was 3,300, most thought it was 6,000, and English commentators considered that the Scotch journo who estimated 10/12,000 had had too much whisky. The gate was little short of £150. John Woods, perhaps with a wager at stake, was glimpsed dodging round the ropes to get to North End's umpire Sudell. Was it a cup tie? Sudell gave the game yet another name: 'a cup-tie played under protest.'

Renton played hard, to the delight of a partisan crowd. Jamie Ross equalised, 'his clever shot was a neat piece of work, but not a cheer was heard.' Renton scored twice more as Preston increasingly relied on their goalkeeper's 'great adroitness': 'Wharton never had so much work to do since he joined the North End.' Before half-time reporters were tipped off: 'we just learn on the quiet that the game is after all a friendly, and when the spectators learn this there will be another scene.' Some had guessed: 'what is it now?' 'A friendly with another name.'

They did not know in Preston. The telegraph worked, although the six hundred long faces of North End supporters in the Town's Fishergate wished it had not. But North End prompted relief by equalising in the last minute. Papers reported the contradictory outcome: 'the result being A draw of Three Goals Each. The match was not a Cup Tie.'

North Enders returned 'badly cut and bruised', and not a man escaped 'without a memento of what was a gigantic and cruel farce'. In the week following Preston developed another excuse. It wasn't easy to articulate. Despite their injuries Mr Secretary Dewhurst said North End 'did not try until the last thirty minutes … none of the players turned a hair during the whole game'. Then why try at the end? After all, the cup-tie as cup-tie never happened: 'whatever the result, it would have to be replayed.' Yet North End could not deny trying in ordinary fixtures without undermining their bread and butter – their livelihood was based on such matches. So the cup-tie-that-wasn't continued to pose a problem of what it had been: 'whether regarded as an ordinary fixture or not meant little.' It was almost as if its lack of status was the problem: 'the visitors attached no value whatever to the match, which was neither one thing nor the other.'

From 1888, the League's achievement, almost accidentally, was to find a third way between ordinary and cup fixtures. Ordinary matches meant a lot. There was money on them. People paid to watch, players were paid to pay, punters bet. Betting depended upon both teams playing hard. National Cup-ties were of a different order. When you lost, it was the end of matches. The passing of the seasons gave this loss greater depth through an appreciation of history, but clubs and communities were not comforted by having another chance next year. There was real pressure on clubs. Instability was evident. It was a matter of life or death. Barely three seasons after winning the Cup, Blackburn Olympic's life was fast running into the sand. If they had won it again, or if Rovers had not won three triumphs, perhaps Olympic would be Blackburn's club today.

And cups were not just played on the pitch. Others could play their part. Club committees could protest to the Association, and often win. There was plenty of room for argument: the physical parameters – pitch size, its playability, the height of goalposts. So was the process. When clubs had to toss for venue, they arranged 'our "calls" should cross each other by post' and be authenticated by bank managers. When their captain lost a toss for venue against Blackburn Rovers' committeemen, Darwen repudiated it, because the rules said 'rival captains should spin but ours did not'. Above all, the regulations of players' eligibility were neither understood nor respected.

The League would stumble upon something that had tangible consequences, and regularity. Protests messed up cup competitions. The routine and frequency of league matches would pre-empt protests.

League matches, home and away, resolved the question of venue. Two months after they were drawn together, Renton, Preston and the English Association were still arguing about where to play. Hampden was chosen, from which North End only just escaped with their lives weeks before. This put Jamie Ross back into the centre of attention. Jamie talked to 'a boy' reporter, and what he wrote led junior to 'threaten to annihilate' him if their paths crossed again. Ross denied any Preston doubts about playing him at Hampden after that 'unfortunate demonstration' the previous October. William Sudell spoiled the scoop, and further wound up the atmosphere by an interview with an opposing paper, read avidly on the morning of the match. He criticised Renton's roughness; acknowledged that Scotchmen were the best footballers, but said North End reached their scientific apogee because professionalism had allowed the same group of players to play together; anticipated a scientific future for football; called the Scottish Association foolish for turning the public against professionalism – he knew from his players that Scotch clubs made payments; and, coming full circle, if there was no professionalism in Scotland, where does the money go – Renton made £100 last week.

The reporter suggested clubs might share out end of the season profits. 'Precisely, and what do you call that?' Sudell advocated England's formal class system. Would the Scots ever accept professionalism? 'Yes, when you consent to call a spade a spade.' Elsewhere, left-winger Geordie Drummond was accusing amateurs of being 'vulgar persons', and Jamie Ross was holding court ('showman fashion') about his 'hair breadth escape … and pointed to the direction of his frantic flight on that bitter day'. North End were up for it.

'The match is the talk everywhere,' so the Association sent their top man, President and Major Marindin, as referee. He found North End's spikes were one-sixteenth over regulation length. The 'gallant major' read the players the 'Riot Act' beforehand, and then took out a brand new ball. Afterwards he called Renton 'brutes' and Scotch amateurs 'cads'. This time Hampden's groundsman stopped Ross junior, Dewhurst and Wharton from running impromptu races. Preston quickly went two up in the 'moist, almost warm atmosphere'. Renton fought hard. The English press complained they took 'ball or man unflinchingly', that full-back Andrew Hannah practised 'scurvy dodges' and half-back Bob Kelso was not only 'very guilty of vile play but resorts to the pettiest of tricks to annoy an antagonist'. When Fred Dewhurst lined up an easy third, Hannah deprived him by 'unscrupulous trickery'. This was a Cup Tie.

Two-nil never felt safe, because it meant so much. Behaviour that characterised the top man of other Lancashire Invincibles a century later showed how much it mattered. In the 1990s Alex Ferguson became renowned for his attention to timepieces in the closing stages of Manchester United games. On January 22nd, 1887, John Woods noted that Sudell spent the last fifteen minutes holding his watch.

A large police presence prevented a third 'unfortunate' Glaswegian football 'demonstration'. The gate (shilling minimum) was at least £300 from 6,782, plus Queen's Park and Renton members who got in free (Queen's Park took another £97 from those in the stand) – 10,000 overall. On the same Saturday, another National Cup-tie was played at Chirk, a mining village near Wrexham. Their previous highest gate had been £7. Now, for Darwen's visit, 1,500 turned up – a £17 10s gate.

Afterwards, the presentations. A Newcastle reporter gave Jamie Ross a 'ferocious-looking stick' to remember his escape from Hampden Park. 'Jamie says he will hand it down from sire to son, in memento of the event that never came off,' i.e. his death. North End had overcome their biggest obstacle. Champers was in order. At their victory dinner, 'Mr Sudell was so pleased that he stood "cham" all round.' 'Oh, what a surprise.' Then a telegram informed Howarth and Dewhurst they were selected for England. Big cheer. 'Oh, what a surprise.' Another telegram brought news about next week's tie. The London Swifts, featuring many Corinthians and England internationals, had lost to Old Foresters. 'Oh, what a surprise.' Unfortunately the confident Swifts, but not the Foresters, had reserved The Oval. North End offered £75 to come to Deepdale, but the Foresters preferred Leyton in deepest Essex. On the downside, right-winger Jack Gordon was suspended for a fortnight for using 'improper language' to Hampden's Scotch umpire. Having appointed neutral officials, the English Association was quick to back them up: 'Gordon did well to get off with a fortnight.' North End defended their men: 'Sudell says he can take his lads anywhere, and he has never had reason to be ashamed of them.'

SHADY AMATEURISM

Having defeated both their champions, Preston's class softened Scottish hearts: 'no words would be too extravagant in praise. They played football as it ought to be played.' North End once symbolised the 'satanic sin' of professionalism, and there were still some sour comparisons of the professionals (ie. North End's renegade Scots) versus working men (Renton's villagers) type. But lately, 'our sense of wrong and outrage desperate' had been 'considerably moderated' by the 'world of fact', i.e. the growing awareness that amateur clubs were paying players. Was 'open professionalism' preferable?

Scotch 'shady amateurism' was only just visible. One week later Vale of Leven charged Hibernian with professionalism. Hibs were the form Scotch club: undefeated since August, they had played more games (24) and more wins (18) than anyone else. But they trained the week before they beat Vale in the Scottish Cup semi-final. The freedom to practice distinguished the professional from the amateur, and 'it is a well-known fact in Edinburgh that the Hibs have not been working for a long time'.

An initial hearing was all smoke and mirrors, and Vale were challenged to provide proof. So they hired 'our most experienced and successful private detectives'. The second hearing teased out the minutiae of the lives of young working footballers, encompassing: a factory pay book, workers' testimony (the whistleblower was sacked, and threatened with violence), cash books, receipts from a hotel suspiciously far from Hibs' normal hangout … and even 'the girl at the bar'.

The amateurs claimed that 'glory' answered questions of dedication: 'where is the football man that has not sacrificed a £1 or 25s. in the pursuit of the game.' Third Lanark's William Crerar, who had recently spent a weekend with William Sudell arguing an offside decision, was sceptical about players giving up a week's work to train without sustenance: 'I have not come across the footballist yet who will give up his bread for the cup.' Hibernian did not challenge the facts – 'our players have had some idle time lately, it is true' – but blamed trade conditions or the weather preventing building work. 'Others, again, are off early in the day, being engaged to the Fish market.'

Vale targeted Willie Groves. Groves became one of football's greatest players of the 1890s with West Bromwich Albion. In 1887 he seemed sure to get his international cap, being compared to England's famous dribbler William Cobbold. His 'rare speed' and 'graceful' runs won Hibernian the Scottish Cup, knocking out successively Third Lanark on Christmas Day, the Vale in January and formidable Dumbarton in February's final, after Groves ran the length of the field to set up the winner. He was 'simply grand'. But, otherwise, the Scottish Association asked, 'what does Groves do?' 'Mr Groves was at his work up to the New Year holidays, when he was idle for a little, but that is a common occurrence with most people.' Groves was 'only an apprentice' boot finisher, so how had he survived several weeks off work? He gave evidence. Groves was nineteen, and on piece-time, earning seven to ten shillings a week, but, during better trade times, had once made 27 shillings a week. 'How can you exist on eight shillings a week?' 'My mother and father keep me for this sum. If I worked from six in the morning, Monday to Saturday, I could earn 15s.'

Groves was unconvincing about his football money. Hibs never paid him anything, or maybe they had, but not for lost wages, or only sometimes. He took his holidays, between the Christmas Day cup-tie and playing Villa on New Year's Day, touring Middlesbrough (where he received ten shillings from Hibs' secretary 'to go to a ball'). The factory wages book indicated he did not return. Groves denied this, then remembered being ill. He was in bed for three days before the Vale cup-tie, and was 'quite sure' he had not played in a practice match, nor dined at Wallace's Suburban Hotel, on the preceding Wednesday. Then he remembered doing both. Hibs were represented by 'facetious' secretary John McFadden, whose cash-book seemed 'written all in one day … but we must accept McFadden's word.' Not least because 'humourist' McFadden was an Association committeeman himself. A year before, he had been a hardliner advocating cancellation of The International if the English did not forswear their professionals.

McFadden actually argued for sitting in judgment on his own case, in his other capacity as the Edinburgh Association secretary. Hibs' cash-book for December 27th, 1886 recorded fifteen men being paid 7s 6d at Middlesbrough and Groves separately 5s. McFadden denied this was extra payment. The secretary explained who got paid when – he never paid anyone anything unless he was asked: 'the exception' was because he was 'more easily "bounced" than the older heads … Groves would not ask for more. It would be unlike him'. Similarly, referring to Hibs' tour of Lancashire the previous Easter, McFadden confirmed five committee men received 35s, the players 25 or 27s and, separately, 'Groves £1.' Sarcastic committeemen commented it was 'curious' Groves 'always got a special rate'.

Hibs were banged to rights: McFadden even acknowledged 'when a fellow played a good game they would be a little liberal'. Asked if he had given the players money lately, he replied: 'I have not been near the players for a fortnight.' Hibs' Scottish Cup final (the first win by an Edinburgh club) was their first match at Hampden Park and produced a gate of £435, but apparently Groves did not even get his usual 3s 6d. McFadden heard of the triumph after refereeing in Dumfries.

The committee grumbled. How on earth had the Cup sub-committee allowed the final to go ahead? Now they were sitting in judgment on the holders. Defining professionalism was like dancing on the head of a pin, but Hibs had paid players' 'lost wages' when they were on holiday; paid them more than they would have earned; and, for some the original sin, they paid for practice. Nine voted for disqualification, another nine against. Hibernian were only saved by the chairman's casting 'not proven' vote. Having done so, he told Hibs they had 'seriously erred'. The English papers cried chicken, the disgrace of banning their Cup holders being too much for the Scotch authorities.

The sums involved indicate Scotch vulnerability to English depredations. In the summer Groves, offered 36 shillings 'and a good place' rather than 3s 6d, ran off to join Birmingham's St George's. McFadden brought him home, minus 'bag and baggage'. Vulnerable also to Celtic, the rapacious Glaswegian newcomer in 1888. Willie Groves went in the first wave.

At the same time another suspected shamateur was being similarly examined – William McLeod, Scottish international and Queens Park's back in the 1885 National Cup final, sometimes Cowlairs' main man, and more recently of Aston Villa and the Nottingham clubs. The English Association's sub-committee asked McLeod how he could afford to 'leave his work to play football?' He pulled out his wad and showed his credit was in three figures.

ONWARD CUP SOLDIERS

Meanwhile, back in the Cup, Glasgow's Partick Thistle played Old Westminsterians at The Oval (where the smell of the gasworks 'knock you down'). A London visit was a treat and Thistle marvelled at the bargains in Petticoat Lane's Sunday morning market: 'overcoats at 1s. 6d. and trousers at 3s. are not to be had every day.'

North End enjoyed greater style, staying at Hazell's Hotel in the Strand, a fine and large establishment distinguished by labyrinthine passages. West End shows Friday and Saturday nights, Saturday morning billiards. But, in between, the Leyton ground's threepenny gate did not produce much 'oaf', i.e. a crowd of 3/4,000 donated £41. Both teams wore white, so Old Foresters had a whipround and appeared in rainbow hue. The ball was like India-rubber. Otherwise match reports of North End's 3-0 win were sparse. Despite promises, Leyton's telegraph was the size of a 'band-box, fitted with a one-horse wire and no batteries'.

Back in town at London's nightspots, Preston's Scotch pros and Thistle's amateur workers met up in the early hours. While Jack Gordon ('a tall, lanky fellow, all legs') sat nearby smoking the pipe of indifference, Jack Ross, Preston's captain, held court in maudlin if irascible mood. He said even if professionalism was recognised, 'he'd see them ***** first before he'd play for [Scotland].' Ross's beef was that he should have been picked when he was still with Hearts. In those days international sides were almost exclusively Glaswegian/Queen's Park. Edinburgh didn't get a look in. At two in the morning Ross revealed the immigrant's sadness – he had never played better than for Hearts – and his perfectionism – 'the North End only really played once' this season, that 12-1 against Bolton. His assessment of Scotland's current backs? Jack Forbes was the best; Queens Park's Wattie Arnott was nowhere.

William Sudell and his team were back at the hotel and, 'like all right-minded people, they enjoyed themselves immensely overnight. In the early hours of the morning they awoke and called for drinks. The bars were not open!!! Just at this moment a barmaid was heard calling out – "Mr Sudell, your bath is ready". Said a droughty member of the football crowd "Bring the bath here and we'el drink it". The bath was brought.'

Despite many 'with a head like a box of toys and a throat like a starch-work gate', North End celebrated church on Sunday's return train. They were still on track for the Cup. But these endless journeys were taking their toll. Next day, Monday, they were still suffering from their Alhambra 'indulgences', and ran out of steam in Fergy Suter's benefit. The Scotch pro was much loved: no one had done more for Lancashire football. Like Ross, Suter never played for Scotland. After leaving Glasgow for Darwen he stopped following his stonemason trade, giving rise to rumours he was being paid for football. Suter had helped 'humble little Darwen' challenge the aristocratic Old Etonians in 1879 in a three-match National Cup-tie, 'an event that shook the nation' [Green, 1953, p.45]. Blackburn Rovers caused an outcry by paying Suter £100 to leave Darwen. He won three Cup-winners medals 1884/86 (one of which was auctioned at Sotheby's for £6,500 in 2000), but in 1888-89 played only one League game … as Rovers' goalkeeper.

All Lancashire football's grand men joined Suter's organising committee – Sudell and Woods from North End; Morley and Gregson from Blackburn; former Bolton secretary Jack Bentley; Joe Hartley from Accrington … They needed John Woods' financial wizardry to turn a crowd of 1,000 into a benefit of £120. Suter could still play, for he blanked North End to help Rovers win 2-0.

So The Invincibles beaten? It depends. North End could find excuses for their non-invincibility – it was a benefit, and anyway they never backed themselves on Mondays. Similarly, that early Third Lanark defeat was pre-season. They had still only lost twice. Another thing the League eventually clarified was what matches counted.

North End felt stronger about the crowd's insults and aggression, out of keeping with their generosity in supporting a Rovers benefit. This conflict escalated, to set in train events that nearly aborted the proposed League in 1888.

In February 1887, North End and Wanderers faced small clubs Witton and Padiham in the Lancashire Cup semi-finals, the second most important competition in late 1880s football. Bolton played at Preston, Preston at Bolton. Witton had been undefeated for months, but North End led 5-0 by half-time. When Deepdale learned the news, Preston wits, remembering their 12-1 Christmas win, chaffed Wanderers goalkeeper Trainer about how many goals he would concede in the final. These semis were attractive enough for some to think a 'captive balloon suspended midway between the two towns and furnished with 40-horse power binoculars wouldn't have been a bad idea'. Preston won by 12-0, Bolton 4-1.

Jack Ross's London nightlife 'cold' turned into rheumatic fever as the matches came thick and fast. North End played their already traditional Shrovetide Tuesday match against Sheffield Wednesday, stopping over at Lincoln the day before. Railway companies valued the good business matchdays, so planned a Monday morning route circumventing Manchester. Unfortunately they forgot to take the brake off, so soon North End's carriage 'threatened a conflagration'. Their party crossed Manchester by cab convoy, before the Manchester, Sheffield & Lincolnshire Co 'courteously placed a luxuriant first class saloon at their disposal'. Preston beat Lincoln 2-0 Monday and on Tuesday (Sheffield) Wednesday 5-0 (8,000 crowd). Then a fourth match of the season with Blackburn. Five thousand Prestonians were not pleased that Rovers did not bring their strongest side (goalkeeper Herbie 'King' Arthur and winger Joe Lofthouse were away with England), and even less so when Rovers led 2-0. But North End came back to win 8-2, the six-goal margin as usual fulfilling a popular bet.

Old Carthusians refused £100 to come to Preston for the National Cup's quarter-final on March 2nd, and hired The Oval for London's grandest match so far. The semi would follow on March 5th. North End had reached the sharp end of their season … Make or break … Invincible or …

They would take the first step on their own. March 2nd was also the club's AGM, so Sudell, Jolly Sir John *et al* stayed in Preston to celebrate their footballing and financial acumen. As the financial year ended on

January 3rd, 1887, the latter would have been even better had they played the lucrative Deepdale fixture with Queen's Park. Hence their pre-Christmas annoyance. Starting January 1886 with a balance of £267, North End's total income was £2,909 and expenditure £2,752. £1,455 went on wages. Among the small items were £56 on jerseys, boots etc, and the £44 spent on police costs dwarfed the £10 on footballs. In a developing theme, they had played more away than home games. Despite twenty long journeys (including three visits to Glasgow and twice to London), travelling expenses (minus hotels) averaged £16.

Another journey already loomed. North End had been selected to play the Corinthians at Kennington Oval on March 12th before the Prince of Wales as football's contribution to the Queen's Jubilee. It would cost Preston £70, because the 12,000 gate would go to the royal charity, Imperial Institute. North End reckoned they could cope: 'all their stands were paid for, they were practically free of debt,' and should have enough to carry them through the summer.

But Proud Preston weren't in it for the money. Cups were the thing, and their Achilles heel during years of invincibility was that they had won nothing. Now 'if there were not "a slip betwixt cup and lip" ... With ordinary good fortune, both cups ought to come to Preston, because they had the best team that ever put toe to leather'. Serious confidence. No fear of hostages to fortune. The Executive also resisted reducing the annual membership fee: 400 members were quite sufficient. One egalitarian contributor looked forward to the team and members dining together, 'after the cup has been won.'

North End struggled against the Old Carthusians, and 8,000 Oval spectators – the 'usual crowds of hansoms conveying the crutch and toothpick brigade' –- enjoyed their discomfiture. North End took stick most places. In Blackburn it was intra-Lancashire jealousy. In Glasgow it had been anti-professionalism. In London, it smacked of class prejudice, as respectable London disdained the North End 'professors'. Some were more upfront: 'the spectators shrieked and screamed and yelled as only Cockney sportsmen know how.' However, the Londoners knew quality. There were snobby crowds who mistook the loose-limbed Scottish pro Sam Thomson running smoothly down the wing as 'that's Dewhurst', North End's only amateur, he's 'so gentlemanly' compared to 'the others'. But London also recognised the real Fred Dewhurst's proletarian effectiveness: ''cos 'e plays wi' 'is helbows has weel has 'is 'ed and feet.' Amidst their Scottishness, Dewhurst was North End's only concession to English traditions: 'for close dribbling, neat dodging, and all round excellency, no forward in the team approaches him.'

The Old Carthusians had pedigree. Cup-winners in 1881, they had England's top backs, the Brothers Walters, and the 'magnificent' William Cobbold, fresh from scoring twice in the 4-0 win over Wales. Their quarter-final captured a clash of methods. The North End marked Cobbold closely, not easy as he ran 'with arms outstretched like ostrich wings'. This gave space to others. Carthusians' speedy right-winger got clear, but as he steadied himself to shoot, 'Ross got on to him from behind.' For their part, Preston could not get past The Brothers who, although also capable of 'shady tricks', proved 'very effective, but it is at times cruel, though it may be well within the rules'. When a Brother tackled fellow amateur Dewhurst, the top-hatters screamed: 'Play at him! Jump on him! Kill him! Do anything with him!' Towards the end, 'inimitable' Cobbold 'threaded his way through the backs' and shot past Wharton: 'deafening cheers greeted this brilliant piece of play, but the North End were not done with.' PM Walters fouled Jamie Ross on the goal-line seven minutes from time and Graham headed the equaliser. In extra-time the Carthusians were done with. Cobbold was limping, North End were 'playing up harder', and AM Walters conceded the winning own-goal: afterwards, 'like the man who fell out of the balloon, the Carthusians were not in it.'

Preston had arrived at Euston 8.30pm the previous evening. After dressing for football at the Covent Garden Hotel, the Railway Company's bus took them to and from The Oval, and back to Euston. Cabs home from Preston station in the early hours of Thursday morning. The following day it was off for the semi. Their railway journeys in the National Cup alone already comprised 2,038 miles.

And in the end, reminding contemporaries of Queen's Park's fate as favourites in 1884, they were travelled out of it – 'long journeys and strange grounds'. North End were heavily fancied (Corinthian 'Pa' Jackson bet a pile). West Bromwich Albion's path to the semi-final had been persevering rather than convincing, and they had never left the Midlands. Nor had they played extra-time days before. Albion spent the week training.

North End pulled out their last financial stop. They planned to travel to Nottingham matchday, but the players wanted to stay overnight, so they did, at the Flying Horse Hotel. Travel-tiredness or not, 'football is full of uncertainties, though the North End have reduced it to as near a perfect science as one can imagine possible.'

The Trent Bridge crowd was over 15,000, made up of 12,313 paid, 500 members, 2,000 ladies allowed in free, and the swells with their carriages and drays: a near-record £479. Trying to see for free was always dangerous. Sadly, Joseph Walter Pym climbed an elm tree, lost his grip, fell off, and landed on his back across a fence. The young man left a widow and four children. It deterred few others.

It was David against Goliath – '3 to 1 or even 4 to 1 were freely laid on [Albion's] chance'. Sam Thomson put North End ahead but Albion goalkeeper Bob Roberts had 'a hundred hands', enough to win England's goalkeeping position against Scotland. Albion took out Jamie Ross off the ball, and the game stopped for eight minutes. Half-back Sandy Robertson went off injured, out for the season. Albion equalised. The second half saw persistent attacks by ten-men Preston but they were 'palpably stale'. Into the last five minutes, Albion captain Jim Bayliss had an inspiration. Shackled throughout by Davie Russell, he changed position, 'came along at a rare bat,' and set up two winning goals.

Referee Marindin's post-match question is often reported: are you all English? Albion's answer is recalled less often: 'We are Throstles.'

North End had been throstled out. Everyone could see that. The Brothers Walters felt it. One wrote in sympathy to fellow Corinthian Fred Dewhurst: 'I am truly sorry about Saturday, but I was sure, after Wednesday's game, you would not be fit by Saturday. My brother and I tried to play ourselves on Saturday and were ghastly failures.'

Geordie Drummond had wanted to 'rest' during the game, but Jack Ross would not let him. Afterwards, in the sickening reality of disappointment, an 'indignant maiden' confronted Drummond with the consequence of his weakness: 'Geordie, what's t'bin doin'? I'll kill thee, I'll kill thee.' Otherwise there were no recriminations (although North End's players were rumoured to take a ten-shillings wage cut). The nearest to a scapegoat was goalie Arthur Wharton, whom the Lancashire press adjudged as – 'no flyer. He was never really tested till last week.' North End stuck with him. It was a very tight unit. Apart from changing goalkeeper frequently, they rarely deviated from twelve outfield players – John Goodall was the reserve forward, and Bob Holmes played back as need be, but that was about it. Sudell did not need to bring Wharton back to London for the following week's showpiece game before the Prince of Wales, but he did.

The 1887 National Cup final would be all-Midland. Birmingham papers had raised visions of Villa facing a virtual Scotland XI in the other semi (recruited from all the non-competing clubs). In the event, only two 'foreigners', including Vale of Leven's Jack Forbes, strengthened Glasgow Rangers. To no avail. Villa won 3-1 at Crewe before 10,000. The Lancastrians felt, never mind the Scots, they couldn't fathom their own failure. 'The Rambler' was one. He was at Crewe, as usual preoccupied by how he would get his copy out (posties on tricycles). He was also drinking 'sma' Scotch to keep out the cold, and noting 'the inhabitants of Brum may be said to be suffering from football mania'. It was worse when news of North End's defeat came: 'I felt lonesome. Not another Lancastrian could I find – nothing but Brums getting boozed over the dual victory. I had a sorrowful journey home.'

'NOW THE SEASON'S SLOWLY WANING'

Still North End were making tracks – 'another tiresome railway journey to the metropolis'. When they awoke to snow and sleet Saturday morning they felt sorry for the loss to the 'Imperial Imbecile Institute'. It would cost 5s in the stand. They were presented to the Prince of Wales, who watched the rugby contribution but confided he liked 'the old fashioned game with the round ball the best'. A royal reception indicated the football pros had come a long way in acceptability in a short time. William Sudell, similar in looks to Prince Edward and himself a major in the Preston Volunteers, had bought a new top-hat, whereas Jack Ross, in chocolate and blue kit, impatiently shook hands with a leg guard in his hand. Marindin generously introduced Jack as the country's best and most gentlemanly player. But the future king wanted the real celebrity: 'Where's Ross junior?' Jamie Ross was unhinged, for when he 'got clean through' he missed, 'owing to being nervous through a remark the Prince had just made.'

Gentleman Cobbold complained of Player Ross, 'I wish you would not kick me on my ankles' – 'Keep your feet away from the ball and I wont' [Hunt, 2000, p.62]. North End dominated but drew 1-1. Wharton had little to do, whereas Corinthians' Mills-Roberts' many saves were 'again and again cheered. I have never seen better goalkeeping'. The good doctor had kept Jim Trainer out of the Wales team for two years, even though Trainer would walk into the England team. North End still needed a cup goalkeeper. 1886-87 had shown that 'neither [Arthur Wharton nor Billy Rose] is a wonder when pressed'. So when North End reached the sharp end of their next two cup campaigns, Dr Mills-Roberts was between the sticks.

Having outplayed this team of internationals, no one could believe North End lost the National semi. Outstanding centre-half Davie Russell was a particular favourite, if 'rather dangerous, but I suppose he has as much right to kick a ball as an opponent has to head it'. Now, against the Corinthians and England centre (1886/91), 'Russell twirled his foot around Tinsley Lindley's head in very uncomfortable fashion.'

Afterwards North End enjoyed their evening on the town. The Prince of Wales missed them at the 'Cri' (he had another engagement), so they went from the Criterion to the Gaiety to the Pavilion. Jamie Ross was the draw and 'two young ladies took the liberty of knocking our table over' to get his attention. Monday morning they left London for Stoke. Another snowstorm, but 5,000 on a bitterly cold afternoon. North End strolled to a 5-1 win: 'I never saw them exert themselves less. They relied on passing and almost walked the ball through.'

They were still hungover for an ordinary fixture against Bolton at Pike's Lane on March 19th. For once they were not centre-stage, overshadowed by the England v Scotland game at Blackburn. Preston didn't much want to play, and no one wanted to referee. Seven candidates preferred to join 12,000 at The International. North End played another 'lethargic, go-as-you-please kind of game', and Bolton won 3-0.

The Invincibles, beaten again. 'How are the mighty fallen!' Surely they were no longer 'moral certs', or 'dead snips', for the Lancashire Cup final against Wanderers on March 26th. Others asked North End, 'is your star set? Another and we will begin to lose faith in you.' But few were fooled. Like fancied horses that had a run-out before the big race, North End were likely to 'come again in a remarkably short space of time'.

If 6,000 had watched the rehearsal, an ordinary fixture, 14,500 attended the final, contributing a gate of £335. Preston were two up in twenty minutes, and neatly reversed the previous week's win – 3-0. The stats are interesting: Bolton's Trainer made 22 saves, North End's Rose nine; Wanderers made 23 goal-kicks, Preston fifteen; Bolton had two corners North End ten; Wanderers made two fouls, Preston one. Up the line, where they had played The International the previous week, 700 watched Blackburn versus Accrington.

Bolton felt a sense of 'profound humiliation, a distinct loss of prestige to the town', but had they been fooled as well? Had the Invincibles acted vincible just to make Bolton's fall all the greater? In Preston, they knew how to keep things in proportion. 1887, the year of Queen Victoria's Jubilee. A small thing, compared to North End finally winning something:

Can Sudell, the mighty, guide his people,
Till breakers dwindle, and specters vanish,
And North End, champions, claim both cups,
To grace a brighter, greater Jubilee.

On April 2nd, North End beat Walsall Swifts when they should have been in the National Cup final: Villa 2, Albion 0, watched by 10,000. 10,000 watched North End against Bootle on the following, very wet

Monday afternoon. OK, it was the city's half-day, but this was impressive – football was gripping Liverpool. One day, it might deserve a Saturday fixture.

On Easter Saturday, North End beat Scottish Cup finalists Dumbarton 2-0. It was a send-off for Scotland's captain James McAuley. McAuley had been his country's keeper for five years and never lost a game. But now he was off to the Empire, in Burmah. But first, Dumbarton helped celebrate North End's Lancashire Cup. Four thousand were in Preston's Public Hall. As gold medals were presented to the players, and Mr Sudell accepted the Cup, someone shouted 'Why didn't you protest?' (i.e. the unfair circumstances of their National Cup defeat). Sudell's special friends were there, like Jack Bentley and Third Lanark's William Crerar. No expense was spared. There were entertainers, music hall artistes and serious singers. Harry Yorke, proprietor of the Gaiety Club, even came from London to sing a specially composed song in tribute. The evening made £50.

North End's fixtures picked up pace at Easter. Those dramatic January games with Renton were played faraway, with Preston people tantalisingly on the end of a fragile telegraph line. So North End brought them to Lancashire. However the crowd did not 'roll up' on Good Friday, largely because North End doubled the admission price to sixpence. North End won again and couldn't resist asking what amateurs Renton would do with their Easter tour bounty: £50 from Preston and £35 each from Bolton and Burnley. A Scotchman said he got 10s per match on tour.

An Easter tour was also an individual opportunity. Along with Willie Groves, Alex Higgins won the popular vote for a cap against England after a scintillating display for the Improbables against the Probables in the Scottish trial: winning 'golden opinions from all sides by his really clever and judicious centre play, and especially by his quick and deadly shooting'. Higgins did not win the selectors' vote but the 'rejected dribbler's' profile had increased significantly. The Kilmarnock forward accompanied Hibs on their Easter tour, and played against Bolton. Then 'they wouldna let me awa'.' He played for Wanderers next day against Third Lanark, and also promised himself to Halliwell.

Wanderers' humiliation in the Lancashire Cup final provided an opportunity for their local rivals. Halliwell thought they could do better than Wanderers' 0-3 against North End. In fact that's all they wanted to do, and that's why Wanderers and Halliwell wrestled over the services of a visiting Scotch 'amateur'. Halliwell's chance was improved by only half North End's 'cracks' being available (five were playing for Lancashire in

Belfast). But Alex Higgins did not turn up. Five thousand watched Halliwell's 'day of disaster': 'what a rope of sand is public form.' Their crowd affected disappointment: the 'public are not so keen' at visitors fielding less than their full strength, but they were compensated by seeing one of Jamie Ross's 'electrifiers' in North End's 7-1 win.

Edinburgh. On a very cold Thursday afternoon 7,000 of his 'brither' townsmen much admired Jack Ross as North End 'did not seem to care' to score more than 5-1 against his old club Hearts. The following Wednesday meant a trip to the seaside. North End went fishing, but the seas were high. Reassuringly, the coxswain of Fleetwood's lifeboat was at the helm, but half the players 'fed the fishes', and one of their entourage, a Preston pork butcher, threatened the crew with violence if they did not take him home. Back on firm land, the Invincibles With Sealegs (or not) had time for dinner before, at 6pm, beating Fleetwood Rangers 5-0. Their full team again.

North Enders were always missionaries: for example in Lincoln, exhorting adoption of their scientific football. For the team, their advice was 'work as an unbroken body'. For the individual: 'they should pass clear and sharp, seizing the opportunity directly it presents itself, for dalliance, in almost every case, simply means placing one's self in the hands of the enemy … Pass low, pass quickly, pass with judgment, and seldom try to dribble, for few men can cope with more than one man, and dribbling often means coping with many.'

Lincoln City were inspired to beat favourites Grimsby Town in the Lincolnshire Cup, which in turn had consequences that came back to bite North End. The 'gentry' supporting Grimsby had been full of 'loud braggadocio and general intemperance' beforehand, and afterwards, they 'went about crying Wolf! wolf! when there was no wolf'. This 'gentry' would not be humiliated again: they recruited a whole new Scotch team that gave North End a mauling in 1889 (see Chapters 10 and 12).

Saturday, April 30th 1887: a big match, fittingly for the last of the 'legitimate season'. At last Queen's Park fulfilled their much-delayed return fixture. Deepdale looked fine, a new set of flags flying high. A lady correspondent came with her husband Charlie, who explained that Queen's Park 'were once the greatest team in the world'. She heard a lot of grumbling about the sixpenny gate, and noticed, compared to her last visit (when Bolton were humbled 1-12 at Christmas), that the stands featured fewer 'big guns of the town'. Mrs Charlie cast her appreciative eye over the North Enders. There was Geordie Drummond, the 'funnyman with the nice moustache'; that 'lively youth' Jamie Ross; Davie Russell's 'very long legs'; and of course there was 'nice-looking' Sam Thomson, after whom Charlie had named their young son in hope he would become Preston's centre-forward. But their impact was nothing compared to North End's perfectionist captain. Thomson put Preston ahead, but then went off injured (he scored five goals in his comeback six months later, but it didn't count for much, as they won 26-0!) and the rest eased off. The crowd started to feel 'North End had not tried', and Jack Ross 'got riled ... and no wonder'. The captain told Drummond to get forward from half-back, and then tried 'hissel', but no use. Charlie's lady noticed how Ross took his feelings out on two 'very little fellows', whom she noticed doing some delightful 'dodging': 'once the big back of the North End, who never seemed to smile, came between them with great force and sent them flying. I did not like that, but Charlie said he was obliged to do it, and hadn't hurt them.'

That season Queen's Park made £2,852 and spent £2,827. More than North End, for all their non-stop travelling to earn their crusts. How, the home of the honest pro asked, had amateurs spent £3,000? The other big winner from 1887's big games was the English Association. They started the season with a balance of £597, and gained £940 that spring. The England v Scotland match at Blackburn made £381; the Cup final £402; and above all the North End v West Bromwich semi-final £479 (and was the most profitable – £314).

May 7th, 1887. North End against Aston Villa. 'The Champions and the Cupholders.' Another score to settle. Could the Invincibles vanquish the usurpers in a 'Grand Finale'. Strangely there was 'no immense concourse'. Villa, astonished at the thin crowd, reflected on too many showdowns: 'Deepdale imitated [the] device of the Home Rulers and went in for boycotting' because the charge was doubled to sixpence. North End gave them a 'taste of whip': 'seldom Aston Villa got over the half-way line.' Flagrantly partisan flag-waving prevented them conceding thirteen goals, at the cost of Villa's umpire (William McGregor) 'inviting the ridicule of the spectators'. North End won 11-1, and Villa's National Cup win suddenly appeared a 'huge leap of wonder'. Was it because Villa's Cup eleven had returned to work after the official season's ending, or had they found the temptation of 'grabbing' the 'loadstar of the flesh pots too much for them'? Now comeuppance: 'they will find the bitter end of reflection like a piece of American gum,' and be stuck with North End's 'bitter sarcasm for years to come'.

This was an epic deserving the iconic style of the Chronicles, plus an undertow of fear about what Preston had to do to attract a paying public. Story: North End had lost the National Cup to Albion, who in turn lost to Villa:

When the elders of the Palace of Deepdale heard of this
they marveled greatly, saying
'we must get the henchmen of the great city of Brum to visit us.'
And after much trouble and travail it was done …
But the men of the city of the Priests said unto each other,
'Why do our elders demand six pieces of copper.
It is not just, and we will not go.
And they did not go all, but about three thousand.

North End left for Edinburgh again Friday morning, to beat St Bernards 5-0 that evening, Jack Ross 'fairly astonishing his old schoolfellows with his clever play'. Next day, specials ran from Dumbarton as North End defeated the remaining Scotch champions Vale of Leven 2-1. Vale played tough: they 'not only went in for "bashing", but for using their hands'. A week later, in Birmingham, Aston Villa got quick revenge – 2-1.

Villa had gone back into training for this joint benefit of heroes Archie Hunter (who gained £73) and 'amateur' Howard Vaughton (£68). North End's passing in front of goal was 'extremely puzzling and wonderfully clever … what struck was the extraordinary amount of control the North End have over the ball. Every kick or bit of heading had an object'. Otherwise they were 'clumsy', typical of playing straight from a four-hour train journey. Injured Jack Ross reminisced to journalists about their last, tempestuous visit two years earlier: having 'simply romped round' Villa, they were 'tooled off', causing 'the fastest fly for life I ever remember' – as their four-wheeled coach 'spun around the corner on two wheels'. Now it was official. Comparing the two Villa matches, at the highest level, Ross was worth eleven goals!

One thing was clear – a Villa v North End decider, in January 1888, would be a 'big event', the match that did more than any other to provoke the League.

North End's penultimate game was at Anfield. The city of Liverpool was becoming football's 'El Dorado'. Everton and Bootle had joined the fringes of the elite. Summer football had a future there. An hour before kick-off the stand was packed to overflowing, 8,000 in the ground, plus overlooking vantage points outside. 'Meteoric' Everton felt ready to test themselves against the best. The betting was generous (George Fleming was 1,000 to one against scoring for Everton) but not only was North End's passing 'utterly bewildering', but Jack Ross led a 'supreme effort' on a 'too hot' day. 'North Enders put an astonishing amount of freshness and vigour into their play', and won 5-0.

A JOKE WITH THE LORD HIGH EXECUTIONER

North End had played 69, won 58, lost seven games – 'pre-season' to Third Lanark, ordinary club fixtures to Bolton (twice), Albion and Villa, Fergy Suter's benefit … and a semi-final. Their last game (the 70th) was on July 16th. Elsewhere football's establishment were doing all they could to assert a close season, free of football, from May to September. North End became a summer attraction at Blackpool. About this time the sea-side town's 7,000 dwellings supported nearly 250,000 visitors. Raikes Hall Palace Gardens had started in 1872 as Blackpool's answer to Morecambe's Summer Gardens, but being a little further from the sea needed desperate efforts to compete.

The Great Football Match between North End and Lancashire (Jack Bentley's selection) was advertised alongside The Toboggan Slide! Skating Rink; Great Whale's Jaws; Chinese Pagoda; A Switchback; Sea Lions; A Monkey House; Open Air Dancing; The Gold Room; William's Hobby Horse and of course The Burning of Moscow and Napoleon's Retreat. There was great interest: specials were run from Manchester, Burnley, Bolton, Blackburn and Preston. By kick-off at 6.30pm the football field was lined many deep, and a 7,000 crowd saw North End win 6-2: 'their exhibition of scientific football is almost perfect.' The venture was a great success. Afterwards, fireworks at 9.30.

The Invincibles continued to risk personal appearances: Ross junior and Sam Thomson ran across James Berry, Her Majesty's Lord High Executioner – they 'hoped he'd let 'em down gently if they ever made a closer acquaintance'.

Chapter Three

'Mangling done here'

August 1887 – March 1888

North End are the best football team the world has ever seen, let the world find another.

MISSIONARY WORK

On Wednesday, August 19th, 1887, North End reprised their 1886 Scottish tour. Competitive from the start, they won 16-2 but still complained that Strathmore's second goal was palpably offside as three forwards were on top of temporary goalkeeper Jim Trainer. Preston impressed Dundee: 'I understood they were rough, but I never saw them charge once; they just stop 'em, and take the ba'.' Next day they were rough and beat Arbroath 2-0. Arbroath would have the sixth best record during 1887-88, behind only Britain's very best – North End, Renton, Villa, Albion and Wolves. The pitch was a 'cinder path, with a few stone buildings promiscuously thrown in'. Arbroath 'floored them unmercifully', so Jack Gordon committed 'the most wretchedly base act of violence ever seen on a football field'. North End's retaliatory fracas brought the 3,000 spectators onto the field and afterwards a stone 'crashed through a double window' of their cab.

But hard though they fought it was too late. Invincibility was already lost – 1-2. Beaten first time out, on August 13th, before 6/7,000 – Easter Road's largest ever crowd. Scottish Cup-holders Hibernian had James Lundie at the back, Willie Groves forward, and half-back James McLaren, a future Scotland captain, scored the winner. North End were missing five first-teamers. Afterwards, Mr McDonald, Hibs' patron, 'a gentleman of immense stature, attired in kilts, inquired if they would allow him to stand a few bottles of "fizz". The visitors had no serious objection, the corks were soon flying about.'

'Free Critic', Lancashire's top football writer, told his readers 'I've been gangin' awa'' with North End and reassured their invincibility was intact because 'football has not started'. North End won their next 42 games and reached the 1888 Cup final, still undefeated. 'Free Critic' had an eye for detail. In Dundee they stayed at a teetotal football hotel, The Imperial, but never mind, directly underneath somebody had opened a bar. He was also politically *au fait* and knew that the Association had just abolished summer football to stymie those entrepreneurial efforts of

North End and Jack Bentley in Blackpool's pleasure gardens. The Association, which celebrated assets of £1,700 gained from pro football, disqualified from their Challenge Cup anyone who played between June 1st and August 31st. No one knew when this took effect.

On to Glasgow, where North End opened Rangers' fine new ground at Ibrox, which cost a daunting £12,000. William Sudell took pity on hard-up Rangers, foregoing half the gate proceedings, and accepting just their guarantee from a record Scottish crowd of 20,000. Ibrox was enclosed by a corrugated, galvanised iron fence, eight foot high, presenting an insurmountable barrier to freeloaders. The pavilion had a spacious verandah, and inside two apartments, two bathrooms – each fitted with 'Braby's improved spray baths' – and a row of wooden lockers. North End dressed at the Royal Hotel, and travelled in an omnibus. The handsome grandstand was 300 feet long, and held 1,200 persons in six rows. John Goodall scored five goals as, for the second time in 1887, North End beat Rangers 8-1.

North End came home to defeat Third Lanark 6-1. Fixtures with the Volunteers captured Preston's emerging dilemma. The Deepdale gate was £50 whereas the return, on Glasgow's Fast Day in October, was £250 (10,000 spread around much-improved Cathkin Park). The North End party got there quickly, 200 miles in two stops, but found Glasgow's Fast Day was a 'slow day and a very slow day too'. George Drummond quickened the pace – he enraged the stands by glorying in holding a bottle of whisky aloft. Lancashire reporters admitted Drummond took a little brandy to recover from a severe charge, then counterattacked: 'has the writer ever been down here with Scotch teams? If so, he will have seen not one bottle, but many bottles in use during a match.' 'Rambler assures me that in all his experience he never saw a football team [i.e. North End] take less.' Like 'Free Critic', 'The Rambler' had an authority that was vouchsafed.

North End's characters were becoming folk heroes. Their deputy umpire borrowed Sudell's massive gold-headed stick to wave and resisted three attempts to give him a flag, whilst combative winger 'General' Gordon was named after the archetypal Victorian imperial martyr of the recent Sudanese war.

Compared to 1886-87, the British dimension to big football was becoming marginalised. The Scots were now excluded from The Cup, a combination of the English Association seeking a tidier format and the Scottish Association resenting the offence to their jurisdiction. But North End's missionary instincts knew few bounds. When news came that Australian football had attracted a crowd of 35,000 there was talk that, like English cricketers, North End would play exhibition games down under.

Sudell received his gold-headed stick at Scarborough before North End's seventh game, starting the season, on Thursday September 1st. It was a brave act to open another new ground in competition with the Victorian Age's greatest sportsman, WG Grace, playing for MCC against Yorkshire next door. They received a civic welcome of 'enthusiasm and ceremony', and Sudell responded with North End's driving credo: 'their endeavour, their pride and their boast that they played the game scientifically.' As a true Victorian missionary, Sudell hoped that football would profit. Scarborough imported Arthur Wharton in goal, but Jack Ross played 'a strict game' – 6-1. Grace and other famous cricketers (many soon off to Australia) watched. Sadly the mission failed. A year later a journalist judged that Scarborough 'don't seem to know the game'.

With Wharton back on board, railway high jinks returned. North End pretended they were accompanied by an imaginary band and, waving their 'leader's baton' (Sudell's gold stick), convinced sceptical porters into wiring Wakefield station where a big drum was supposed to be lying, lost, on a platform.

Back in North End's goal, Wharton was accused of 'Whartonesque posturing and sensational acrobatics'. He was under pressure, pompously dismissing queries about his amateur athletic status as 'nothing more or less than unwarrantable liberties'. The 'ice-cool feller' was overdoing it. Wharton's 'nonchalant as if the game was a mile away' style was no longer admired: 'when he wasn't posing in stained glass attitude he was rushing twenty or thirty yards from goal.' North End's driven captain was not amused: 'Jack Ross never plays football but he plays to win … what does Ross think of Wharton as a goalkeeper?'

Wharton returned because of a growing goalkeeper problem. Billy Rose had played in the summer football show at Blackpool, but a few weeks later his wife died. Rose went walkabout. Work was not on his mind and, when rumours spread, Rose opened up his heart to the press. After his wife's death, 'whatever situation I might have held, whether as a football player or something more exalted, I most certainly should not have been able to follow it for a time.' Furthermore, Rose complained he had been short-changed on the original inducement that persuaded the four-times English international to turn pro. Rose wrote an 'extraordinary letter', moaning about North End to the Association.

Sudell retaliated: Rose was paid £2 a week in summer as well as the football season (Rose might have queried this distinction, playing in Blackpool on July 16th). When his wife died, Rose simply disappeared, but sent a letter written in lead pencil: 'Dear Sir, I shall not care to play football for a time. I think of going away somewhere until I get more settled, and will see you when I return, Yours obediently, WC Rose.'

North End added to Rose's public embarrassment by revealing an earlier begging-letter: 'I think you will see me clear of the difficulty … even if I have it deducted from my wage a little at a time.'

North End advanced Rose a 'considerable sum of money for a private reason' and, needless to say, it was not repaid. He turned up too late to sign his season's registration. They went their separate ways. When Rose petitioned to be reinstated as an amateur, the Association put him on three months probation. He would come again.

North End did not wait for long. Bolton were warned to 'have Trainer chained down or you will lose him'. But Wanderers were skint. Then the Association were slow to accept Preston's registration, so observers –

Ask … is North End gainer / By having captured Jim Trainer

Trainer would be ineligible for cup-ties for two years. From our world of League and Cup, it seems strange that the world's best goalkeeper could not play in any 'worthwhile' matches in 1887-88. Would they miss him? Not initially. In their first competitive game, they won 26-0.

The referee for this cricket score game was, appropriately, RG Barlow, batting hero of England's Test win at Sydney Cricket Ground in March 1887. Barlow had refereed an earlier ordinary match, when Sudell was generous. Opponents Derby arrived one short, but Sudell agreed that both sides play with ten men – 8-0. North End are 'billiards pure and simple', said County. Similarly the following week Sudell took pity on a sparse crowd watching North End take on Davy Weir's Halliwell. It was bitter, so cold that their two reserve teams played only twenty minutes each way in Bolton. Journalists could think of only one colder day in four years of top football in Preston. So cold that even Jack Ross led the players' resistance: 'a petition was signed and presented asking that the match be adjourned sine die.' Contrary to its name, Deepdale 'forms the summit of a hill, enjoying the full advantage of the breeze from all sides'. The problem for the pros was that nearby, 'two mill teams were already braving the storm.' The players wore three jerseys and long knickers. When Sudell invited the frozen crowd to 'enter the deserted stand, there was a laughable stampede of spectators standing in the cold rain'. Halliwell took their 1-10 'licking' as a matter of course: 'it was North End'.

THE ENGLISH CUP

During Liverpool's dominant years a century later, opponents were intimidated by the warning: 'This is Anfield.' In 1887 the message at

Deepdale was 'Mangling done here'. That was before winning 26-0. Sudell showed no mercy. Hyde had turned down their chance to scratch so that North End could arrange a more lucrative fixture. It was not amusing when Hyde proposed switching the cup-tie to their 'big crowd'.

North End aimed to give a lesson. There were 149 clubs in the Cup's first round arranged in geographical divisions to prevent a repeat of North End's travails in 1886-87. But that meant the best could play small fish indeed, unless they scratched. Hyde were not hopeless: they later beat Derby County 4-0 during a 'wonderfully successful season'. When they wouldn't scratch, Hyde knew what to expect: 'the Preston men are going to try to break the record' (they bet on it) but 'they wont get half'. However, North End's humble secretariat made the kick-off 2.30pm as they 'may have to play an extra half-hour, you know' in the event of a draw. Even early on there were 'very amusing episodes as the plucky Hyde lads tried in vain to get the ball'.

Only 2,000 were present but 'a loud burst of applause greeted the twentieth goal', plus Sudell's beautiful smile. He had been generous after all, allowing his opponents a second-half substitute. Hyde's reporter growled 'they need not put it on quite so thick'. Apart from retreating behind his post for North End's record 25th goal, goalie Bunyan (who later played for Derby in the League) played as true as a puritan, and the jokes were on the theme of *Pilgrim's Progress*, written by another Bunyan, one of the most popular books of late Victorian society.

There were also jokes in Liverpool. That very morning two Scotch amateurs left Bootle in the lurch and joined Everton (who had trailed their Cup eleven as a 'profound secret'). They were 1887 Scottish international half-back John Weir, 'a veritable Tom Thumb', and his friend Izatt. So the excruciating puns went something like: 'Iz-zatt true Bootle lost two players? Weir are they?' Weir had initially impressed by chivalrously doffing his cap whenever his play was applauded: 'he's a fine fellow.' However, Weir had now distastefully passed his cap around all three Liverpool teams (Stanley, Bootle and Everton) in just two months. Izatt was plain 'intractable', and only accepted as 'inseparable' from Weir. Everton and Bootle were in 'open feud': when they meet, 'Dar'll be razors flying in de air.'

Scratching was not a joke, rather a trade-off between finance and reputation. Bootle had recently scratched to North End in the Lancashire Cup, then lost a club fixture 2-6. Too many of Bootle's first-teamers (like Weir and Izatt) were ineligible to field a cup side doing justice to their status pretensions. Similarly Notts' English Cup opponents, Basford Rovers, 'have either been persuaded or paid to scratch.' County had previously beaten them 13-0, so, by scratching, Basford 'saved what little reputation they have got and pocketed a little '"ooftish".'

The scratching freed Notts to appease their disgruntled membership by challenging North End. Once a top club, County had declined during Preston's rise. But their members momentarily 'ceased growling'. The negotiations said a lot about pre-League fixture-making. Under the prevailing etiquette, it was Notts' turn to play at Deepdale but no return was likely until the spring when there would be no good gate. County's 'elastic-minded committee' solved the problem by offering North End half a Trent Bridge gate, rather than a lower, fixed guarantee.

Nottingham lacked a 'gentlemanly spirit' towards 'Sudell's death dealers' (since their 26-0 win). North End's 'machine-like precision' drew no crowd applause, which was 'right to expect and obtain justice from Britishers'. North End continued the lesson, using full-backs and half-backs 'as a sort of connecting link'. But they missed injured Jack Ross, and it was the nearest they came to interrupting a seven-month winning run. Notts led 'with fifteen minutes to go but they were done, whilst North End were fresh as daisies'. One impartial Lady Spectator responded viscerally to the 'unchivalrous' atmosphere: 'Oh, I am glad Preston have won. I never came across such a prejudiced lot in my life.' Since early 1885 Preston had won all seven fixtures with an average score of 5-1.

In fact, cup fixture chaos enabled a Deepdale return in December. There, Notts' aim was only to better Nottingham Forest. When they merely equalled Forest's 2-5 defeat, Edwin 'Nun' Browne, County's frustrated secretary, conducted a press argument with Sudell alleging that Notts had 'really' won 4-3. Sudell threatened not to play them again, but the respective gates were £120 at Trent Bridge and only £60 at Deepdale.

North End were improvising fixtures because their season entered quietus, awaiting their second round Cup opponents. In the end, extraordinarily, they would amass fifteen goals against serious Lancashire opponents, both Everton and Bolton – only eleven short of the 26-0 record. But first they had to wait. In a welter of partisan crowds, controversies, feinted and actual protests, exclusions, emergency rulings and dictats from the Association, Everton and Bolton played four close matches spread over six Saturdays during October and November (see Chapter 4).

If anything set the conditions for the League this tie did. Their neighbours and local rivals, Bootle and Halliwell, fumed. For William McGregor's Aston Villa and North End, 'Cup ties are a nuisance'. Their fixtures disrupted, all lost money. And why the effort? Everyone knew the survivors faced certain exclusion from the Cup, in fact a mangling from 'the North End bloodhound crouching in the path, its fangs double sharpened, its tongue lolling out, its cruel eyes bloodshot and bleary, its breath coming in short, thick gusts, crouching impatiently, with an occasional low growl, for the inevitable prey'.

However for weeks North End lacked their sharpest fang. Jack Ross was one of nine Prestonians in two elevens representing Lancashire on October 22nd. One opened Villa's new £360 pavilion, and beat Birmingham 3-2. Ross's other Lancashire team was beaten 1-4 by a Dumbartonshire eleven full of later League stars. Future Everton legend Alex Latta found Ross 'a rather fearsome fellow ... it was both you and the ball – if he could take the two'. But once Ross dislocated a wrist, Latta was freed to be 'a beggar to shoot on the run ... I loved to get a goal. It was the salve of many a wound'. In Birmingham, Lancashire's secretary Gregson thought the telegram reporting the defeat was kidding: 'Send correct result. Don't like chaff.'

Ross returned for an ordinary fixture, North End v Albion, the first since that 'ever to be remembered Semi-Final' eight months earlier. The crowd was one of Preston's 'old sort', maybe 10,000, making a gate of £108. The football was 'almost perfect'. Albion's teenager Bassett got through until Ross 'unceremoniously grassed him on the touchline'. North End led 3-0, but injured back Bob Howarth spent the second half standing by his goalkeeper. That left Ross on his own, roaming 'from one side to another ... Never had a finer specimen of back play been seen at Deepdale, or anywhere else'. Albion goalkeeper Bob Roberts said he would back North End against England, Scotland, Wales and Ireland for a thousand pounds. The devil had come snarling back.

At last their Cup opponents emerged, and still the wild beast motif prevailed. The Fixtures Net had trapped the North End Lion, prevented from 'roaring about, preying at will'. Would it be Everton the 'cheeky, bad, bold mouse'; or Bolton, 'Mine Old Enemy the decrepit wandering Rat whom I vowed to chew up?' Mouse it was. North End 'never gave them a chance'. Everton's forwards, confusingly, were 'all up a gumtree'. Their defenders were distinctly un-mouselike – Alec Dick's 'unmanly proclivities' amounted to attempted manslaughter: 'let Everton purge herself of the sore spot.' They knew they were walking a tightrope with their tough Scotch back: 'Dick will certainly get into trouble sooner or later ... thousand pities for he is a brilliant player when going square.' Everton's response was that of many teams accused of intimidating North End: 'it's enough to make a horse laugh.' Preston could be manly enough, especially when Drummond was urged to 'rouse up and do your work properly or be supplanted'. Four goals in 25 minutes, 6-0 altogether. Moral: never tease a lion when he's chained up.

North End always got serious as the Cup-ties became imminent. The previous Monday, they had an ordinary fixture scheduled at Burnley, but they preferred not to play. So they sent a telegram on the morning of the match: 'Match must be postponed as ground is not fit to play on, Nuttall.' Burnley's secretary-goalkeeper Jim McConnell replied: 'Thawing air; have just been on ground and find it in splendid condition and certainly shall expect your team for this afternoon.' Unfazed and knowing they had the upper hand, North End stated definitively at 12.45: 'Committee will not risk our men on present state of ground.' It caused bitter disappointment for the hundreds who left work early. 'The Rambler', as usual 'in the know', tried to tell 'thousands' alighting at Bank Top Station that the game was off. He was told 'go to hell'.

Halliwell were next. They had sneaked through the previous round at Liverpool Stanley, for whom Archie Goodall, usually North End's utility player, moonlighted under the name Brown. Davy Weir was not fooled – he had toured Scotland with Goodall for North End. Weir lodged a protest, then changed a losing team around, scored a hat-trick and won 5-1: 'Weir was first, the rest nowhere.' Halliwell supporters pondered recent lessons, and advised that to avoid 'a sound thrashing against the North End they must persistently take the man and prevent them settling on the ball.' Preston won 4-0.

Then chaos. Amazingly the Association completed a confusing series of enquiries by retrospectively disqualifying Everton and reinstating Bolton, then took up North End's 'courtesy' offer to replay the second round (with a bye, North End were now through to the fifth round). Truly, the Challenge Cup competition was causing football's troubles.

Wanderers were now truly decrepit rats: they would have scratched but for appearances' sake. Both teams wore white, so North End retired to find other togs, returning in many colours with a 'washed out' look. Bolton waved the 'white feather'. In the Deepdale stand, a Prestonian wagered: 'I'll bet the Wanderers are licked by five goals.' Brave Boltonians took him on at five shillings each. Into the second half, with the score only 3-1, the ante was upped: 'I'll bet North End win by seven.' No takers this time, because by then Preston had begun 'to show the game – the passing game – which bodes no good for opponents.' The headline read: 'Slaughter of the Wanderers' – 1-9. Still Bolton's worst ever competitive loss. Really, that 1-12 defeat in an ordinary fixture at Christmas 1886 was more competitive. Everyone knew this Cup match was a joke. What round was it if Wanderers won? Would they go back (or forward) and play Halliwell? There was an even greater joke: they might go further back and offer Hyde (beaten 0-26) a replay – as a courtesy.

Preston had now scored 45 goals in three rounds. With five against Bolton, Jamie Ross was demonstrating 'as near infallibility in the direction of his shots as we shall ever attain in football'. He was modest: 'them shots of mine will come off one day.'

At first Christmas meant fun with the amateurs. The Corinthians brought seven internationals who helped clear the snow off the pitch, before finding some handy to bring round Jamie Ross when he 'spread himself comfortably on the ground in a swoon'. Association secretary Alcock thought North End were at their most scientific, whilst the Corinthians' too-frequent claims of offside were mocked by the 'behind-goals' spectators: one amateur was 'so wrathful that he made a very ungentlemanly gesticulation'. On Christmas Eve Queen's Park came bearing reconciliation: a 'very strong team represented this once powerful club'. North End won 7-2, after which Queen's Park's President magnanimously addressed a Deepdale stand 'full of nobs' (for this class of opposition). In contrast to those riotous games in Glasgow a year before, this time there was only one foul, for hands. He attributed earlier misunderstandings to their not knowing each other: now that had changed.

Then things got very serious. North End were drawn against the holders. Barely a week ahead. Villa were stronger, a raid on Albion being recorded in a celebrated telegram: 'Have got Tom Green, going for Bob Roberts.' 'Offside Tommy' Green struggled to stay onside with his colleagues, being 'unmistakably eccentric in his habits'. For example, earlier Villa had played Shankhouse. Unlike the wholesale Scotch importations practised by the top North Eastern clubs, Shankhouse Black Watch represented the English way forward, a talented team of real miners. Villa's veteran captain Archie Hunter bet Green ten shillings that they would win by ten goals. They would have, except Green, 'having the goal at his mercy, when nine had been scored, deliberately kicked the ball in another direction.'

Returning from post-Christmas Black Country wins (Walsall 8-0 and Wolves 3-1), North End held a war council on Thursday evening at Shelley's Arms over the featured dish, hotpot *à la* Sudell. When the Association refused to give them more time to qualify a new goalkeeper, they decided their reserve team would fulfil the New Year fixtures with the touring Scots. Cowlairs (who included three sometime Scottish internationals in William McLeod, John McPherson and Tom McInnes) thought playing North End reserve beneath them, but they were reassured that their substantial guarantees were unaffected. The reserve drew 2-2 with Cowlairs and beat Hearts, with another three Scottish internationals, 4-1. North End had to eat the lost gate money.

Villa went further. Cancelling their Christmas tour smacked of panic, fearing to encourage players' 'over indulgence' – they 'are as safe in Scotland as in Birmingham'. Villa hired trainer Gorman and retired to Holte Fleet by the Severn. Archie Hunter thought they got the balance wrong: too much running, 'too little practice with the ball.' On return, they were 'handed over to ... the medical official of health in whose care they remained'.

Preston's call went out for Concannon, the famous Widnes long distance trainer. 'Preston has so far not trained an inch:' now it was 'cold water treatment, shooting seagulls, and playing football'. The only question was who would keep goal. It was sourly noted that Trainer was having more holidays than work. No call for Arthur Wharton; Billy Rose 'could not be found'; Mills-Roberts ineligible. That left 'five foot nothing' Addison. Concannon could not save him from Villa's tough forwards.

Where had North End gone? 'The Grumbler', investigative reporter, went in search. At Southport Hydropathic Hospital he enquired of a man on crutches. No, he said, no North End, only five invalids. Next the Palace Hotel, Birkdale, whose advert read 'all the hygiene of the hydropatheries with the comforts of the hoteleries'. 'The Grumbler' asked an ''aughty menial', that is hall porter, who replied, 'Yes, sir, they're here, having the Turkish bath, I think, just now; but I'll see.' As the boys were out for a stroll, 'Grumbler' rambled around upstairs, where their 'apartment is the essence of comfort'. There was the detritus of serious training: 'senna leaves', 'Epsom salts' and Jack Concannon's 'Turkish towel on a chair'. North End's return was impressive: they 'present quite a formidable appearance, armed to the teeth with double-barrelled guns, with which they toy as to the manner born, occasionally taking aim at a harmless "brid", then follows the "flash, bang" and down drops the feathered victim.' With something thus secured for the pot, 'Grumbler' got an invite: 'Sit down and have a bite after the bath.' Jack Ross took the longer view and tipped him to 'have a bit on us'.

Meanwhile 'feeling runs high in Birmingham'. Fred Dawson, who a year earlier had gone into an Edinburgh crowd and attacked an innocent reporter, was 'told often and long to keep cool and steady'. Or would North End create a 'disturbance ... as once before' (causing a two-year break in fixtures).

But the crowd caused the trouble. With 20,000 expected, Villa members lost their reserved seats. When these were put on sale for an 'unheard of' ten shillings, £1 was promptly offered. This Cup-tie was more than the match of the season: in paving the way for the League it was a match for all time.

Newsboys called out one outcome: 'Riot of Perry Barr. Military Called Out.' But it wasn't all heavy: there was the (near) streaker, a lady who scampered across the pitch towards Perry Barr's fine new pavilion. She did 80 yards 'in evens', 'thirsting to be among the classes,' and giving spectators the opportunity to 'see more of her red stockings than we had paid for'. She found the lowest level of the pavilion (where 600 nobs sat) six foot about the ground. The plebs stayed in front. When the sixpenny gate was divvied up the crowd was 25,827. William McGregor later thought 'there were quite 35,000 in the ground' [McGregor, 1905, p.38]. Take away the mere £73 expenses (hence the eventual match ruling that Villa did not take sufficient precautions carried some validity) and North End's share was £365. With stand income (and 75 people in personal carriages) thrown in, Villa made an astronomical £740. Hindsight said it should have been a shilling gate. Maybe next time. Villa wanted that next time to come real soon. North End were less keen. It would not come for over a year. To end the inaugural League season.

Correspondent 'Free Critic' would become a League pioneer. In 'spring-like warmth', he travelled with Association high-ups amongst a continual stream of 'busses, hansoms, four-wheelers'. The legend written above the Wellington Road enclosure warned 'Abandon hope all ye that enter here'. And once in the ground it was every man for himself: 'the magic word "Press" had no effect.' The chaos had a different effect on the team bosses. Maestro Sudell sat impassively, pointedly next to Dr Mills-Roberts (i.e. his goalkeeper for the *next* round). Birmingham folk wondered whether their local hospital's House Surgeon should be quite so pally with the opposition – Mills-Roberts 'is being made too much of a fuss of, and old and tried friends should not be forgotten in the dazzle of the new and shining star which has arisen amongst us'.

Villa's Ramsay and McGregor, responsible for the outcome, were sprinting about distractedly. They had reason for discomfort. Few could see anything, 'a solid phalanx … unable to move any part of the anatomy except his head,' so overflow and delay. Referee Betts withdrew in favour of tough umpire Charles Clegg. Kick-off. Another stoppage. Restart. When Hunter scored, 'the familiar Black Country pigeons begin their flights, bearing the glad tidings to many a frowsey public house parlour.'

Villa's mood brightened towards hacks like 'Free Critic': 'Mr McGregor smiles and wants to know what he can do for us.' 'Rob Roy' McGregor was a public relations man: the 'reporters' guide, philosopher and friend.' The crowd broke in again. Ten minutes. Ramsay knew the game was up. He summoned mounted police but none were near. Sudell told Jack Ross to protest and the referee declared an 'ordinary' game. The crowd did not know of course. 'Free Critic' saw the military intervention for what it was: two Hussars who had been spectators hopped on a couple of cab horses and trotted up and down the touchline. The game was still tough. North End had caused a surprise with the one selection decision they ever seemed to make: who would be in goal. Not Addison, he had, in that special way of Preston goalkeepers, disappeared 'under the Rose'. North End chose instead Scotch reserve half-back James Ferguson, on the basis of one outing a few days earlier. He hardly needed to touch the ball. North End's 'Safety Valve' Graham proved a 'burly bounder'. Villa knew the danger man was Jamie Ross. 'Don't let him shoot,' called out Archie Hunter, so 'Dawson clean knocked out two of Jimmy Ross' front teeth, which have been replaced by two excellent replacements'. Brother Jack played with his usual affliction: an 'immense boil on the side of his head'. Jamie Ross scored and North End dominated – 3-1.

Excuses. Villa knew the game was a friendly … the Association would order a replay. Hadn't everyone agreed it was not a Cup-tie? North End had none of it. Protest was forgotten. The niceties were remembered: their protest was invalid because they had not made a deposit. Without a protest what could the Association do? The Villa were left without legs to stand on. This time Sudell was not helping. When the Association had got into their little bother deciding the Bolton-Everton dispute after both had been knocked out, Preston offered to play the survivors, 'as a courtesy' (and a written protest, plus deposit, just in case). But lately the Association refused to delay this Cup-tie. So Sudell told 'Free Critic' they would not replay: 'we came here to play the Villa, and we beat them.'

It needed a controversial Association meeting to find a way forward. Decision would be too strong a word. Even then, it needed the casting vote of President Marindin, regarded as friend to neither Villa nor North End. Its only clear effect was to settle bets. Otherwise the Council confirmed that the referee could change a match status from cup-tie to friendly. But could the Association change it back? If not, how did North End win? The best the Association could do was to accept that a match had been played between the right teams, on the right day and place. Preston proved 'diplomatists of the highest order. If we lose, we protest; if we win, we forget all about the protest'.

Protests dominated the 1887-88 Cup competition. Birmingham felt cheated (and suspected 'betting considerations' decided some Association votes). Villa were not disqualified, they had lost but it wasn't really the match it was supposed to be. On the precedence of earlier protests a replay was expected, but every protest was different. Villa's failure was to control even an unprecedented crowd. Sudell's refusal to replay cut the ground from beneath Villa. North End needed no 'paltry bauble' to convince anyone, from John O'Groats to Lands End, who was the 'champion combination'. No doubt true, but was it bluff? If the Association had ordered a replay, at a shilling a go, North End could have made £600. The strategy matched Imperial Germany's within Europe: 'Sudell has outgeneraled Mr McGregor who has hitherto supposed to be a diplomatist to whom Bismarck himself is but an infant in arms.' More, 'Sudell is the Napoleon of the Association football world.'

In Birmingham, the Staffordshire police superintendent became the scapegoat. He had had 50 constables available, surely enough for any crowd. Quick as a flash, Preston commented they had only been charged for 40 constables. They had no cause for complaint. The match made £1,100, and North End's share had been more than enough to pay for their palatial training. The English could not help comparing the gate with the big Scotch cup-tie, Queen's Park v Renton: 8,000 made £95.

There was no sensational quarter-final. The favourites were kept apart: North End at evens and Rovers and Albion at 3-1. Still the old Preston-Blackburn rivalry revived. They had not met all season, but two successive Saturday fixtures offered the promise of a Cup final to come. In the first, ordinary club game, both had their international goalkeepers. Rovers had England's 'King' Arthur, while 'Pansy Bottom' Trainer, in a rare outing, wore his Lancashire cap. Rovers lacked any 'fever heated vim' until a late fight-back. They only lost 3-4.

Encouraged, Blackburn looked forward to hosting the Lancashire Cup quarter-final. Trainer was ineligible, and Rovers would have Bill Townley. Townley would score the first English Cup final hat-trick in 1890, and he was already controversial in 1888. Townley's reputation was having 'side', being a 'gallery' player – his teammate Edgar Chadwick gave him 'a lesson in parting with the ball the instant he is called upon or sees an opening'. But whilst 'tainted with selfishness', Townley was now England's reserve forward. He was 'all bone and no flesh', speedy, marvellously clever, and 'promises to be the best the Rovers have ever had, and that's saying a good deal'. Townley destroyed neighbours Darwen in successive matches. It was like old times between serious East Lancashire rivals – in one historical battle, the relative of a Rover had wagered, and lost, a whole street of houses when Darwen beat them. However Darwen were well primed to protest their English Cup defeat, so Townley had to defend himself at the Association in Holborn. He was in double jeopardy. Townley was an amateur, yet Darwen had the man who paid him for playing with Blackburn Olympic, *and* in the summer. Somehow, the influential Association Councillor (and recent Blackburn chief) Dr Morley got him off. It was a close-run thing, but Townley could make a difference. Jack Ross would welcome him back.

There was a massive 12,000 for the Lancashire Cup-tie, which made £284 – Rovers' fourth largest ever gate. The bookies thought North End were playing the same trick as the previous year, when they barely turned up against Bolton one week, only to win 3-0 when it mattered. So it was 5-to-1 on North End winning the match, 2-to-1 on by a two-goal margin and an evens bet on a three-goal win. The match inspired poetry:

Spectators came one thousand strong,
And lined the ropes, an anxious throng,
Tramped through mud and mist and rain,
Trammed by tram and trained by train,
Sat on seat, or stood on stand,
Or shivered in the sodden sand ...

Famously Sudell would suffer a match of 'continuous insults in cowardly fashion'. It started when he sat in the stand, and felt the hand of the law. PC 101 enters the poem:

When a hand sacrilegious on Sudell he laid
And wanted to know for his seat had he paid;
And then, since no red ticket to show,
The officer threatened him outside to throw,
I'm the great Agamemnon his breath away took,
With a 'Sir-do-you-know-who-I-am?' sort of look.

Rovers committeeman Jesse Birtwistle also heckled Sudell, declaiming loudly that North End's wage bill was £30 a week whilst Blackburn paid a mere £8. The Rovers had King Arthur in goal; Preston had a novice. Rovers had 'Townley, from Holborn returned,' whilst Preston lacked Dewhurst, out 'with a bad leg – or two'. Rovers made the first impact:

... Townley quick
Advanced across the heavy plain
And centred neatly, but in vain,
For Ross was there, and punted far,
Beyond the hedge and o'er the bar.
But the corner, neatly placed, came to nought, as corners will ...

And Townley shot – and instantly lay stretched upon the plain,
For Ross, too late to kick the ball, fell foul upon the lad.
(That Preston's famous veteran back should be so rough is sad!)

Ross's late tackle on Townley was the defining moment. Referee Jack Bentley missed the afters. So did reporter 'Free Critic'. But Rovers' crowd saw, and insulted Sudell with venom. Bentley's whistle became 'a shrill warble like an arthritic linnet'. When Preston led 3-1 keeper Ferguson had yet to handle, but then Rovers equalised. Jack Ross had the last word:

... the Demon is a demon, and Goodall is a whale ...
To send it through past Arthur; – which concludes my humble tale.

Rovers railed at North End's savagery: Preston were disgusted at Blackburn 'howling like savages throughout'. It reawakened old hurts. Didn't Rovers win the Cup pretending its players were amateurs (the legendary Scots Suter and McIntyre), when other Lancashire clubs, led by Sudell, challenged the Association to accept honest professionalism? Very personally, didn't Rovers write the letter that got North End disqualified from the Cup in 1885-86?

These squabbles would return to threaten the League before it began, but their rivalry now ended in anti-climax. The following week Townley gave Rovers the lead, but little Derby Junction Street won their English Cup quarter-final 2-1: 'let Blackburn be stranded in shadow to-night.' 'Horror-stricken supporters' were left with the horrible feeling of 'lamentation'. Dr Morley – renowned for lambasting 'lying, deceitful and scheming semi-amateurs' – protested. Junction's members, encouraged by their unprecedented progress, had subscribed to send their hitherto-amateur team on a week's training. That made them professionals, said the doctor with the inside track on Association decisions. But the Juncs second-guessed them. On the Association's advice, they registered the whole team as pros. The protest failed. Blackburn was 'a place of such black desolation', and when they lost 0-7 the following week, 9,000 Prestonians enjoyed reminding Rovers of their junking. Rovers remained real gluttons for punishment: Halliwell went to Deepdale with 'W K Amateur' on the left wing. Bill Townley. Well Known Amateur?

PLAGUE

North End's quarter-final was in another football city that Preston had eclipsed. Sheffield had done nothing since they lost the 1881 semi-final replay. Wednesday aimed to show 'there was life in the old dog yet'.

They improved their new ground at Olive Grove, and had a Cup run: 'it is not impossible the old Association capital will win over again the glory of its former days.' Although they had lost to the future League clubs Albion, Villa (1-6), Burnley (0-6) and Accrington, Wednesday had won fifteen of 23 games: a record Sheffield thought showed 'indisputably that Wednesday may take first rank in football'. They had been Cup underdogs at Nottingham. When their occasional Scotch player William McLeod offered to come down for the Cup-tie, Forest wired back: 'shall not require you till the next round.' England's amateur centre Tinsley Lindley quickly put Forest ahead before an 8,000 crowd but Wednesday overhauled ten-men Forest to win 4-2.

Preston had yet another obstacle to win the Cup: 'contagion they defied.' 'Sheffield is not very tempting just now. Too much smallpox.'

This fear postponed the tie from Saturday until Monday, and even on Sunday North End were trying to get the Association to transfer the game to Preston. Sheffield countered, unconvincingly, with death rates. The average of 28 large English towns was 23.3 per 1,000 people: the worst was Manchester at 35 and Preston was 25, Sheffield a little higher at 25.3. Editors found that reporters, or their families, were not reassured, and offered feeble excuses. 'The Rambler' was used to going away: he travelled a thousand miles a month. Now, in an 'unguarded moment' he told Mrs Rambler he intended to go to Sheffield. 'She swooned: "What, you wretch, and kill me and this dear little cherub with small-pox!" and rushed for assistance. At the present moment I am strapped down in bed, with my wife's brother standing over me with a rolling pin.'

He went, of course, prudently risking the 'small 'uns' in the company of Preston's Cup goalkeeper, Dr Mills-Roberts. The good doctor might have been wiser to reassure his new teammates, ensconced in railway sidings with their saloon carriage, 'sending out odours of camphor.' Afterwards mockers claimed a small fortune in camphor was wasted, but at the time it was 'solemnly divided' as North End 'anointed themselves' with care: being 'rubbed well into those parts most likely to come into contact with the Sheffield players'. Some went further: James Ferguson had a 'charm sewn up inside his waistcoat'.

Eventually they braved the 'bills on the walls' proclaiming small-pox, and reached the Royal Hotel. There Concannon 'drew the line at pudding and insisted on nothing more than a plain lunch'. The unnerved Lancastrians expected only a small crowd in the circumstances, but for Sheffield the match was a 'historic sight'. 'It was very cold. There was no doubt about it,' but the ground was full – nine or ten thousand – half an hour before the start. There was a biting wind and a blinding snowstorm.

The 'croakers were busy' in Sheffield – the grandstand was not safe, the ground was not large enough, Preston would not turn up. It was cold enough 'to freeze the most brilliant spark of sportsmanlike ardour'. Snow poured down and a young man up a telegraph pole came down to retrieve his cap, and then shinned up again. Wednesday's Committee, conscious of how Villa forfeited their tie, distributed a 'printed entreaty' to the crowd against encroachment.

When the North Enders arrived, big men still wearing their 'topcoats' and handsome Lancashire caps, even Wednesday's keenest supporters were discouraged. 'Oh! I suppose it is only a case of the number of goals.' This was no drawback for some. One Sheffield visitor found Preston so confident that he laid £3 to £6 that North End would not win by four goals. North End kicked off uphill on a sloping surface with a thin covering of snow. This proved something of a leveller. Wednesday's initial threat was offered by veteran Billy Mosforth, England international since 1877: 'same old walk and I daresay the same old boots.' Home hopes – 'Billy's with him' – were promptly dashed – 'he's with Billie'. Thomson's two goals and 'a beauty' from Jamie Ross put North End 3-0 ahead. Wednesday's supporters kept going, and their players were 'frantically entreated by the love they bore them to mow down the Preston men like wheat before the sickle'. A sole brave Prestonian responded: 'play up, smallpox.' Billy Ingram pulled one back, and the 'spectators were a surging mass of throbbing humanity almost mad with excitement'. 'The Rambler' got on his bike to create a new record. The match was over at 4.10pm: a ride of a mile and a half, and a telegram conveyed the result to Lancashire at 4.25, and was on sale 4.35pm.

Preston relaxed on the way home. They always took their shoemaker on Cup journeys and he suffered the same fate as the gullible Bob Howarth: the two were 'unwittingly left' at Guide Bridge station, near Dukinfield on the eastern outskirts of Manchester, a long way from Preston. It brightened up an otherwise tedious five hours trip.

Preston had survived their close brush with the reaper and Rovers had lost – 'Rejoice that their pathway is clear'. But wait … 'Sudell does see the grim phanthom appear'. Was that a dread Throstle ahead?

'All honour to the railwaymen of Derby and Crewe,' but neither surprising semi-finalist got a sniff when the League's Twelve Apostles were selected a few weeks later. Anfield as a venue represented rehabilitation for disgraced Everton after their month's suspension. 'One of the most unpromising pieces of land imaginable' had been transformed into something impressive, 'tier upon tier twenty deep' in a vast stand. Everton's 'King John' Houlding, 'Lord High Everything,' hosted football authorities, the Mayor of Bootle, pretty well anyone who was anyone except the President of the Liverpool Association – presumably because his casting vote kicked Everton out of the Liverpool Cup as a consequence of their national punishment. The gate was good, £340 from less than 10,000.

But the pitch, so 'muddy and treacherous', made it enough of a farce for Crewe to protest their 0-5 defeat. They were bought off with the promise of an ordinary club fixture. Preston kept their word, playing on the Saturday before the final. And at last North End's 42-game winning run came to an end. This one draw reduced North End's status to 'well nigh invincible'. Their Cup goal-difference was now 56-3.

Despite the imminent Cup final, Preston's season continued at pace. Five games in eight days, starting with a 6-1 win in the Lancashire Cup semi-final. Monday was snowy Sheffield for Billy Mosforth's benefit, with England's Tinsley Lindley and Arthur Wharton augmenting Wednesday. Mosforth scored, and it was still 1-1 until North End's 'exceedingly fine' passing, 'like a piece of machinery,' created seven goals in the last 30 minutes. 'Wharton came in for some booing' as his 'ineffective' goalkeeping took the blame. Lindley faced North End again on Thursday for a Cambridge University Past and Present team, and five England internationals lost 0-5. Then back to face a Bolton Wanderers rehabilitating under restored secretary Jack Bentley. North End were ready – 5-1.

Preston's last Saturday win had been a long-awaited fixture with undisciplined Burnley. Burnley failed football etiquette tests thrice over. First they sent no wagonette to collect North End from the railway station. Second, the Burnley Reserve was a no-show so that, rather than return the admission charge, Preston Reserve played a team of spectators (this soon after North End had played a benefit for a disabled Burnley player). Finally, although this was commonplace, the Turf Moor spectators abused Sudell as umpire. One of Burnley's Scotchmen also tried it on, appealing to the touchline for surgical assistance with a dislocated neck one moment and then racing back into the fray. All the 'big guns' of the district turned up, and a 6,000 crowd produced a healthy £94 gate.

Otherwise North End were in 'final' training at the Grapes Hotel, Southport, with a daily regime tramping around Formby Lighthouse. They left for London Friday afternoon, March 23rd, their party including 27-year-old Bolton secretary-Association Committeeman-professional referee Jack Bentley. He was always a busy man. Could he persuade William Sudell to attend the League's inaugural meeting that evening? The next morning Bentley watched Albion arrive, and afterwards produced the definitive account of a shock result. He had a way with words, writing as 'Free Critic' and 'The Rambler'. Jack the Rambler.

Chapter Four

The Other Eleven

ASTON VILLA

Everyone knows Villa's William McGregor founded the Football League [McGregor, 1906, pp.170-74; Williams, 1994, pp.102-06]. He had the thought bubble and wrote the invite. Or maybe.

Later the spin took over. He created something as 'near perfection as any competition can be'. He lifted the game from its 'precarious position in the [18]eighties' when friendly matches were failing to attract the public and attendances were rapidly dwindling. He was the champion of the onlooker, a 'great believer in the doctrine that football is a game to be watched as well as played'. He was clairvoyant: no one 'scanned the horizon with more clearness of vision … no man ever looked further into the future'.

The creation myth began one winter's evening when two small Birmingham businessmen discussed the football business. They knew the importance of predictable cash-flow and product consistency, and its unpredictability in sport. William McGregor, draper, and Joe Tillotson, coffee shop owner. Despite five-shilling season tickets supplying 37 fixtures, customers complained that too many were one-sided or disrupted by cup-tie postponements. The public needed a 'fixity of fixtures', reliably punctual matches between first-class sides. Villa player Charlie Johnstone remembered the response of his father, Vice-President Fergus Johnstone, to McGregor's idea: 'Mac, you've got it; you've hit the nail on the head. Work it out man; work it out. It will be a grand success.'

McGregor's actions hardly did justice to this encouragement or to later visionary claims. On Friday, March 2nd, 1888, he wrote to four other clubs proposing a system of mutual fixtures, and suggested a friendly meeting to take it forward. As one insider said: 'That is all.' Four is not many and it was not worked out. Mutual fixtures, home and away, were already part of football club etiquette. Failure to honour return obligations was frowned upon. And it already made sense for leading clubs to play each other because they were generally attractive fixtures. Interestingly, McGregor chose Bolton and Blackburn, neither reliable for sending strong teams.

McGregor wrote from a position of growing weakness. Villa had one more day as Midlands champions. Albion had murdered Villa in an ordinary fixture on February 25th, and would surely dethrone them as

Birmingham Cup-holders on March 3rd. Both matches provided opportunities to engage Albion to the League. But McGregor's need was urgent and selfish. At stake was more than local bragging rights. Weeks earlier Villa had been national champions. Then North End knocked them out of the Cup, outflanked them politically at the Association and openly coveted Denny Hodgetts, 1888's top English forward. Aston Villa's other great star, Archie Hunter, 28, was now 'old and slow'. Were Villa sliding out of first rank? Their raids for local players became increasingly panicky. Throstles threatened to dump 'Kenrick's famous soot bags' over Villa secretary George Ramsay when he 'hovered about Kenrick's Foundry' before swooping on Albion's captain Bayliss; Unity Gas aimed to tar-and-feather 'bodysnatchers' Ramsay and McGregor and dump them in the canal running through the gasworks, whose waters were 'slightly thickened by the remains of numerous specimens of the feline and canine species and various other carrion'.

McGregor was canny, later famous for his strategic 'misdeals' when playing whist. His circular was as much about keeping Villa's fixtures with the big clubs as anything.

In his decade of senior football William McGregor had seen local clubs decline and fall – Wednesbury Old Alliance (1882 National Cup quarter-finalists, beating the other senior Birmingham clubs – St George's 9-1; Small Heath 6-0; and Villa 4-2), Stafford Road Works and Wednesbury Strollers. All now much-reduced. When 23-year-old William set up a drapery business in Aston in 1870 his first love was Calthorpe FC. But nearby Aston Villa had more Scots, like Ramsay and Fergus Johnstone. Ramsay reeled him in carefully. First, McGregor was attracted by Aston Villa's 'uniform dress. He was always an admirer of neatness.' Then, he was occasionally allowed to keep goal in practices. Ramsay realised this 'intensely practical' man would be great on the committee, and even better supervising Villa's notorious Scottish tours. Deeply religious, a serial teetotaller, he 'stood for strict temperance in all things', yet tolerated Villa's inveterate practical jokers 'letting themselves go on a tour'. Denny Hodgetts 'led a few expeditions of the hilarious order'. The charabanc excursion in which a wheel 'accidentally' came off. The 'good feast off a spread that was intended for a wedding'. McGregor routinely paid two hotel bills: one for the stay, the other for the damage.

McGregor bailed out Villa during their hand-to-mouth days. Twice he paid 'the bailiffs put in by the landlord', and when they pounced anyway Villa's 'goods and chattels were taken to McGregor's business'. He could not overcome a 'financial racket' practised by Villa's gatekeepers: gate receipts were 'queerly distributed, and he knew it'. But McGregor was a tough as well as 'cute Scot'. Once, the tenant of the house where Villa held their committee meetings was 'forced to make a sudden departure from Birmingham', but had time to take the club's piano. McGregor was undeterred: he pursued the offender and recovered Villa's piano.

He was a true fan. After Villa's 1887 Cup semi-final win against 'Scotland' (i.e. Glasgow Rangers), he and his supporters 'joined hands and capered in a sort of fandango'. In the final, after their second goal, 'good old Mac' performed the whoop of a clan chieftain, threw his bonnet high and led Villa's other committeemen in a Scottish reel, causing referee Marindin to 'stare and gasp as he whistled the men off the field'. As Villa's umpire, McGregor was sometimes regarded as too impartial. When he missed a game, McGregor's replacement was an improvement: 'he would rush up and harass the referee, and throw down and trample [his hankie] in his indignation … [which] took with the crowd mightily … he was a lot better than old Mac.'

In his maturity William McGregor cut an avuncular figure. In fact when he died, just before Christmas 1911, the image suggested by his benevolent appearance – 'flowing silvery beard, beaming eye, and resonant voice' – was irresistible: 'Santa Claus. By his creative faculty he has filled the stocking of many a player and enriched many a club.' By then too he was 'as full of reminiscences as an egg was full of meat'. One told of his overcoming the Harding Street gang that made Aston 'a dangerous quarter' in the 1870s. The gang featured in a Parliamentary enquiry into 1884 political riots between the followers of leading politicians Randolph Churchill and Joseph Chamberlain at Aston Park. But McGregor saw them off. He described offering to fight in a Glasgow Fair boxing booth but the boxer, a Harding Street gangster, knew he was overmatched: 'No, Mr McGregor, I shan't take you on.'

Finances are a tantalising part of club histories. In Villa's, Andy Hunter was a shopman in McGregor's drapery. McGregor 'treated him like a brother', and had to withstand his real brother's complaints that the licence given to Andy to play amounted to neglect of business. McGregor himself claimed that the club lent both Hunter brothers the very large sum of £200 to set themselves up in business … as drapers [McGregor, 1905, p.8].

Essentially McGregor was a small trader, and events in February 1888 left him feeling the need to act. His anxiety was longstanding. A confidant, labouring under the pseudonym 'Old Fogey', remembered that 'for years … he used to growl about and lament the way in which match-cards went awry'. Fergus Johnstone's son remembered the financial edge to this frustration: whenever Mr and Mrs McGregor paid a social visit 'the subject of guaranteeing matches was sure to crop up'. McGregor's own story of the League stressed his personal responsibility, and hence financial vulnerability, for the lease of Villa's ground [McGregor, 1906, p.171]. He was co-guarantor along with the richer George Kynoch, MP. Villa's governance was often described as McGregor and sympathisers moderating the effect of Kynoch's autocracy. And in February 1888 Kynoch walked out in a fit of pique: 'Gentlemen of the Villa club … disgraceful puppies.' Kynoch's grievance was that he had not been allowed to place his carriages exactly where he wanted them for the Preston Cup-tie. The press pooh-poohed Kynoch's financial contribution as just comprising a 'few "feeds" which he has treated the players'. McGregor knew better, that now he was isolated and in sudden and urgent need of reliable income. So he wrote his desperate letter.

William McGregor got help from Lancashire. Appropriately, because he had came to their aid, unexpectedly, in the Association's 1885 special general meeting to accept professionalism. As Villa's representative, McGregor was expected to maintain Birmingham's pretence as the home of amateurism. So 'Lancashire delegates, who were strongly in favour of professionalism, greeted his opening remarks with jeers'. But McGregor 'up and told the truth that professionalism existed'. Lancashire cheered him as a 'champion of the open slate'.

THE COMMERCIAL IMPERATIVE

The founders later claimed they saved football from ruin. The League gave class to each fixture, and provided clubs with predictable income. But at the time there was no generally expressed financial crisis. The League was presented as a positive choice.

That individual clubs rose and fell was a natural tension. In Victorian capitalism, a few businesses prospered, others survived and some amalgamated. No one was comfortable applying this to football. Advocates of a purer vision of sport opposed the 'present deadening spirit of business'. They looked forward to bankruptcies: 'by the wild expensiveness of the system, commercial football itself will fail … [and football will] return to healthy conditions of sport.' Their hope lay in limiting the season. Professional clubs who paid their players needed to impinge on the summer, and whilst people paid to watch, why not? The purists anticipated financial ruin would follow the enforcement of an October to April season. The League in effect endorsed the Association's compromise (September to May) by limiting its fixity of fixtures to each 'season'.

A counter tension lay in community. Clubs grew out of, and represented, communities. Progress depended upon that community's investment. The League was seen to threaten community because it made selections: 'self interest just now is the ruling passion in football as between club and club, and there is no love lost between clubs in the same town, who may be considered trade competitors for public favour.'

McGregor wrote to four other clubs but wanted more. Who else? Blackburn suggested Burnley and Accrington; and Bolton's Jack Bentley proposed Notts, Wolves and Stoke, and three surprises in the light of what the League became. First, Old Carthusians: amateur, London, who rarely played their strongest side – the Brothers Walters, uncle Will Cobbold and all. Bentley was professionalism's champion and a football romantic. He also suggested Halliwell (Wanderers's neighbours) and St George's (Villa's nearest rivals). Neither progressed. No reason was given, but McGregor later developed the rationale of one club from each town.

Given that Bolton would not long sustain two top clubs, Bentley was either generous, risk-taking, or he savoured Halliwell/Wanderers' big gates. McGregor was more cautious, hard-nosed or selfish. In 1906, when the Dragons, as St George's were wittily known, had breathed their last, McGregor apologised: if 'the first league ... made itself somewhat unpopular by its selfish methods during its early history, then I will grant there was much to deplore' [McGregor, 1906, p.170].

McGregor immediately briefed *Birmingham's Mail*, but their first comment was Fools Day, April 1st. They wondered rhetorically why St George's – as good as Derby or Stoke – had been omitted: 'football is now a commercial speculation ... The League was started by the Aston Villa, and St George's are neighbours, therefore commercial rivals. It was hardly likely that the Villa should invite them to share in the advantages created by the League.' Birmingham's Small Heath, National Cup semi-finalists in 1886, got no look-in either. Aston Villa's sensitivity was also indicated by the existence of significant other local clubs: Aston Shakespeare (with the inevitable nickname 'the Bards'), Aston Victoria and Aston Unity. These were all good enough (their capture from 'the Bards' – with the Shakespearean name 'Bartholomew' – played in Villa's League debut) for poached players to go straight into the first team.

Of course, an exception was made. Albion. In fact, if 'Birmingham' was allowed only one club, it might not have been Villa!

McGregor's policy ignored an abiding feature of British football, the immense appeal of local rivalries. A League that glorified the intense Villa v Albion clashes, and included Nottingham, Liverpool, and Bolton's 'derbies' would have had even greater impact. Nottingham's County v Forest was typical. In 1887-88, before a 12,000 crowd (gate £243), 'Notts supporters dropped their money in wholesale fashion.' One laid £100 to win

£35, another £20 to win £5. Unsurprisingly, when Forest led late on, 'a run and a goal by Gunn would be worth £50.' Unfortunately, not this time. *Sans* miracles, as a double football-cricket international, and as a pro, William Gunn was 'blamed for everything'. After Forest's win, Gunn was 'very severely criticised, not to say grossly libeled', took it to heart, and three days later 'Gunn still disconsolate, and his amiable better half ... informed me they have never enjoyed a meal since the match. Of such is the glory of football.'

Another '12,000 roaring, bellowing, hooting, cheering, fanatical partisans' attended their Boxing Day return (£229 receipts).

Instead of embracing this intensity, the League chose one club from these towns and Blackburn (Rovers, Olympic or Witton), Derby (County, Midland or Junction), and Stoke (or Burslem Port Vale). The League's commercial imperative became overt in Nottingham's case. County, Forest or Notts Rangers? Both Forest and Rangers had recently proven stronger than County, but County occupied the Trent Bridge ground, which promised a good gate. That was the thing: 'no one can object to the search for big gates and the strangling of the demon debt.' These local choices reinforced a growing image of selfishness: 'cliqueism in the hope of starving out thriving and dangerous rivals.'

The spin went on. The St Peter of the League legend required that McGregor had 'considerable difficulties in getting the clubs together', and that disappointingly neither Bentley nor Sudell attended Anderton's Hotel, Fleet Street on March 23rd. William Sudell's attendance would surely have been remarkable, the evening before North End realised their obsession of winning the National Cup. He knew the others needed him more than he needed them. Bentley was different. He was in nearby Covent Garden, with North End. So far Bentley had run with the League. Why wasn't he there? Maybe somewhere else was more important.

McGregor's conference was small beer. Trailed as a meeting for secretaries to fix the magical 'fixity of fixtures', few turned up. Tom Smith's presence betrays its junior status, because Albion's power brokers were still in West Bromwich with the players for the morrow's Cup final. The paucity gave Stoke's Harry Lockett no opposition as the League's secretary. Blackburn were represented by committeeman Jesse Birtwistle, a recent aggressive heckler of Sudell during North End's contentious fixtures at Leamington Road. Notts, Wolves and Burnley also sent committeemen rather than their secretaries. Derby were observing only. The High Rip Gang leaders were elsewhere. Jack Bentley knew the venture was doomed unless North End were on board, so he was with Sudell, encouraging, persuading.

March 23rd was terrible timing. Only the week before, in Glasgow, the Associations had decided 1888-89's fixtures: representative games, including internationals; and cups, city Cups, county Cups, English Cup – every week from October until late April 1889.

The name itself reveals McGregor's weakness. As a Presbyterian Scot, he wanted 'Union'. Not only politically more correct, 'union' carried the subtext of clubs 'binding themselves' to each other. League 'did not please me', carrying too many echoes of the Irish troubles, where the National League and Land League were bad news. Yet he gave in, a price for the group arranging to meet again on April 17th at the Royal Hotel, Manchester.

Another parable is McGregor as Prophet in the Wilderness, proclaiming the future in vain, being met with 'apparent indifference' when he briefed Birmingham's sporting editors. Is it surprising they were supremely underwhelmed by such itsy-bitsy news, hours before Albion challenged the Invincibles for the great prize? Was this the action of a surefooted spinner? Albion were now unequivocally Birmingham's top club, and journalists might reasonably have regarded McGregor's Union as a transparent spoiler. Any other time would have been better.

On April 17th the deal was done. Derby moved from observers to insiders, and most interestingly, Everton were added: 'the original idea was to pool gates, and that was the reason why Everton were admitted, because they were not so powerful as the other clubs' [McGregor, 1905, p.173]. McGregor's favouring of Everton renewed the 'heartburning' of other Birmingham clubs. Halliwell, Nottingham Forest and Sheffield Wednesday turned up but were rejected.

Notwithstanding, the meeting ended in true Victorian artifice, 'utmost harmony'. The symmetry of six Lancashire and six Midlands clubs was later stressed but contemporaries noted absences: no Yorkshire, Cheshire or Lincolnshire club and none from the North East. No Southerners and no 'Scotch'. Other commentators wondered whether it was feasible for Midlanders to 'travel all the way to Lancashire': 'will it pay them?'

Before March 23rd, only Birmingham's *Sport and Play* mentioned the movement 'to ensure the fixtures of all the prominent football clubs of the country can be carried out as they appear on the cards'. Understandably, since the underlying obsession was with fixture lists, the author was Villa secretary George Ramsay. Perhaps Ramsay was founder all along. He was good at pulling strings from the background. So, McGregor as frontman. At this stage it was neither union nor league: 'it is proposed that sixteen clubs should form a compact to carry out the fixtures arranged by them, at all costs.' The Football Compact? Cup-ties were the enemy, making the fixture list 'a dead letter'. In Birmingham especially there was 'no end of grumbling': 'the everlasting pot-hunting will not keep the ball rolling, and football followers can do with a good deal less. What they want is first-rate matches.' Ramsay was not at the March 23rd meeting. The next day Villa played Everton at Anfield in front of 7,000. Ramsay might have thought Everton were becoming first rate.

Sport and Play reported the inaugural meeting in subdued tones. Not McGregor's clarion call of first-class elevens. Instead what sounded like a secretary's cautious briefing: 'so far as possible the system of playing the second-class elevens should be avoided.' Reporters had trouble with the mathematics: twelve clubs makes 24 games, right? There was no mistaking their pretensions: 'National Football Association League is a high sounding name for a dozen clubs to take to themselves.'

The League started to matter when North End spoke up, saying it was surprising that powerful clubs had not acted previously against the 'topsy-turvy' interference that rendered their fixture lists 'worse than useless'.

The biggest myth was the last: that McGregor gave the world competition and saved it from friendlies. On June 5th Mac explained his League to Villa's AGM. It was about finance and fixtures. A 'large amount of money has passed through his hands', headed by the epic North End Cup-tie (which, by the way, we never lost). But Villa's Achilles heel was that 1887-88's record number of fixtures had lacked quality, and 'the greatest cause of loss' (£153) was Mondays. The University types provided socially attractive but costly matches. Mac sought a different class of fixture: 'The Football League had been formed for the purpose of creating more interest in friendly matches … Birmingham people had a keen taste, and only turned out to see really good matches. This was the reason why the league was established, and he thought the prospect of any heavy losses to the club on friendly matches was very much minimised.'

The League was about class. That it was a distinct competition, something later taken for granted, is absent. No talk of determining a champion. Competition was primarily a means of defining the unworthy. Although no 'mode of reckoning' (i.e. how results would be computed) was decided, the bottom four clubs, a third of the membership, would withdraw. They will have lacked class.

As the spring wore on, the League assumed a combination of hard-hearted commercial risk-taking and messianic imagery: 'the millenium [sic] at hand. No more debts. Both ends to meet. Plain sailing.'

So the happy group was called The Twelve Apostles, exhibiting a very unchristian attitude to their neighbours: 'without a care for those unhappily shut out in the cold.'

THE TWELVE APOSTLES

Aston Villa, with William McGregor as St Peter; Bolton Wanderers, with Jack Bentley, chief lieutenant as a fisher of clubs; Wolverhampton Wanderers the Schoolboy; Notts of Ancient Lineage, with aristocratic patrons; Everton the Moneybags; Burnley the Errant Scotchman; Albion, Victoria's Factory Boy; Blackburn Rovers the Old Man; Derby County of Uncertain Identity; Accrington the Poor Boy; and Stoke the Lost Soul.

OUT IN THE COLD

The model was not exclusive. Crewe's secretary 'somewhat unwisely whipped out a circular suggesting a second league' (called the Combination), but that was no problem for the Apostles. It failed. Twenty was too many, and only seven eventually became League clubs – Crewe Alexandra, Grimsby, Sheffield Wednesday, Port Vale, Nottingham Forest, Lincoln and Newton Heath (subsequently Manchester United). Bootle initially scorned the League's 'irresponsible and self-constituted authority', viewing a future based upon a negotiated fixture-list with 'utmost complacence', but eventually joined the Combination.

So exclusiveness stayed the central issue. Who was in and who was out? Why twelve, and why this twelve? The League acknowledged that whilst some members 'are not first-class, the majority are without doubt the pick of English football'.

The class of London clubs was unreliable: they could be strong but were often weak. Scotland posed many problems, mostly deriving from its separate and sensitive jurisdiction. Clubs from the North East (especially Sunderland and Newcastle), and Lincolnshire (the triumvirate of Grimsby, Lincoln and Gainsborough) were being driven along by fierce rivalries, but local competition could only go so far. All these areas were far away. Away teams were at a significant disadvantage after wearisome and expensive travel, and could these costs be offset by gate receipts?

Clubs of urgent ambition needed Scotch imports. Most of those on the edge of the League had leading Scots, whose inspiration and recruitment skills determined their level of success both locally and against class visitors. Grimsby Town had Macbeth. Like Jason of the Argonauts, Bob Macbeth became mine host of Ye Golden Fleece, Grimsby, in the summer of 1887. He had made his name as Accrington's star forward but straightaway went poaching in his native Edinburgh. He came back with big game, notably Hibernian's James Lundie, Scottish international (1886) and Cup-winner (1887). Lundie stayed until 1896. Macbeth himself had an eventful few months: 'McBeth [sic] went to Grimsby, fell in love, got married and became a widower in a very short period of time.' At

Christmas, Hugh McIntyre, legendary Scotch half-back from Blackburn's four Cup finals, came to cheer him and was promptly put in goal on Christmas Day. Macbeth represented a tough tradition, even his admirers reflecting ruefully that he had found 'apt pupils' in Grimsby for his invariable advice: 'go into them' and 'as we all know he is a glutton for that kind of business'.

Macbeth's Grimsby were among England's top twelve in 1888-89 (but outside the League), and strengthened, for the English Cup campaign, by younger Edinburghers. Dan Doyle joined Lundie to become 'almost the best backs in England' [Lincoln, 1912, p.322], fit to challenge North End in 1889's definitive English Cup-tie. Grimsby's shot at the League went the day they beat Bolton. Jack Bentley had just taken over Wanderers again. It was a 'terribly long journey' fuelled by copious amounts of sandwiches and bottled Bass. Bolton survived until a long ball floated wide of goal. Then 'a gust of wind came off the sea at Cleethorpe and put it between the posts'. Bolton lost 0-2 and rushed, half-dressed, to catch their train. 'Grimsby's boss' sent Lundie after them with a bag of fish for Mr Bentley. Not enough. Football sandwiched by endless railway journeys was 'not bad work, but too much for any team to do'. When Bentley pondered his additions to McGregor's A-List, Grimsby did not feature.

West Bromwich Albion

The Throstles had to be Apostles. Yet they contradicted at least two of McGregor's principles. First, Villa and Albion came from the same town. Second, Albion loved cups.

The League's fixtures required clubs to limit their participation in cups. Cups were particularly unpopular in Birmingham. The Lancastrians had the Lancashire Cup, and Everton and Bootle only played each other when they contested the Liverpool Cup. Birmingham had too many cups.

Nevertheless, McGregor asserted his loyalty to the Association: 'of course, this is no way to interfere with the National Association; even the suggested matches might be played under cup-tie rules.' Was this naïve or disingenuous? His plan's first argument was that 'through cup-tie interferences, clubs are compelled to take on teams who will not attract the public'. Associations drew their power and finances from cups, and cup-tie rules severely restricted professionals' participation (under cup-tie rules, for example, Everton had too few eligible players to join the League).

McGregor genuinely intended no challenge to the National and Birmingham Cups. His aim (until someone unwisely proposed a Warwickshire Cup) was getting Albion to bump the Staffordshire Cup.

Yet the 1880s was Albion's Cup decade – thirteen final appearances and six trophies … including four Staffordshire Cups.

In the long run the ploy worked. Albion, officially crowned English champions on the day the League was announced, have only been champions once in 120 years since. McGregor's League gave Villa a head start.

In 1888 Albion had achieved the unprecedented feat of reaching the finals of the National, Birmingham and Staffordshire Cups for three successive years. Their fame began by beating Villa in the 1883 Staffordshire Cup. Strangely, as McGregor proposed the League, Villa criticised Albion for opting out of a cup. Albion rejected the Mayor of Birmingham's Charity Cup because their existing club 'engagements are so important that they will not be able to spare the time; and I believe it is also a fact that shekels are not so very plentiful in the Albion exchequer at the present time'. Albion's finances were something of a puzzle. They famously paid their players little and commanded good guarantees. After refereeing a match with North End, Jack Bentley commented that Albion were well managed and 'ought to be rich in funds'. But he did not say they were 'rich in funds'.

Albion snubbed the Mayor of Birmingham in retaliation against Villa's refusal to enter the West Bromwich Charity Cup. Relations between the clubs and their partisans were uneasy. Tense rivalry pervaded the two matches (February 25th and March 3rd) straddling McGregor's March 2nd letter, with a third game on March 10th. Three matches to decide the championship of Birmingham, as important locally as the national final between Albion and North End on 24th. Albion trainer Joey Law, the Birchfield Harrier, gloried in the first, ordinary fixture, 4-1: 'you should have heard him crow … after they walked through the Villa! I don't know anybody more competent to give them a good cross-country spin.' Villa were 'utterly disorganized'. For the following week, Denny Hodgetts was back, which meant a fair fight: 'when it was seen that the full teams were in evidence supreme satisfaction was expressed on all hands.'

The welcome given to the League reflected an intuition that football needed to change. But it was a complex mix. Nostalgia for a lost past accompanied many big matches in the late 1880s: Fergy Suter, Lancashire's original Scotch import, said, despite contrary evidence, that 'the day for big gates has gone by'. The Birmingham Cup final was one such: it 'put one in mind of old times … the exciting events of former years.' Villa v Albion events were not old times. Albion had National Cup victories in 1883 and 1884 (10,000 watching) and Villa unexpectedly beat Albion in the 1887 final.

Newspapers provided a 'full, true and particular account of the warfare' on March 3rd, 1888. The Aston Lower Grounds, setting for recent National Cup semi-finals, lived up to its name. A big ground, a new grandstand, the pitch shifted, but still an old meadow. It was snowy, so 40 bags of sawdust created the 'perfect quagmire', four inches of clinging sticky mud: 'the ground came in for a good deal of inspection by the players, and wry faces were made.' The leisure grounds were rushed and the switchback railway, skating rink roof and the great tobogganing slide all became viewing platforms.

Albion started quickly – 'the Throstles came down like a wolf from the wold'. Then a fox terrier intervened: 'Tom Green chucked him among the spectators, but he wriggled quickly back again, and was scampering across the meadow, and came across the dark and gloomy Timmins, who soon finished his football career with a brutal kick, and laid him out prone and stiff in the muddy meadow, for which he was soundly and most deservedly hissed.' Albion scored, to their supporters' pleasure: 'I say you, that were a regular good cock throstle, that were.' But Hodgetts' brilliant late goal won it: 'hundreds of folks stood with their watches in their hands counting the seconds as they flew … the Villa left the field, many of them being carried shoulder high, amidst the excited and triumphant cheers of their partisans, after about the hardest and closest game they had ever played even in their exciting career.' Albion 'took their defeat in anything but a generous mood, and grumbled and growled at their luck.'

There were 10,000 for the decider, the thrashing that proved Albion's superiority, 4-0, with captain Bayliss 'mighty fond of playing pick-a-back at opponents' expense'. Albion scored whilst he was 'potting the keeper in his well-known fashion'. Harry Yates was another target: 'throughout the play [Bayliss] had been hacking him, frequently charging, turning around and coming down with his heels on his legs.' Eventually, Yates snapped and kicked out. The forward made the most of the retaliation and the defender was sent off: 'Bayliss did not forget to make a tremendous fuss about the matter … he is not the most gentle creature in the world, as every goalkeeper against whom he plays is aware.' If the reporter exuded subdued indignation, four or five Villains laid in wait and beat up Bayliss – blows to the body and his legs badly kicked – whilst a policeman refused to help. There were two weeks to the Cup final.

WOLVERHAMPTON WANDERERS

If McGregor wanted the strongest teams he would go to the Wolves early. Bolton and Blackburn had reputations, but Wolves had the fifth-best record after North End, Renton, Villa and Albion. Villa's weaker fixture list provided a hundred more goals than Wolves' 132, but Wolves had a strong defence getting stronger. Half-back Albert Fletcher was 'without doubt a coming man in his position, and some of his opponents know when he is coming too'. He and Arthur Lowder would also play half-back for England in 1889, adding to Wolves' other internationals, full-back Charlie Mason and centre-half Harry Allen, the 'impressive' star of England's 5-0 crushing of Scotland in March 1888. What the Wolves lacked were quality forwards, especially as talismanic Jack Brodie missed most of 1887-88.

Brodie and Jack Baynton were two pupil-teachers who helped form St Luke's FC in 1877 after schoolmaster Harry Barcroft made the famous record in the school log: 'Let boys out earlier on Friday Afternoon and they had a Football Match.' They eventually became Wolverhampton Wanderers and another original scholar, John Addenbrooke, established the club on professional grounds. With a new ground on Dudley Road, they overtook the previous top local club Stafford Road, yet even in 1888 a cohort of these schoolboys – Brodie, Baynton, Baugh, Mason and Lowder – were still going strong.

McGregor knew Wolves were first class. His complaint about disruptive cup-ties was a bit rich, because the worst had been Villa's toughest hurdle in their triumphant 1886-87 National Cup campaign. Four sensational matches with Wolves in seven weeks. After two periods of extra-time in three draws, the last game attracted a then-record 12,000 to Perry Barr, clinging precariously to temporary wooden stands in a raging gale.

Wolves also provided the best story justifying the League. A big crowd gathered to see the Druids' Welsh internationals, but they sent a weak team who were 0-11 down at half-time. Wolverhampton was small market: £821 gate money; 'wages and loss of time' cost only £396; and a loss of £158 in 1887-88. Six years later gate money had risen four-fold and wages six and a half times [McGregor, 1905, p.62].

WHERE NEXT?

After Wolves, it was anyone's guess ... on merit. Villa's journeys around March 23rd were instructive. In a short Lancashire tour, Villa beat Blackburn Rovers 6-4 and concluded they were 'not what they used to be'. At Burnley, they found five Rovers playing again, with Fergy Suter as a controversial referee: 5-5, and Villa thought 'Suter was worth all the five to Burnley'. That Saturday they played what became the most important fixture in Everton's history. The club had risen since local brewer-politician 'King' John Houlding purchased and developed Anfield in 1886.

Now his investment could pay off. But there were fourteen prospective Apostles already, without Everton. On March 24th Villa came to Anfield. It was heaven-sent. The team competed – Villa only won 2-1 – and Everton's crowd turned up – 7,000 was like Villa versus Albion. Could 'King John' find a sweetener for McGregor or Ramsay? He could. In McGregor's later history, the League only became openly commercial with Everton's late inclusion [McGregor, 1906, p.173]. 'King John' offered sharing Anfield's gate money as Everton's entry price: it had been their practice over 1886/1888 anyway.

Many clubs had better records in the National Cup. Sheffield started in 1873; Darwen 1877; Nottingham Forest 1879; Bootle 1881; Halliwell and Grimsby 1883 and Sunderland 1884. Arguably, Everton had only played one match, one cup-tie, of any significance outside Liverpool. Ever. If Liverpool was the newcomer, Nottingham and Sheffield were the first Northern football outposts, with cup battles since 1877. But their respective star youngsters, and later England internationals, Harry Cursham and Billy Mosforth, were still playing a decade later, and both cities had only partially recovered from crises. Cursham's aristocratic self-regard captured County's complacency: he 'shook his leonine locks, curled his moustache and showed his profile in good style'.

Their fortunes revived when the famous cricketer William Gunn switched from Forest, and County began playing on Trent Bridge's cricket ground. With Gunn running through defences, Notts reached the National Cup semi-finals of both 1883 and 1884. In 1888 they were Nottingham's richest (a balance of £600) and third-best side. They only won eleven games in 1887-88, and Forest won the derbies. In January 1888 Notts Rangers beat County 8-0, with star centre Fred Geary scoring five goals. Notts Rangers had a very talented team: Geary, goalkeeper George Toone and brothers Charlie and Alf Shelton all became internationals. When County joined the League they put Forest's Frank Guttridge into the 'Porter's Rest', and poached the Sheltons (paying fifty shillings a match) and Rangers winger Hodder. But County could neither secure all the local talent nor enough Scotchmen. Internationals came but did not stay: Tom Robertson 'could not find a situation' and became 'unquestionably [Scotland's] strongest and best right half'. County went after Jamieson of Dumbarton, the latest hot Scotch centre, but Bootle lured him to Liverpool … via the workhouse (see below p.92).

LANCASHIRE

Lancashire begat professionalism; professionalism begat the League; and the League ate up Lancashire. Something like that.

Lancashire became the northern centre of football in the early 1880s. Billy Struthers remembered his Scotch view of Lancastrian football in the late 1870s when he visited with Partick and Glasgow Rangers: '[we] considered it mere child's play to meet a Lancashire club ... [no] serious thought ... a jolly outing.' In July 1880 Struthers answered a Bolton Wanderers advert wanting footballers and offering employment. So 'were you a pro?' asked the interviewer. 'Certainly not. I did bookkeeping in a mill.' Another Scottish pioneer recalled those times from the different world of the Great War: '[we were] very unpopular I can tell you. There were no machine guns then or we should have been popped off very quickly'. Struthers regarded Wanderers as raw recruits: 'they were all for dribbling, and it was a big job to get them into passing with anything like accuracy.'

During Struthers' career Lancashire became the dominant English region; persuaded the Association to accept professionalism; and paved the way for the League.

The 1880s was a period of controversy, of alliances and deal-making [Green, 1953, pp.46-50; Williams, 1994, pp.88-95]. The Association survived, given stability by its triumvirate of senior officers – Charles Alcock as Secretary, Arthur Kinnaird as Treasurer and Francis Marindin as President. They rode the waves of change as Lancashire advocated professionalism against the opposition of Scotland and English provinces overtaken by Lancashire and its Scotch imports.

The pace quickened when Accrington and North End were disqualified from the Cup, and William Sudell openly proclaimed professional recruitment as the road to excellence. Richard Gregson, secretary of the powerful Lancashire County Association, entered the shark fields of national football politics to steer professionalism through. His first effort was countered by London's 'Pa' Jackson and Queen's Park, who proposed 'all Associations should unite to stamp out professionalism'. By October 1884, 31 Lancashire clubs were on the brink of seceding from the Association. With this iron fist inside his velvet glove, Gregson persuaded an Association sub-committee to propose legalising professionalism. Birmingham's resistance was undermined by William McGregor's surprising conversion and despite Scottish objection, it was approved, 113-108 – but way short of the necessary two-thirds majority. It took two more votes before Dr Morley of Blackburn Rovers, Gregson's front man, carried professionalism at a Special General Meeting on July 20th 1885. Opposition was not so much overcome as faded away (the final vote was 35-15), but the price was the irksome and illogical restrictions on professionalism that caused much irritation between 1885 and 1889.

Lancashire embraced professionalism avidly but its meaning and future was controversial. Tom Hindle, the father of Lancashire football, claimed it started by accident. Darwen's first imports were not paid to play, because they had real jobs. For him, professionalism started when unemployed Fergy Suter proposed to return to Scotland, so Darwen arranged 'another job'. The slippery slope became steeper. Hindle's ambivalence was typical. He brought in residential qualification for the Lancashire Cup to obstruct professionals, but Bolton Wanderers kept on importing 'foreigners': 'Oh, that doesn't matter. It's the English cup-ties we want; they draw the gate money.' The national Association was slow to take the hint.

The county's main personalities debated professionalism endlessly. Few had sympathy with class shamateurism, Jackson promoting the Corinthians' exploitation of expenses whilst mocking Scotch amateurs as corrupt. Did it matter whether a Scotchman's job was real or illusory, or one paying more than the going rate? Expenses posed similar issues. Lancashire tried to draw the line. In November 1888 their Association defined 1s 6d for 'tea' expenses as reasonable. Whilst Hindle wanted the player who saved a bit on his meal expenses kept out of the professional ambit, William Sudell mocked the paid amateur, the semi-pro, the man 'cobbling' a few coppers.

Sudell instead championed the full-time footballer, whom Blackburn's Dr Morley opposed in principle. For Morley, professionalism meant football was a 'recreation to be paid for', but nobody's business. Football earnings should be lost wages for the youngster, or a supplement for the established player. Where Sudell saw uplifting science, Morley saw decadence: full-time professionals 'became a source of degradation to all concerned … [and] ruin to football was not far off'.

Dr Morley was Blackburn Rovers' Grumpy Old Man. In 1886/88, Blackburn Rovers felt like the Old Men's Club. Their two famous Scotch imports had declined – Fergy Suter still ran The Castle, the Rovers' house, but he and Hugh McIntyre were effectively retired. As their team fell away, the town fell out of love with football.

Blackburn Rovers' 1887 AGM was an important moment. Financially they felt better than for eight or nine years. Years never bettered footballwise. Rovers' National Cup run began by losing the 1882 final after beating previous top Lancashire club Darwen 5-1. The following season Darwen got their revenge. Then came Rovers' three successive Cup wins, still a record. Their reward after all this success was paltry. They had a balance of 18 shillings and owed their treasurer £70. The gate money had been £973, and they paid £516 in players' wages. Despite this, it was said 'they know now how they did stand, and previously they had not done so.'

Jack Lewis was one of the club's founders and for the next twenty years a powerful figure in football, as a fearsomely autocratic referee, politician and syndicated newspaper columnist. Eighteen years later Lewis bemoaned 'the old days [when] there was very little financial profit to be got out of the Cup. The Rovers played in three, possibly four finals without getting a cent from the gate receipts.'

In 1886-87 Lewis had presided over Rovers' worst ever season – 56 matches, only twenty wins and 23 losses – likened to an advanced 'stage of consumption'. Dr Morley returned because of 'the chaos into which the club had been plunged'. He had retired after the three Cup wins, but Morley's involvement had been recent: it was only five years since the Rovers committee asked for help with a presentational matter and, as a middle-aged man, he watched his first match and was hooked. As a convert he thought he knew it all.

The League fitted Dr Morley's views in a strange way. Like Villa, Morley did not like Mondays. But whereas William McGregor's concern was that Monday fixtures did not pay, for Morley they symbolised the evil of the player without a proper job. Full-time status was bad for the player, bad as a moral example to other young men, and bad for clubs. Because they needed to pay players, clubs took on too many fixtures, hence Mondays. But the more fixtures, and therefore travelling, the harder for a footballer to do real work.

So Dr Morley puffed on his cigar, surveyed Rovers' AGM and pronounced 'they had too much football'. It was a popular message. 'Hear, hear.' He warmed to his theme. He was sorry there were not more players present. This was moral loss: in earlier days the players would be active club 'members'. Now they were 'loafing about the town all the week doing nothing'. And Blackburn was not a place to 'loaf about in'.

Rovers recommended two other Lancashire clubs for the Apostles. First, Accrington. Blackburn had recently attracted Accrington's largest ever gate, but Rovers queried the seven guineas the home club had spent on posters. The result may have been bad news for Accrington's England winger. Joe Lofthouse had won the Cup for Rovers in 1884 and 1885 (and would do so again in 1890) but was now hopefully taking bets on Accrington winning. In any event, afterwards, Joe was seen settling his bets at the station.

Accrington were the League's 'poor boy'. Suspended Everton, who missed a lucrative month of 1887-88, still reported twice their opponents' gate receipts and expenditure. Accrington would go where the money was for fixtures, to Liverpool and Newton Heath in Manchester, as 'that's where the shekels flow'. They also had scampish characteristics. Like Burnley's, 'the Accrington umpire is a professor in the art of claiming,' and they famously riled opponents and onlookers by their regular lateness. At Bolton, on a bitterly cold day late in 1887, journalist 'Grumbler' grumbled. Everyone grumbled: 'even the pigeons grumbled beneath their basket-lid at being dragged out of their snug cote to act as winged messengers.' But the pigeon was still sent with dramatic news to be included in the evening edition: 'there was one redeeming feature, and one only, about the general gloom which damped out gaiety. Let it be writ up in the biggest type you can afford, Mr Master Printer; let it be blossomed forth to the four winds of heaven, let it be recorded amongst the marvels of the Nineteenth Century, let it for ever remain the event of the year of grace and jubilee – Accrington were on time.'

Accrington had a respectable record in the National Cup except … respectability. Their disqualification in November 1883 for professionalism looked like dishonesty-found-out until William Sudell dignified North End's similar exclusion with the virtue of honesty. Accrington were disqualified again in 1884 as Lancashire's challenge to the Association developed. Earlier they had lost to the winners Blackburn Olympic in 1882-83; and only 1-3 to powerful Darwen in 1881-82. In 1886 they were only beaten 0-1 by top Scottish club Renton; and in 1887-88 beat Burnley before losing 1-3 to Blackburn Rovers.

Accrington had the best English half-back in George Howarth and he was dedicated enough to give up an international cap to play an ordinary fixture with North End (see below p.107). The Reds (25 wins out of 41 in 1887-88) were more likely than most to be wholehearted: 'when the Accrington boys go in to win a match, it is time that the opposing side put forth all it knows … when these wonderful forwards … get swarming around a goal, its downfall is generally a sure thing.'

Accrington's few Scots tended to stay. Burnley however was famous for its ever-changing cast of often-errant Scotchmen. Ever since professionalism had taken hold, Burnley had had more Scots than anyone. But to less effect. They rarely stayed and usually showed less discipline. Even Dannie Friel, who had run The Footballers Arms since October 1883, frequently preferred professional sprinting. In one race, for a £10 stake at the Bull & Butchers, he ran a dead heat. He lost the re-run for £35. Burnley's highlights included beating both North End and Blackburn Rovers (5-0) in 1884-85; earning £250 for an October 1886 Royal charity match before Prince Albert Victor, second heir to the crown; and a 4-1 home win over the disgruntled Corinthians on their Christmas 1887 tour. Their 1887-88 record was 59 played, 29 won and twenty lost. They lost £210, spending £500 more than Rovers, including £330 more on wages.

Burnley were ambivalent about the National Cup. When they didn't lose (0-11), they were disqualified. Their 1887 committee pondered, was it worth it?, and announced they would not enter the English and Lancashire Cups because of 'serious pecuniary loss'. They eventually relented, and won their first ever tie, before losing a real battle, 2-3, with Accrington. That was another notable betting coup: Burnley had been 2-0 up at half-time.

Burnley had some talented Englishmen as well, especially their 'perfect' half-backs. Captain Jack Keenan, 24, came close to becoming Burnley's first international. When Rovers' Jimmy Forrest dropped out against Scotland in March 1888, Jack was reserve, but they sent for a Corinthian instead. England won 5-0, and Keenan's replacement was the only failure: 'Holden-White did not kick quite straight.' He could take a mean train however: he left London at 9pm on Friday, played his international and got back 7am Sunday. Keenan never played for England.

Frank Sugg was Burnley's emblematic star, the archetypal Victorian sportsman, Test all-rounder. Interviewed in the autumn of 1887, 'the man of three counties lit his cigar, twirled his moustache' and held forth. Born January 1862, dad a solicitor, brother Walter equally sporting (they opened a sports outfitting shop, courtesy of Everton and the League, in November 1888). He exuded laidback confidence: 'I don't go in for the breakneck game ... I like steady play and prefer heading to kicking.' Burnley's journalists, used to erratic Scotchmen, appreciated his 'admirable co-operation with the front line ... such nerve and steadiness ... perfectly safe'. A man of the 'most immovable good nature', Frank Sugg had already played for Yorkshire and joined Lancashire CCC because 'there is no credit attached to playing for' Derbyshire. That rankled. He fell out with Burnley early in 1888, either because of refusal to train or play on dangerous ground; or a reported fight between players. Soon afterwards, goalkeeper James McConnell resigned the secretaryship and Burnley's ground-keeper was so disgusted by lack of effort that he locked the changing room door and would not let them out. After Test heroics against Australia in August 1888, Sugg was anybody's for 1888-89, and much coveted.

THE AFTERTHOUGHTS

Stoke had history and Derby County had none. Founded in 1863, Stoke had had a chequered past. Their first professionals, including later internationals Tom Clare and Billy Rowley, were paid 2s 6d a match. They led the first strike of football pros to earn 5s. In their first year of professionalism, Stoke's gates included £27 (a National Cup-tie), £24 (Cup-holders Blackburn Rovers) and £20 (Scotch tourists Third Lanark), until North End showed what was possible: £115 [Cockbill, 1905]. Stoke were still cheapskates: 1887's wages amounted to only £153.

There was little to choose between Stoke and near rivals Burslem Port Vale as Apostles. Was it Stoke's longevity, or their better reputation for reliability and fair play? Or because their secretary Harry Lockett had been fingered for League secretary? Secretary was a key role if the League was to work – fixing fixtures. So no chance for Vale. The two clubs had already clashed in the County Court, and did so again in the League's early days. Vale had successfully sued over Billy Rowley's registration, and Stoke retaliated regarding Staffordshire County forward Joseph Lewis Ballham. Ballham had signed an agreement on September 3rd, 1887, committing him to Stoke for thirteen months.

Harry Lockett was pulling a fast one, securing him for two seasons because the Association viewed any registration effective on September 1st as binding the player for the ensuing season. After complaining of fraud and oppression, Ballham accepted summer wages but ignored Stoke's registered letters requiring him to attend matches. Instead, Ballham signed another agreement with a 'private gentleman' (Vale's Vice-President) 'to play with any club the latter might direct'. Stoke won the case, but complained that Port Vale, rather than Ballham himself, would pay the £20 compensation. The Judge said 'well and good. Port Vale are very well to do, I believe [Laughter]'. £1 a month.

Who were Derby County, and how come they would not take no for an answer? They were 'wolves in sheep's clothing', formed in 1884 as an offshoot of Derbyshire County Cricket Club, to make money in the winter. Their footballers were often cricketers – Will Chatterton, the 26-year-old County cricket captain, and his friend Will Cropper. Frank Sugg was their first football captain but the authorities did not appreciate his playing football for Burnley the two subsequent winters. Before the 1887 cricket season the Cricket Club said they would not play Sugg unless he turned out for the Football Club. He called their bluff, and left amid acrimony. Members complained: 'if you speak to any of the Committee you cannot get any information, no-one seems responsible for anything.'

County had done little (they were 57th in one Order of Merit), although they had won 75 of their total 150 games in four seasons. They lost 0-7 at home in their first National Cup-tie; reached the 1885-86 third round after beating St George's and Aston Villa; and did little in 1886/88.

Derby Midland and Junction Street were equally deserving of League status, if any Derby club was.

THE WARRING APOSTLES

Bolton and Everton were contrasts. Bolton Wanderers had reputation but insufficient money to realise their ambition of challenging North End. Everton's reputation was for big-city money and potential. Wanderers were obvious Apostles but doubtful successes. Everton were last choice but most likely winners if the League had any legs.

They inadvertently helped establish the League. The Association failed as a football authority in managing the 1887-88 Challenge Cup competition, and particularly two ties, Bolton v Everton (in October and November 1887) and Villa v North End (in January 1888). It created a vacuum of authority providing fertile ground for change.

The Bolton v Everton tie hinted at a change in the guard. Wanderers had tailed away after their 1-12 Christmas 1886 defeat to North End, when they were challenging for England's best. By the season's end they were tired, demoralised and broke. Wanderers went to Albion, lost and were so impoverished by the gate that the Albion President gave them £10 to get home.

By autumn 1887 Bolton had 'unquestionably dropped from its once dizzy pinnacle'. Even England forward Kenny Davenport was showing 'more discretion than valour'. The week before the Everton tie another loss confirmed their decline: 'a very bad effect – will have to pull themselves together or they will be in a hole.' Wanderers and Halliwell were playing 'worse than at any previous period in their history'. The moral seemed obvious: there was no room for two first-class clubs in Bolton. Wanderers had their backs to the wall.

'Grumbler' was told to 'get on' and back George Dobson's boys (Everton) to win a 'pile'. 1886-87 had seen Everton's 'phenomenal growth in public favour' and on paper they were stronger for 1887-88. But their new Scotch amateurs did not match Bootle's, and disappointed. Everton were worse, with uneven results against undistinguished opposition – the losses included St Oswald's and South Shore. They were still struggling to break into the elite: 'Mr Evertonian' found he 'cannot dictate terms to big clubs' despite offering Anfield's 'big gilded plum' gate. Even a status jump – being admitted to the 32 clubs competing for the Senior Lancashire Cup – ended badly, losing 1-4 at home to Blackburn's fourth-best team, Witton.

Bolton beat Everton 1-0 in the explosive first English Cup match on October 15th, 1887. Five hundred Merseysiders made a bigger rumpus than 5,000 home spectators: 'had the game been played at Everton I'm fairly convinced the Wanderers would have lost; they would have been shouted out.' 'A fight was imminent' when Davenport and Everton's tough Scotch back Alec Dick exchanged blows. Later, with Wanderers leading and Davenport writhing from another blow 'below the belt', Everton supporters made the call of unsympathetic opposition fans through the ages: 'Get on with the game; he's only wasting time.' Despite their earlier bravado Everton felt honour was satisfied. They could compete with Lancashire's Old Guard. But the Association would not leave well alone, and they were 'not good law-makers'.

The Association allowed sixteen petitions following their Cup's first round, most 'arising from some informality in registration'. One London club put out a completely unregistered eleven. No disqualifications. Replays were ordered. Other petitions were disallowed. Detectives' enquiries and bribes were defeated by armies of affidavits. Burnley threw the book at Joe Lofthouse: born in the wrong place (his mother said different); he lived more than six miles from Accrington's base (a surveyor measured five miles, four-and-a-half furlongs); and he broke his residential qualification by emigrating to the States (he only got to Liverpool).

Everton did not protest their defeat. It would have been impolitic: they turned up with two defectors from Bootle that very morning. However, the Association spotted that Wanderers' Billy Struthers' registration was five days late. It was a piece of sleuthing that eventually cost secretary Fitzroy Norris's job, and his replacement by someone who made the League work.

Nothing 'ever stirred the Liverpool public' as the Anfield replay. Seven thousand attended – 2-2. Everton protested a Bolton goal. A shot hit the post, ran along the line until 'keeper Joliffe kicked behind. Goal, claimed Wanderers. Everton's umpire simply spluttered, No goal' (the guidance stated umpires 'are bound to give a decision one way or the other when appealed to'). If the umpires made different rulings then the referee decided. Referee Gregson, the Lancashire Association secretary, asked Everton's ump, what are you claiming? If he had counterclaimed 'corner', the referee would have agreed. But without that option Gregson awarded the goal and demanded a new umpire. The Association pondered that eternal question: is 'no goal' a positive claim? The protest was thrown out. Understandably the tie produced a parody of a popular Gilbert and Sullivan refrain:

When a great National Cup tie's to be won, to be won,
A referee's lot is not a happy one, happy one.

Another replay on November 12th. Jack Bentley, the contracted referee, was appointed Wanderers' secretary, so the Association sent Major Marindin instead. The newspapers wondered whether the protest game was played out, but it was only just beginning. Scrutiny would be total. The Association notables were astonished by Everton's cheek. First they arrived late, and in batches. This raised a 'slight cheer' from Pike's Lane's 8,000, who blamed the railway as usual: 'oh, you trains. You Lancashire and Yorkshire trains, when will you come up to time, to time.' In fact Everton had arrived in Bolton half an hour earlier. The advance guard faced the major's patrician displeasure: 'Where's the rest? 'They're coming, sir.' He responded with martial precision: 'three minutes to fall in.'

Even Liverpool journalists expressed uneasiness at Everton's team. 'Where's Joliffe?' 'On the stand.' Bob Smalley, North End's reserve goalkeeper, and both Bootle's defectors, Izatt and Weir, were in the side. They cannot be eligible. 'Why, they've chucked the game away.'

Everton took the lead: 'Izatt comes along beautifully. Farmer takes the ball, and with a screaming high shot affects the Wanderers downfall.' It was a pure Everton moment: 'no such mangy tricks as howlding the goalkeeper while the ball was goin' thro'.' Darkness was imminent at half-time: 'a minute's rest and they are off again.' Twenty minutes from time 'Brogan returns and the thing is done.' Too dark for extra-time but surely Everton will be disqualified … if Bolton protest. Other clubs (especially Villa) were enraged by the fixture havoc: on November 19th, Wanderers had two cup and two ordinary matches scheduled. These replays had 'proved a boon' to cash-strapped Wanderers. Everton gained £300, and Bolton's only downside was disputes over the distribution: Anfield's had been a 'big gate with a mysteriously small income when the divi came to be made'. New secretary Bentley was cast as having Hamlet's dilemma: 'whether it is better to protest or play on and risk the slings and arrows of outrageous fortune, that is the question.'

The Association lost control of the protests. Their weakness caused both teams to include their ineligibles for the fourth game – Wanderers actually played Billy Struthers, whose late-registration started the whole thing off. Meanwhile, acting on information received from Bootle, Bolton charged professionalism against Everton's Scots. This needed investigation, but there was no time. The Association dictated 'play again at Everton and begin early enough … [and] play on until one was knocked out'. Ten thousand people, including 800 'colleens … dainty maids, clad in minks and victorines … came rushing through the portals – a sight for gods and mortals'. Bolton came in cream and crimson jerseys and the roar went up:

Two places, since the earth was created,
For noise and confusion of tongues celebrated,
… [The Tower of] Babel must yield
In the matter of uproar to Everton's field.

Everton scored two quick goals and hung on. At last it was over. Bolton dropped their protest but they had handed the Association an opportunity to pay back Everton for their uppityness. 'What will the Association do?' Would Third Lanark 'disclose uncomfortable particulars' – the Glaswegians were in debt to Bootle's secretary. The following week, 'as all the world knows,' seven Scots were declared 'veiled professionals', including Dick, Izatt and Weir, and Everton was suspended from all football for a month.

The Association's judgment effectively asserted precarious new tests for amateurs: their employment had not been their normal trade, and they had been paid too much. Thirty shillings a week for bottle-washing and barbers! Such refinements carried great potential for newspaper mockery: why shouldn't a man better himself 'if he is a football player'.

Afterwards, by what paths did Bolton and Everton arrive in the Apostles a few months later? In both cases it is best seen through their rivalry with their respective neighbours, Halliwell and Bootle.

SCOUSE GOSPEL

If Liverpool was 'hot for football … to the winners the spoils'. Everton versus Bootle. It was 'not pleasant, not wise' that they only played cup-ties, not ordinary fixtures. In their last match before suspension, Everton faced Bootle in the Liverpool Cup. The crowd was 12,000 despite increased prices: the 'toiling masses' had no time for their dinner or a wash after work. The players 'shake hands like plucky pugilists before the fray'. Everton v Bootle was not even sport: 'flying razors' had been promised. The bitter enemies produced many injuries – Alec Dick finished with black eyes. Everton won and were carried off shoulder-high on a triumphal march to their Sandon's Hotel headquarters. A few days later, after the Liverpool Association followed the National in disqualifying Everton, secretary Lythgoe completed the humiliation by arriving in a cab and taking the Cup. It was doubly galling that Lythgoe's club was Bootle.

Londoners thought Everton had got off lightly, but were finished. The Corinthians' 'Pa' Jackson adjudged the punishment as absurdly lenient and lambasted Bolton for their connivance at the illegality all along. Midlanders prophesied Everton would now 'sink back to the ranks of a medium club from which it sprang by illegitimate means and somebody will lose a "pile" – serve them right'.

Everton's appeal to the Association 'magnates' at their London offices with its 'pretentious-looking brass plate' failed. The outcome held a ridiculous contradiction. The seven Scots declared pros would have to satisfy the two-years residence qualification before they could play. Everton felt like scapegoats for shady amateurism: 'oh, no, this terrible plague which has been winked at so long, must be crushed out, and so poor Everton have to remain with the official thumb screws on.'

Secretary Alex Nisbet blamed jealous Bootle for the incriminating evidence. Already the knives were out. It was not 'King John' Houlding's fault or the clique of robber-barons on Everton's committee. Nisbet was 'responsible in great measure [for] the club's suspension'. Nisbet counter-attacked the restrictions on professionalism as 'protection in its worst form', introduced to mollify the Scottish Association and limit importation. Unusually for the period Nisbet openly promoted the principle of 'importation' against commentators who wanted clubs to field 'bonafide' local teams, as Birmingham did. Lancashire papers were ambivalent: there was 'much to be said in favour of legalizing importation, but there is far more to be said against such a system'.

Everyone agreed that Everton were scapegoats. Others broke those rules, like Grimsby's team of Edinburgh men. Lundie and Lee, from Hibs' 1887 Scottish Cup holders, were not practising their normal trade: 'Lundy and Mooty Lee are employed in a cooper's shop. They have a good screw, and rare old times of it. Lundy lights the fire, and Mooty carries the wood for him.' Who else, Mr Nisbet?, inevitably asked the journalist: 'if you come some other day with a bigger piece of paper, perhaps I may tell you.' There was a consolation. Nisbet ended his interview with a mischievous smile. At least 'we lived long enough to beat Bootle'.

Everton schemed a charge of professionalism against Bootle – who had Izatt and Weir first? Had not Bootle helped Weir 'honourably discharge any obligation to Stanley' by repaying his former club's 'loan'? Bootle's Andy Watson was caught up in the charges.

Thirty-year-old Watson and Rob Calderwood, both internationals, illustrate the precarious circumstance of the Scotch amateur. Rather than Arthur Wharton, Guyanese-born Andy Watson was the first significant black footballer and administrator (as Queen's Park's honorary secretary, when the 1881 census described him as 'warehouseman'). Watson's 1881 and 1882 appearances for Scotland against England produced an aggregate win of 11-2. A Scottish Association Vice-President even threatened to drug Wattie Arnott to get Watson into Glasgow's side [McBrearty,

2002]. Although winning three Scottish Cups with Queen's Park between 1881 and 1886, Watson spent 1882/85 in London, appearing for the Swifts and Corinthians, and ironically was still a committee member of the pukka amateur outfit when accused of being a Bootle shamateur.

Everton fingered Bootle secretary Harry Heard because he had form as a snitch, as star witness at a Scottish Association Inquiry. Third Lanark initially charged Cowlairs' McLeod and Robertson with professionalism, focusing upon frequent trips to Nottingham. 'Foxy Billy' McLeod was 'as cool as usual', so nothing stuck. Instead Calderwood faced the 'Capital Charge'. He answered Bootle's advert because, like McLeod and Robertson, he had been unemployed for twelve months and had no prospects. In August 1887 he signed: 'I hereby agree to accept a situation from Mr Sim Jones for the next seven months at the rate of 26s. per week – Signed Robert Calderwood.' This was pay for 60 hours as a dock labourer, unloading grain ships and working a small machine called the 'Devil'. Andy Watson was employed in engineering at the same time.

Calderwood also received £5 from Bootle to pay his debts and bring his wife and family to Merseyside. Back home, Cowlairs bought him back with 30s and a Postal Order for 15s. Calderwood's error was not to repay Bootle's £5, thereby making him 'one of the very meanest types of Scottish professionals'. He denied everything, even his signature, but was forced to provide a damning specimen. The hearing got out of hand. Tom Robertson called out: 'It's a downright, deliberate lie. Don't believe [Heard]'.

Robertson later became the leading referee of his generation, controlling 22 internationals and five Cup finals. But once, playing for Queen's Park against Corinthians, he was pulled up by the referee, Major Marindin: 'Do that again, Robertson and I'll send you off the field.' When the player walked away muttering, Marindin asserted his authority: 'Pay attention, sir. I think you do not know who I am.' Robertson recalled an old Scottish grievance: 'I ken verra weel who y'are. Yer the man who robbed Queen's Park of the Coop.' His 'dark eyes flashing', Marindin could hardly credit the impertinence: 'What's that?' Robertson yielded: 'I was saying a' recht, sir. Dinna "fash yersel".'

There was a postscript. Third Lanark's protest gained a replay, for which there was much betting. Their goalkeeper Collie took a £15 bribe, and Cowlairs won.

Izatt and Weir wanted revenge for their suspension. Out to get Harry Heard, they tried to spill the beans. The stakes became higher: Bootle's future depended on their credibility. It was recalled that Izatt and Weir left Bootle on the morning of an English Cup-tie, an act of 'purely malicious spirit', so their word should be regarded with 'utmost caution'. Bootle survived. Andy Watson was cleared.

In Liverpool, even the Police Athletic 'have gone in for the prevailing fashion of seeking eligible football players, before admitting them to the Force'.

Before suspension, Everton had at last reached the desired level: 'Everton are just now good all round ... Every man fitted for his shop.' Afterwards, they were in chaos. For their first post-suspension match, they straggled out in detachments to start with a 'motley collection' of nine men. There was a rounders bowler; an old Park player; on the right, a reserve partnered by a stranger 'rather plump and not very fast', and 'on the left – no, surely not ... was AN Other,' in fact Arthur Jones, who 'retired some time back, and who has vainly sought a place' in any Bootle team. 'Never did such a queer combination do battle for the club.' The 5,000 crowd felt cheated, the membership had a 'very bitter feeling' against the ruling clique: 'someone has blundered.' Of course the seven Scots were missing but so were others. Billy Briscoe was suspended for playing during the suspension. Having been 'fairly galloped round' by Notts Rangers, Everton suffered 'drastic dribbling' by Liverpool's third club, Stanley 0-3. As the football quality quickly deteriorated, other attractions had to suffice: a 'spicy bully in front of goal caused the few spectators to bristle up a bit'.

Former warriors like 'Black Prince' Fleming returned but captain George Dobson was injured: attributed to dancing two or three times weekly. 2,200 watched Darwen make 'ducks and drakes out of the taut little Liverpool barque'. Everton members' view of their executive was compared to the Irish political economy: like 'all Irish tenants: they have so much to grumble about'. Soon Halliwell dumped their fixture as not good enough. Everton were 'out in the cold'. The joke was that the Stock Exchange was panicking because it was Thursday and there were no posters advertising an Everton match. At the last moment Burslem Port Vale (notorious for doing anything for a guarantee) cobbled a side together. None of this was 'first class'. 'Everton in Mourning.' They were rumoured to pay village team Witton to throw their Anfield game – secretary Eccleston admitted they received a 'consideration' – and 'fortunate to induce little Padiham to come', for the tamest match in years. How did Everton join the League only weeks later?

Bootle looked like the League-club-in-waiting. They 'intend to rise'. New half-back Jack Holt showed 'amazing pluck' and was proving the 'perfect glutton' for all kinds of football work. He already looked the ten-times England international he became between 1890 and 1900. At 5ft

4in his battle with Burnley's six-footer Frank Sugg caused infinite amusement. Within months, Holt and Sugg were rivals for the centre-half slot in Everton's League team. Bootle secured two top new Scotch forwards including twenty-year-old Bob Jamieson, famous for two goals helping Dumbartonshire beat Lancashire 4-1 in October 1887. Bootle's offer outbid future League clubs with jobs on the Workhouse Casual Ward. Did this meet the new Association test for amateurism? At their own trade?

Everton's policy of appealing on behalf of the Anfield Seven looked doomed in comparison. Archie Goodall came and went. But slowly senior clubs were persuaded to come back. Just about. Five thousand waited for Derby County to arrive 45 minutes late. A week before the League was announced, Notts were so uninterested that lacklustre double international '[William] Gunn never went a yard out of his way to get the ball'. No surprise that Everton did not feature in the first League list. Secretary Nisbet got the boot.

WHICH WILL GO TO THE WALL?

Wanderers' relations with Halliwell were equally dangerous, for an amalgamated Bolton club might challenge North End. Preston differed from other Lancashire towns in having no serious local rival. Halliwell had risen as Wanderers declined in 1887, on the back of charismatic goalkeeper Oliver Fairclough, Scotch back Jim 'Golden Slippers' Lucas and ex-Wanderers midfielder Davy Weir.

They met in the Bolton Charity Cup final. Halliwell's ground, Bennetts, was a caution: 'the lane is steep, circuitous and rutty. It is a pull which takes the wind out of you, however fair it is, and even in summer time, though your stockings may not be splashed, you are apt to think.' Nevertheless 4,000 'clomb' the hill to see the eye-catching goalkeepers: 'Trainer simply marvellous … in the midst of this wild encounter … Fairclough wonderful … stops ball after ball in a manner which simply opens the eyes and unlocks the throats of the bystanders.' Davy Weir won the game after Wanderers' equaliser was controversially disallowed: Fairclough and Brogan's 'respective heads going like a couple of bantams in a dunghill argument'. More dung was thrown afterwards: the policeman who saved referee McIntyre from violence reported the official's view that Wanderers were a 'most scampish lot of professionals'.

Oliver Fairclough – 'the bow of Goliath' – had provoked Wanderers with his usual sackcloth and red paint attire, whereas Bolton were now in sackcloth and ashes. Wanderers' 1887 AGM brought no retribution. 1886's AGM had seen a palace revolution ejecting secretary Jack Bentley.

His committee had enjoyed football success but the finances were horrible: £356 debt. 'William the Popular' Struthers became secretary but soon resigned. The 'redoubtable' Fitzroy Norris took over on £35 per annum – his predecessors had been paid £66. Fitzroy's annual report 'had not got a sunny corner'. The three Cups from 1886 were lost, and Wanderers were even worse off financially. First-team wages were £715 but gates were £447 less. Norris had been 'sore pressed owing to the shortcomings of the late secretary'. Bentley had cooked the books and Struthers left a 'terrible state of mystification and chaos'. Everyone was jumping ship. No one would be President or Treasurer. When a member stood up to complain he was immediately promoted to the committee.

Bolton Wanderers were in trouble for 1887-88, and very doubtful contenders for any new premier competition six months later. Their fixture list 'smelt of gate money', there were worrying gaps and, a crucial test of validity, North End had yet to confirm their fixture. But Norris could talk Wanderers to the 'top of the tree', the 'team is kept a profound secret by the wily Fitz who, by sundry winks and hints and shakings of his curly locks, conveys the impression that it will be "a warm 'un".' Four internationals had signed, and the fastest centre in Britain (Dundee Strathmore's Billy Dickson) was on his way. Emperor's New Clothes? Norris also obtained new jerseys that 'sets off the figure'. No one arrived, the forwards got slower and figures were mixed. Every penny had to be watched. Wanderers visited Port Vale on a Monday afternoon. They later complained that lunch served by the Burslem Coffee House broke teeth. Moreover they expected to pay 8d as before, but had been charged 1s 10d which was only with difficulty beaten down to 1s 6d. The proprietor responded by detailing their pre-match meal: 7½lbs loin chops; 15lbs potatoes; 12 glasses milk; 12 glasses ginger beer; 1 large damson tart; 1lb tomatoes; 3 cabbages; 6 large coffees; 1 large tapioca pudding; and sundry confectionery. He said they 'left nothing for a mouse'.

Norris was 'always in trouble over some real or imaginary error of judgment'. Ultimately Wanderers lost the Everton Cup-tie through his 'oversight' in not registering Billy Struthers in time. This was really another sign of Bolton's vulnerability. Struthers was no fly-by-night. He had been a Wanderer for seven years and had retired. Norris found himself short as his 'incompetent men' were 'ruthlessly pulverised' by Burnley and Halliwell. Struthers was asked to get himself fit and Norris took a chance on the registration. The 'Hon Fitz' was usually most principled. Another nail in his coffin came during the first Everton match. Wanderers scored, the Everton umpire protested 'offside'. Had Norris, as Bolton's umpire, stuck up for his team, a goal would have resulted. But no, Norris dumbfounded his crowd by proving to be an umpire with 'conscience'.

Worst of all, he fell foul of the Association. Norris took Wanderers to the Manchester Exhibition celebrating Queen Victoria's Jubilee. No one could play for medals without the Association's permission. Their opponents Newton Heath apologised and nothing happened. Wanderers didn't, and risked being suspended for the whole season. The hint was taken and the 'indefatigable' Norris was gone. He returned to the profitable practice of refereeing and became a familiar figure on League grounds: 'the blue lounge jacket, the watch chain suspended prominently outside, the short knickers.' One season, he travelled a record '5,460 miles to fulfil his duties', renowned for being 'quite capable of following the play throughout a game' [Lincoln, 1912, p.345].

Jack Bentley returned as secretary, with radical action to resolve Wanderers' financial plight – a Grand Prize Draw. He mobilised his network: Preston's Jim Trainer sold tickets at his 'Football Rendezvous' and so did Burnley's Dannie Friel at his 'Footballers' Arms'. These draws were potentially profitable but legally problematic. There was the legend of Father Enoch, Witton FC's patron saint, presiding over their not-so-Grand draw: 'Blind Mike will fish the tickets out. Now you are aware that Mike cannot see, but he will pull out one of mine for the sheep.'

Bentley found even Scotch sides treated impoverished Wanderers casually. Cowlairs sought a replacement fixture for one with suspended Everton. Yes, said Bentley, but then Cowlairs started playing games. We can't confirm, they said, because Everton have appealed. OK, said Jack, come if the appeal fails. Bills advertising the match were duly posted but no Cowlairs. Bentley knew what had happened: 'someone gave them more.' Strangely that someone was 'King John' Houlding – £30. He also paid Northwich Victoria to play as Everton's proxy at Anfield, either to spite Bolton, or Bootle, or just to keep appearances going. Unsurprisingly, Wanderers were hereabouts best friends with Bootle. After an enjoyable Christmas game, Bootle's captain Tom Veitch complimented his fellow Scot Brogan, not realising the stick they were taking back home: 'Why Jimmy, your chaps have improved this season.' 'If you told that in Bolton you would get paddled.'

There had never been such an 'unfortunate season'. Wanderers were 'pretty well towards the bottom of the averages' of first-class clubs. They only won twenty of 57 matches, whereas Halliwell won 27 of 52. It 'cannot possibly get worse … they don't like the idea of shutting up'. Wanderers were being 'snuffed out … where will the fixtures come from next season?'

The crunch games were against Halliwell. One Halliwell player boasted winning £14 in bets from their Charity Cup win. Now the placards around town asked 'Champions Who?' Davy Weir steered Halliwell to a 4-3 win. Bentley reacted by copying Albion. No one would call West Bromwich 'a pretty spot, or would care to spend their holidays there', but Bolton Wanderers could follow the diet that made Albion strong. Albion's Bob Roberts advised not to 'eat up the extra larder at the Plough ... though we [Wanderers] disposed of all the meat they had ... a large leg of mutton'. They waited thirty minutes for potatoes to follow until Bentley learnt from the Plough that 'our boys [Albion] did not take any in training'.

Confident too of new funds from the Grand Draw, Bentley strengthened Wanderers. Bethel Robinson, an ex-North End 'amateur', was set up and soon 'doing good trade' in the Crown & Cushion on Mealhouse Lane. Fourteen-stone-plus Walter Flitcroft became his formidable full-back partner, and soon the wandering Archie Goodall played in a 5-5 draw with Derby County, a score that naturally had Test batsman Barlow as referee. Bentley was into his stride and with smart work he got Frank Sugg as centre. It was altogether, for pun-loving Victorians, 'Suggestive of more prosperous times.' Bolton announced Renton as their Easter Monday attraction. 'Good biz.'

But would it be enough? Halliwell sent Davy Weir to Glasgow and he brought back Jardine and Duncan from Partick Thistle. Theirs was not a whimsical move: out-of-work Bob Jardine had long wanted a move to England. Halliwell were ready for Wanderers. On March 17th, their last games before the League was proposed, Weir, Jardine and Duncan all scored – 4-1.

If the League wanted a Bolton representative, it should not have been Wanderers. But once they were Apostles, Davy Weir joined them. It proved enough.

Chapter Five

'Invincibility Lost'

I was a guest of Preston North End, and we were looking across Euston Square, about noon on the day of the match, when we saw a small band of boys emerge from the platform, each carrying a little insignificant bag, and they sauntered across to the East wing. When we were informed that these boys, acting as their own porters, were our opponents at the Oval, our confidence increased. They had a simple two-horse waggonette … we had a prancing four-in-hand.

Jack Bentley

The 1888 Cup final changed everything for Albion and North End. Briefly West Bromwich truly became England's Albion before descending into 'public-house paupers' and over-mighty subjects, and then quarrelsome sulks of the new League. North End, suddenly a second-choice attraction, picked a fight with the authorities and were suspended for the year. What price the Invincibles; without Preston, what price the League?

The final was a surprising thing. North End were such hot favourites it seemed men against boys. There were stories of Preston's complacency, the most emblematic being Jack Ross asking Major Marindin if they could be photographed with the Cup. 'Had you better not win it first?' was the laconic reply. The boys won: eighteen-year-old Billy Bassett led North End such a 'pretty dance' that he walked into the England team that evening.

For some, North End had it coming. There was much pre-match sneering from Birmingham correspondents. Their theme was a powerful one. What did their opponents have to do with Preston or Lancashire? Their team was Scotch. Albion was home-grown.

Brummies did not think much of the capital either: London trains were 'literally choke-full, and with a horrid indescribable sort of fog hanging over the great city'. Timescales allowed the train companies to advertise excursions combining the March 24th final with the morning's Boat Race. Visiting journalists thought the Boat Race a 'poor show' undeserving of its reputation as a spectacle. Bob Holmes, North End's own kid, later blamed their defeat on being 'starved to death' with cold watching the Boat Race, and never got warm afterwards. 'Yes, we were daft' [Hunt, 2000, p.75].

The sporting scene had recently been debased. The bare-fist boxing Championship of the World, between American John L Sullivan (who made £5,000 from his European trip) and Brummie Charley Mitchell had just turned out a 'pugilistic fiasco', subject to much 'ridicule'. Athletics meetings, not so long ago capable of attracting crowds of 10/12,000, had been discredited through betting scams and pretended amateur status. Even the 'Derby favourite may be nobbled'. What was left? Cricket and Football Rule OK: 'all the corruption in the world cannot vitiate its straightforwardness. Football is a grand game.' The 'people are able to distinguish between sham sport and the real article', and the Oval's final, watched by 16,000, was a 'perfectly genuine affair'.

Albion's players had been promised 'a first class traveling bag' for winning (presumably to replace the 'little insignificant' ones described above), but local papers begged, please, no presents for individual scorers. Respect the team. They also travelled down that morning whilst North End stayed in London overnight. Anyone might have thought Albion were short of money.

The final saw North End's 'magnificent' play frustrated. They were 'bigger, quicker and more lithe than the Albion ... the lot of them passed and dribbled as only they can, till they came to the Albion backs. Then they passed and repassed.' North End foundered on the rocks of Harry Green and Albert Aldridge, the latter also earning immediate England selection. Albion's forwards, Bassett, 'Spry' Woodhall and Bayliss proved elusive. Bassett was the 'pick of the basket ... a clumsy, flatfooted runner, but he can go and can double'. North End only intimidated onlookers: 'Safety Valve' Graham acted 'brutal ... once when he came at Woodhall with clenched fists and a look of fierceness I positively shuddered.' England forward Woodhall nonetheless scored the late winner after Jack 'much-talked-of-wonder' Ross did a double somersault and floored Bassett just after he centred. In North End's desperate scramble for an equaliser 'science and organisation were utterly thrown to the winds'. Albion 2, North End 1.

North End left 'with hearts as heavy as lead ... the bitterest and direst blow of their hopes and aspirations.' 'Free Critic' knew from the inside how it felt: 'North End were not smiling ... and from the bottom of my heart I felt sorry for them.' Jack Bentley thought mostly of William Sudell, who proved a model Victorian sportsman: 'a man who cannot lose is not fit to win ... I will try and try again and again until the cup does come to Preston.'

'Everywhere ... the news has been received with amazement' and quickly became a morality tale. A triumph of native man: 'not a fratricidal strife as when the Villa and Albion met' in 1887. North End represented professionalism and importation, yet had been beaten: 'it was legitimate football against moneybag football, and legitimate football won.'

WEST BROMWICH ALBION

The 1888 final reprised the 1887 semi-final. Both times North End 'kept their opponents penned in round their goal'. Both times Albion's goalkeeper Roberts had been superb and Albion's forwards broke away at the end to win. It was more than a coincidence: the 'second signal proof of the prowess of local athletes'.

The English gloried in the triumph of 'our lads' and their 'pluck'. Albion was the ancient name for England. England's amateur centre Tinsley Lindley typically understated: 'a point to [Albion's] credit is that they are all local men.' They were hailed as local Englishmen and as Empire builders: they 'never knew when they were beaten'. Football was beginning to define national quality: 'from a footballer's point of view England can literally boss creation. Imagine a Frenchman …' The great General Wellington thought the same: it encouraged 'the pugnacity that runs in the blood of the true born Briton; and which the Iron Duke once said, when a spectator at a football game, won Waterloo! … Won Waterloo'.

'Intoxicated with their great victory', Albion's weeks of celebrations caused months of trouble. 'Bayliss got the cup, and hurried across to the pavilion with scarcely a bit of his face not smiling.' Even Albion's usually dour financial and general secretaries eased up: 'Ford smiled – a most unusual thing … and Mr Smith looked happy.' Their preparations however had been suitably frugal, with each player given a 'small bottle of champagne' at the post-match dinner. This was not flamboyant enough for Captain Mitchell, President of the Staffordshire Association and soon-to-be President of the 'second league,' the Combination. He ordered the Criterion to fill the Association Cup with their best champagne. Surprisingly it took a hotel well used to entertaining the Prince of Wales 30 minutes to do the deed. Then the toasts started, from players as well as officials, like Albion founder member George Timmins: 'Darkie hoped they would keep [the Cup], and that it would always be as full [loud laughter].' Albion joined North End at the Pavilion Music Hall before getting home at 4am Sunday morning. It had been a long day. Monday saw the town's reception, or 'demonstration', before adjournment to Bob Roberts' Horseshoe Inn. Albion were having a 'high old time … the fun, the frolic, the enthusiasm … imbibing the strong waters of success'.

Imbibing became a theme. Both club and players cashed in. Their first trip was a mistake, to Scotland and 0-3 defeat by Third Lanark Royal

Volunteers. The Albion had the 'good sense to fetch the English Cup which was exhibited in the pavilion window' at Cathkin Park. They negotiated for half a £194 gate. Albion praised the Volunteers as 'gentlemanly' but the Scotch press hardly beat about the bush: Albion 'made fools of themselves' on the 'strong Glasgow air and stronger Glasgow liquids'. Already they were told to 'pull themselves together'. Albion wanted to play Queen's Park on the same trip but they would not oblige, miffed that Third Lanark got there first: '[Queen's Park and Thirds'] feud has been handed down from generation to generation.' Instead Albion stopped over at Newcastle and pulled themselves together by winning 5-1. After travelling a thousand miles, they took their share of Anfield's 'monstre gate' and beat Everton without their three England men.

Then they took to the music hall. One player got ten shillings from the Gaiety in London and later they created 'tableaux vivants' of their final triumph. The Cup was going from pub to pub, for a consideration. If it was all done in the best possible taste it was tolerable: the town was awash with placards announcing the 'distinguished patronage of the Albion' at this or that establishment. But it went too far. Granted the players were not very 'flush with money', but leader-writers were soon waxing indignant that 'the trophy is being turned into a public-house show ... [and the team] a collection of public-house stalkers'. The authorities were not satisfied until the Cup was lodged in a tea emporium window, belonging to West Bromwich Mayor [and Albion chairman] Edward Heelis, a grocer.

Results were mixed. They drew with North End, at home, showing that after 'the festivities, all the dinners and suppers,' their Cup final win was not the 'mystery' that the Scots had concluded. Prices went up – four shillings for a place in the covered stands – so a 6/7,000 crowd produced 'very handsome receipts'. North End started smoothly and were two up until the beast motif returned: Albion's left-winger was 'like a flea upon an elephant' and their other 'greyhounds' caused further [h]itches. Sudell saw the signs and called out 'Stop that short passing'. At half-time Preston's half-backs were 'perspiring like blast furnacemen'. Afterwards, North End were 'besieged' in their own goal to keep Albion out.

Albion were lucky to survive two hours against Wolves in the Staffordshire Cup final replay. More money came in. The Staffordshire Association, having gained enough, allowed the clubs a third each of the second replay's gate receipts. This time disorganised Albion lost, their first loss, to Wolves in seven matches during 1887-88 and at home all season. Bayliss, Woodhall and Bassett were openly quarrelling with each other. Albion were unravelling.

Unfortunately, Albion published their Oval team photograph in May when interest in football had become 'brief'. Yet the biggest game was still to come, and the weather proved very unspringlike. Scottish Cup holders Renton had reacted to the change of guard down south. They cancelled a mooted Easter game with North End, the old invincibles, whose 'terms did not suit'. Instead, Albion. 'Won't there be a crush?' As Scotland had lost the International to England, Renton 'can do the country justice. North End can be dealt with afterwards'. Albion delayed the match until Whit week when they could run a special train. So, on May 19th Albion and Renton contested the Championship of the World. It was a good marketing idea, it might have caught on, if it had not been for the weather, or the League. It was played in an unprecedented storm. McNee put Renton ahead before play had to stop. After ten minutes, they returned to standing pools of water. The rain became a blinding deluge amid more thunder and lightning. James McColl scored twice and even on the flooded pitch great Renton passing had Albion 'puffed' long before the finish – 4-1. Albion were no new invincibles.

Their season was far from finished. The Monday after the World Championship they won another cup … the West Bromwich Friendly Society Charity Cup; next day there was a benefit for Bob Roberts; then a final series of would-be prestigious friendlies – a draw with Villa, at last a win over Third Lanark and a tired Monday defeat to North End at Preston.

Albion were therefore flawed heroes before their AGM in June. Chairman George Salter lugubriously reported last year's successful playing record: 58 matches, 43 won, only eight lost, nearly 200 goals scored at a ratio over 3:1. Secretary Tom Smith advised next year all 'the principal clubs' would be played. Unlike Villa's AGM, there was no justification of the League: it was not even worth mentioning. The local press took this opportunity to note that the champions of the National Football Association League would be the most winners of the '24 matches' [sic] the twelve clubs would generate.

Instead, Albion's balance sheet was the bombshell. In 1887 there had been 'bad blood' between the players and 'the scores of tradesmen – especially the butchers – [who] lost a pile of shiners' betting on Albion's unexpected National Cup final defeat by Villa. They 'wreaked vengeance and spite' by withholding the players' £100 Prize Fund. In 1888 supporters won large sums betting on Albion's unexpected Cup win, but the club again lost money. Despite the frugality of their final preparations: the bounty from the Staffordshire Cup replays; those trips to Scotland, Newcastle and Liverpool purely to cash in their fame, the increased prices for North End matches. And yet a deficit. Then there were off-balance sheet items – the 'Prize Fund' became a 'loan advanced' to the players. They had intended to pay secretaries Smith and Ford, and now could not. Really, they had nearly lost £200! 'One or two of the big wigs grumbled at the deficiency and rather misleading statement of accounts.' West Bromwich's tradesmen were appalled: an income of £2,000 and they could not afford to pay a secretary! 'Something going wrong somewhere.' The balance sheet was not accepted, the meeting adjourned. Only weeks earlier, Albion's telegraph seemed ripe for investment as a 'stage coachey and fossilised system'. Now modernisation was out of the question: rather, there was such a thing as clubs 'drying out' i.e. being disbanded.

Rather than challenge the accuracy of the income figure, in typically Victorian fashion the members charged profligacy. The classic insult was that their committee had shown 'extravagance worthy of a Board of Guardians'. A Board of Guardians was the local management of the Poor Law: the Workhouse. Our folk memory, gained through Dickens, was of a parsimonious group refusing Oliver Twist any more gruel. But at the time they were more likely to be criticised for 'extravagance'. The Albion crisis broke on the back of existing criticism that the West Bromwich Board of Guardians had 'created the impression that there is no limit to their spending capacity'. The reality seems different. The West Bromwich Board of Guardians were at the same time demanding enquiries, answers and a change of practice after learning they had spent £1 more this year than last on out-relief, despite supporting fewer people outside the workhouse.

When the adjourned AGM threw out a second 'inaccurate balance sheet', officers ran for cover. Chairman Salter knew nothing ('little things came to [Salter's] knowledge which did not meet with his approval') and threatened resignation unless the players were reined in. Captain Bayliss saw who would be cast as baddies. Albion's players cost comparatively little – £611 in 'match fees and loss of time' – and contributed far more than the members' subscriptions of £18. But the members held the power, and the players had already been described as 'public-house paupers' during the earlier undignified exploitation of their cup win. 23-year-old Bayliss sought a place on the finance committee! If his play had been criticised recently for an 'old unhappy knack of shooting over the bar', his politics were 'aiming too high'. Players had been members, several founding members, until they became professionals. Bayliss still demanded a stake: his was the Last Stand of the player-as-member.

Now the 'simply abominable' finances were forgotten: even financial secretary Louis Ford kept his head. Albion's power bloc and press united. No one was going to give players, even (previously) 'our honourable worthy captain', a place on the committee. The club united around the principle that paid players had 'not one atom of claim to membership or voting power'. 'The committee should rule.' Payment had moved players into a different class. It was not about sport. West Bromwich's tradesmen knew all about employer-employee relations, and so did its rhetorical local paper, the *Free Press*: 'would any employer who pays a man 10s for a day's work – and the Albion players have often had more than double that.' These employees were 'not allowed to be managers as well'.

The conflict was acute: a heady mix of class, the honour of local associations, and money. There was 'talk and gossip about the probable dissolution of the club, or rather it was in danger of being wrecked on those financial rocks which have wrought disaster amongst so many other football combinations.'

James Bayliss was now styling himself 'the late captain' and half the team were similarly alienated. England's Albert Aldridge, Cup final hero, left for a new outfit, the amalgamation of Walsall's two clubs into Walsall Town Swifts (if they had done that a year previously they, rather than Derby County, might have been original Apostles).

There was talk of Albion's stars – Bayliss, Woodhall, Roberts, Harry Green at least – forming a new club, the West Bromwich Strollers. It was not fantasy. Potentially important clubs were still being formed. But there was no institutional or entrepreneurial backing for slighted professionals. Backers would only promote amateur status. The previous year it was Warwick County (mentioned as possible League candidates). Now it was Wolverhampton Town, formed with Charles Crump as president (a noted anti-professionalism protagonist in the Association battles of 1885). Strictly amateur. The only new development in pro football was elsewhere in Birmingham, where Small Heath Alliance became the first club to take advantage of recent limited liability company legislation (with £150 capital – of course it meant dropping the Alliance bit – too mutual, friendly society sounding).

Lack of confidence in Albion players was made retrospective: it had been 'very widely thought at the end of last season that the team needed very much to be strengthened'. Instead of winning the National Cup, 1887-88 was now remembered for two 'unfortunate blots', losing the Birmingham and Staffordshire Cups.

By mid-August 1888 the stalemate made prospects bleak for the coming season. The new committee was castigated for 'want of firmness' with the players. To the 'all-absorbing' question 'What will they do?' the answer had been 'nothing'. Instead of their voluntary efforts, why not 'place reliance on some experienced official' like Jack Bentley of Bolton. Was this the first media advocacy for a change in management, to a professional outside the club? For sure, Bentley would 'secure the services of one or two sterling good men'. Otherwise, Albion 'may find themselves sliding into oblivion at a more rapid rate than they came into fame'.

Sorely provoked, the committee took the hint. They went to Scotland, tapped their contacts with the 'World Champions' and hired six Renton men. The motivation was overt: to 'scare the other players into submission'. The odd cautionary voice was heard – this was taking an 'appalling risk … over a bogus balance sheet'. The players suddenly found defenders – they are 'looked upon as too much of a hireling'. Now the committee were 'moneygrabbers'. Players make a club and are no 'less honourable', so why not 'give them a voice in the management of their own affairs'.

Representation seemed a lesser evil than 'importation'. It would be a great pity to disturb Albion's 'proud boast' of displaying 'native talent'. The news that Renton's James McColl refused 'undoubtedly the largest sum ever offered to a football player' came too late. Enough Scots accepted to convince. The committee played their trump card. When Bayliss got the bad news he caved in. Albion's strike, or 'family squabble', was over.

The question now was 'What to do with the Scotchmen?' Albion's reputation was restored. True-blood local men were back. 'All seems to be going well again.' But Albion now had at least two world champions available, half-back Bob Kelso and back Andrew Hannah. West Bromwich revived their 'proud boast': 'no foreigners'. Ignoring their obvious recent quarrelling, the team were said to be 'harmonious' without outsiders. Hannah was mocked for being an 'interesting female' and his likely reception from the 'recalcitrants' was obvious: 'won't that youth get some chaff?' The principled answer was equally obvious: the town's prestige was back safe in the hands of local committeemen: 'the foreigners will only play on emergencies so that we shall still be able to boast a playing team composed entirely of "throstles".'

Throughout their 'turmoiled troubles' Albion had played. Predictably they started on a Monday evening in early August against North End. Albion's muscular new executive charged an extra 6d, and 2,000 saw Preston win 4-2. Bassett reprised his Cup final form, but the 'boss' was unappeased: 'why Bayliss should continually keep shouting at him I cannot understand.' August did not really count. September was the time to assess prospects. West Bromwich's *Free Press* imagined the eyes of the football world upon their 'giants of the leather'. Albion had come through their dissension. Andrew Hannah had gone home before Saturday's first League match and before, on a misty September Monday evening, 7,000 (one of 1888-89's best attendances) watched Albion and Walsall Town Swifts play under electric light to open a local Science and Art Institute.

PRESTON NORTH END

On March 24th 1888, Preston's Fishergate was almost impassable. A dense crowd watched, with feverish anxiety, the *Evening Post* offices display telegrams giving a running account of the Cup final. The crush was so great that police struggled to preserve a passage through. The disappointment was received at a quarter to six: 'not a sound was heard, but there was a rushing to and fro in hot haste, and five minutes later, not a vestige of the crowd was to be seen.' As in Birmingham, the moral of defeat was 'endless money thrown away' on North End's professional footballers. It was a plague of biblical proportions: verily, 'wherefore have we spent our money for that which is not bread, and our labour for that which satisfied not.'

Like Albion, the new League featured little in Preston's spring and summer. They had other things to worry about. On Cup final day, West Bromwich's *Free Press* carried no mention of the 'fixity of fixtures' movement. One fixture was reported: North End were postponing their next visit to Albion to accommodate the Lancashire Cup final. It became a near-fateful issue.

This kind of postponement was exactly what the League was designed to prevent. The scene was being set for conflict between League and Association over the *raison d'être* of both organisations: fixtures, and which could command the clubs' best teams when they coincided. And behind fixtures lay receipts and their distribution, and that meant also conflict with the many affiliated county associations. For example, West Bromwich Albion's AGM followed close on that of the Birmingham Association. Their meeting bathed in the confidence that Birmingham was 'supreme with respect to football' and was addressed by Charles Crump, leading football speaker and leading opponent of professionalism. For Crump 'every man who gave up his work for football made a very great mistake … most successful players worked as hard in the shop'. In contrast to Albion's money problems, the Birmingham Association bathed in the confidence of having £1,000 in a large reserve fund, a largesse due to the recent Villa v Albion Birmingham Cup final.

The League would combat the 'caprice of Associations'. The summer brought a dawning view that the League fixtures 'will take the wind out of the cup-ties', and that it would 'virtually sound the death-knell of more than one Association'. Those Associations that saw the 'breakers ahead' became less 'cocksey'. Like Lancashire, the Birmingham Association agreed to exempt top clubs (Villa, Stoke, Wolves and Albion) from the early rounds of their Senior Cup, and for the semi-finalists to divide the proceeds. Despite these significant concessions – the later rounds of regional cups were big draws – 'ungrateful' Albion withdrew from the Birmingham Association anyway.

Affiliation required accepting the primacy of the County cups, providing players for representative games, accepting Association discipline and financial calls. Associations did not always act with humility, or even-handedly. Some officers were in position to promote or defend the interests of their own club.

The 1888 Lancashire Cup, second only in prestige to the national Association's Challenge Cup, ended in a chaos and acrimony that reflected the way fixtures mediated conflict over power and money in the pre-League days. And all manipulated by William Sudell.

The 1888 Lancashire Cup finalists were holders North End and Accrington. But when the Lancashire Association decreed that the final should be held on Blackburn's Leamington Road ground, Sudell anticipated 'a bit of a riot'. He remembered the 'very scurvy' insults, 'vulgar abuse and badinage' during North End's visits weeks earlier, which 'achieved its foul purpose of irritating and disconcerting the players' (see above pp.60-61). North End were overtly conciliatory, offering to play anywhere else, even on Accrington's ground. But the Association's 'autocratic executive' saw Sudell's threats to resign as a challenge. It became a 'war to the knife'. Others took sides: Jack Bentley had refereed both North End's matches at Blackburn in February 1888 and agreed that Rovers' spectators had been 'simply disgraceful'. This was hard to take. Blackburn's representatives resented their identification with a 'gang of rowdies'. And the town was powerful in the corridors of the Lancashire Association.

They confirmed the original choice of ground. North End, acting 'exceedingly childish', scratched. Lancashire, 'all boiling hot and bubbling over with righteous indignation', retaliated. Secretary Richard Gregson wrote, unsuccessfully, to persuade Albion to refuse North End a fixture to replace the final. It was personal, a matter of Victorian manners. Individuals were accused of 'wreaking their jealousy and their vengeance'. Gregson defended his letter as the action of a private individual, echoing Sudell's justification of why he ignored a letter from the Lancashire Association. He said that as the letter was addressed to 'Dear Sudell', rather than his official club position, he took it to be personal, and thus put it on the fire. Similarly he regarded his own communication as private because it was signed Sudell – 'did you ever hear of a man wiring his christian name?'

Newspapers regarded the venue of the Lancashire Cup final, rather than Home Rule for Ireland or the health of the German Emperor, as the question of the day. It got really heavy when Preston wrote to all English clubs complaining of Blackburn's unsportsmanlike crowd, and resigned from the Lancashire Association. The punishment for scratching from the Cup was limited, and had only been applied to withdrawals short of the final. So the Association found Preston, the Manchester United of their day, guilty of misconduct and banned the club from all football until December 31st 1888. The rest of the year. Where did this leave the League? Hamlet without the prince. Cynical Jack Bentley nursed 'a strong suspicion that it is a blow at the New League'. The controversy enabled the opportunistic Bentley to publicise the League.

Birmingham papers immediately saw that the suspension would test the loyalty of the 'Twelve Apostles'. On North End's next tour, Scotch clubs added mischief by offering fixtures throughout their suspension. It was doubtful that other clubs would resign from their Associations to play against North End in the League. Doubtful, but possible. Everton viewed Lancashire's over-reaction with incredulity: 'an official thunderbolt has been launched as a counterblast or challenge to mortal combat hurled ... at the Football League.' Equally, this 'extravagant piece of despotism' increased the appetite for challenge: 'the Leaguers will now have a stronger motive for disregarding these Associations with their absurd pretensions ... next season will witness a revolution in Association football'.

Right now, Lancashire's dignatories had to preside over the ignominious failure of their prized competition. Their coffers suffered: the 1887 final grossed £300, but Accrington versus Whoever attracted only £40-worth of Blackburn rowdies. The grandstand was full of football VIPs. The Association's Donald Woolfall was embarrassed: 'the competition has been utterly spoiled – ended in a regular fizzle. And then look at me giving the cup to Accrington. Wasn't it a regular farce? No wonder the Accrington men did not care a dash whether they got it or not?' Never mind, 'North End would be dealt with afterwards.'

No one was sure whether they would turn up. In Preston on Saturday morning the final was advertised as North End versus Accrington. Accrington attended Leamington Road punctually and did their duty: Captain George Howarth 'tossed himself for choice of ends, and of course won [sic].' They also kicked off, and constructed an elaborate passing manoeuvre to score a goal 'amid loud laughter'. They then sheepishly received the Cup, after which who should trot onto the field and win, by 4-0, 'the final that wasn't' – Witton. This was poetic justice, as Witton were commonly thought to have been 'officiated' out of their semi-final with Accrington. Lancashire's Association lost much authority.

The irony was Accrington v North End would have been a lucrative match. The clubs had not met for two years, since Accrington's 3-2 win on Easter Monday ended North End's unbeaten 1885-86 record. But the clubs would have benefited little. Most receipts went to the Association, hence Lancashire's main argument at the national hearing was that North End pulled out because it was not to their 'pecuniary benefit'. The colloquial explanation was that North End had 'already lost two cups, and they're afraid they'll lose the third'. Sudell made sure they did not lose out. Accrington and North End's two-year-old grievance was now conveniently resolved. They celebrated making-up by playing a match that was so successful they promptly arranged another. So, really, they played the final, home and away, without the Association.

Sudell had needed something to kickstart North End's season after they lost the English Cup final. It was a sensitive time. Would their public desert them? Had 'endless money [been] thrown away' on their scientific pros? The town forgave North End, and turned up in large numbers – seven, twelve and eleven thousands – for the Easter games. The middle fixture, Preston's largest of the season, was against Accrington.

The ground was full an hour before the start. Special trains had brought 1,300 from Accrington. Whilst waiting, supporters 'twitted' each other with 'various incidents' from their respective cup-ties the previous week (the English Cup final and the Lancashire Cup semi-final). Latecomers broke into the ground. Accrington's executive, flush with its Easter egg of half Deepdale's £180 gate, agreed a return the next week.

That match was the biggest in Accrington's history. They had only lost 0-2 at Preston and had a chance of winning. George Howarth turned down England selection against Ireland to captain Accrington. They brought old favourite Bob Macbeth from Grimsby for the game. They charged high prices and forced ladies to pay for the first time. They turfed journalists out of their privileged positions, and the crowd 'brought down their arms upon the shoulders of the unfortunate scribes in a manner the reverse of pleasant, while a shower of rain in no way served to sweeten the temper.' It was nominally an ordinary fixture.

Seven thousand in the Cemetery ground produced receipts of £150. Accrington scored first but Gordon equalised within two minutes. They then battled until Jamie Ross shot over the top but claimed a goal. Referee Jack Bentley said no, so North End 'gathered together in a body, made use of some uncomplimentary remarks … [and] showed a tendency to leave the field'. They 'made fools of themselves and everybody else concerned'. Bentley, so often their defender, was unhappy and Accrington's crowd called out: 'Yo're soft.' Drummond scored, and Bob Howarth preserved North End's lead by handling a goal-bound shot. Nothing came of the free-kick – 2-1.

After these dramas, who needed the Lancashire Cup?

Afterwards, North End set out on another tour of Scotland – five games in six days. Caring not one brass button about the Associations, Sudell perforce became a champion of the League. The agenda had changed from a matter of manners to one of strategic conflict: 'North End don't give a fig about either the County or the National Association if the newly-established Football League will only stick together.' The *Blackburn Times* noted that, curiously, the League fixtures meant North End would play on Blackburn's ground next season. That would be some event.

In London in early May the National Association decided whether these would be the last games Preston would play this year. They laughed at examples of the Blackburn crowd's misdemeanours – 'Give it to the ******s' was translated as 'Pass the ball, please' – then chose discretion by overturning the suspension. Sudell was free to join the League and the Lancashire Association was humiliated. Would his League deliver the 'mortal blow'?

Preston were in new trouble. That Scottish tour was a disaster: three successive defeats, including their first loss to Queen's Park. Could Sudell stop his team breaking up? Billy Rose, their former goalkeeper/reinstated amateur, had persuaded Sandy Robertson and Sam Thomson to join Warwick County; and the Ross brothers were going to Everton. It looked like dunghill-time: 'in losing these redoubtable champions the North End have taken the first step towards the dissolution which many people have prophesied for the mushroom-like organisation.'

Chapter Six

'Where are the Scots, Rob Roy?'

English football has failed, or is in a bad way.

A week before the League began, Jack Bentley took his Bolton Wanderers to face Manchester's best, Newton Heath, and pretended he was someone else again.

It had been a wet summer for cricket, which made football's return all the more welcome to 'Free Critic', a.k.a. Jack Bentley: 'you are apt to wish for football, which you are prepared to see played, no matter what sort of stuff there is flying about, in the shape of weather.' 'Free Critic' had a dig at Newton Heath's itinerants: four were ex-Wanderers, several other Welsh imports; and the Heathens expected two 'name' Scotch amateurs, including Grimsby's Bob Macbeth, but they never came. 'I finished up a pleasant afternoon with an inspection of the Lancashire & Yorkshire Waggon Works, where so many of the players are employed, chaperoned by Mr Farrow, the courteous financial secretary.'

Courteous Mr Farrow may have been diverting Bentley's covetous attentions from his best Welshmen – Jones the back, and centre-forward Jack Doughty. Chaperoning was wise: Bentley evaded long enough to persuade 'Jones the back' to join Bolton soon after, and Doughty flirted with being Wolves' centre in the League. Doughty was the Heathens' star: a scorer for Wales against all three home countries in 1888, including four against Ireland. Like many centres, he was combative. A Bolton goalkeeping save 'was scarcely any reason for Doughty to go up and strike him'. Wanderers' new forward returned the compliment: 'Milne, who is a demon for the goalkeeper, gave him anything but gentle charges.'

The match was not seen as preliminary to the new League, or to anything. It was the new season. Seven thousand watched, twice as many as the average League crowd to come. 'Free Critic' thought 500 supporters from Bolton was most 'encouraging for Mr Bentley and his co-workers'. Prospects were promising: hundreds had watched Wanderers train during the week, more than attended some matches in 1887-88. It was however still early doors: 'one cannot expect men to be in the best of condition on the first day after the holidays.'

'Free Critic' affected a detached interest: 'I wanted to see what these new men the Wanderers have got from Scotland are like.' Jack Milne proved resilient: being ever-present and playing six positions. Bentley's curiosity was echoed elsewhere. Bolton's rivals Halliwell were keeping up with the Joneses: 'three Scotchmen have appeared at Halliwell, but nobody seems to know much about them. However the fact remains that they have three brand-new Scotchmen, and that's something.' Halliwell's Scotch forwards had something all right. Bob Jardine moved to Notts, becoming in October the first League player to score five goals, and McGuinness, ex-Kilmarnock, quickly attracted League offers.

Scotland was the obvious place to search for reinforcements, or in Albion's case replacements for their rebellious Cup winners. Some clubs advertised, sometimes promising real employment, as Grimsby did: 'Wanted, a Boatbuilder; must be good footballer; Forward preferred. Permanent position at good wage.' Or: 'To football players. A clerkship open to a good back or half-back. Good salary to a suitable man. State club, age etc.'

Albion, Bolton and others surprisingly focused on Dundee. A peripheral football centre, yet 'valuables are sometimes found amongst rubbish'. Dundee Strathmore's Billy Dickson was really valuable, 'a fine strapping fellow – just the stamp that centre forwards are made of,' who scored four international goals earlier in 1888. Dickson proved to be beyond the League clubs; beyond the whisky companies supporting some of Scotland's amateur clubs; beyond the 'big sum' offered by the club that stayed amateur, Queen's Park. In the end, 'most unexpected of all, the great, the mighty, the much-run-after-not-to-be got at Dickson has at length succumbed and has gone to – of all places on earth – Sunderland.' The Scotch press reported that a 'very good bargain' induced the 'fatal plunge'.

Davy Weir had come earlier: 'a man named Weir from Halliwell has been knocking around Glasgow recently on the look out for players with a thirst for English gold and English glory. He has conducted his operations so quietly that no one can tell whether he was successful.' Weir soon switched allegiance to Bolton Wanderers. He tried William Paul of Partick Thistle (Dickson's rival as Scotland's best centre) and got Milne and Coupar from Dundee clubs. Negotiations for Alec Barbour included football strategy. Barbour, recent Renton captain, was 'given control of Bolton's forwards and would insist on the passing game'.

Wolverhampton Wanderers followed Albion's tactic of using Scots to pressure established players. Founder, captain and star centre Jack Brodie let it be known that he might not play this season until Wolves showed they could replace him, either with Jack Doughty or a Scot. Wolves' initial imports were dismissed locally: 'we don't know where the last two came from.' When Cameron – Edinburgh St Bernard's 'clever' centre –

arrived, Brodie retracted, to become a dominant personality of the first League season.

Although the Renton men departed after Albion's committee's feint, Jack Hendry, a Scot without reputation, stayed, quickly impressing as 'finished ... passes with utmost perfection and judgement very nearly perfection ... astonishing he has to go so far to be discovered'. Hendry had an eventful season. In his later career he reached two Cup finals with Notts County and provoked the introduction of the penalty-kick offence.

The English were encouraged. If Hendry could be so effective, so might other unheralded Scots. Imports remained numerous and controversial throughout the season, but they were rarely top Scots. Only one 1888 international (Bob Kelso) appeared in the League, and then only one game. The most prominent new Scots were full-back Jack Forbes, capped nine times between 1883/87; and forwards Alex Higgins and Alec Barbour, who both played once for Scotland, in 1885. The top Scotch clubs largely saw off the League's challenge and the biggest attendances of 1888-89 remained in Glasgow. But the writing was on the wall. If the League had yet to guarantee clubs a more consistent income, there were definitely more real jobs in England.

The English attitude was still influenced by Dr Johnson's axiom: 'Sir, let me tell you, the noblest prospect which the Scotchman ever sees is the high road that leads him to England.' They were also as casual about importing Scotch talent as they were exploiting their Empire's other raw material. The attitude was instrumental: could Scotch amateurs be got, and were they any good? Where football importation symbolised conspicuous consumption by English towns, there might be parochially inspired sour comments. For example, a pick up in trade was Lancashire's explanation for Sunderland being able to sign so many Scotch 'bawbees'. When they did moralise, the English castigated them as ultimate shamateurs. The Scotch response was to return the charge of hypocrisy with interest: 'it is only the tempter mocking the tempted after he has yielded to the temptation.' There was also cynicism about the authorities: 'when Scotch players are about to migrate to England, they are told they are certain of International caps.'

In Scotland the exports carried a heavy moral significance, although one full of contradictions. For a decade the English had paid the Scots the compliment of importing their football 'professors'. This implied acceptance of inferiority was not unwelcome to nationalistic Scots, but unaccountably it was not accompanied by English deference. Scotch importations avoided the restrictive rules governing English professionals. For example, Accrington lost Jemmy Lowe, their fancied League centre. Lowe came from prestigious Midlands club Wednesday Old Athletic in 1885 but secretly continued to work in Staffordshire rather than be faithful to his Manchester residential qualification. For his 'deliberate falsehood' and 'unlimited animation' Lowe was suspended for two years.

What the English saw as the easy option, the Scots took as an 'unrelished compliment', which not only betrayed Scotland's 'slow, natural methods of development', but carried an unpleasant sting in its tail. 'When an English club purposes to 'rise in the world', as a great many unfortunately do every year, it takes a third class ticket for the North, and sends a few bank notes and as great many rosy promises in boots to Scotland ... The baited hooks too often prove only a delusion and a snare ... they pamper him, and spoil him, and finally cast him adrift.'

'Bastard professionalism' was condemned in Old Testament terms: 'Reverend Smith knew nothing more satanic than the sin of making gain out of our amusement. It is a prostitution of the most heinous sort ... poisoning of the wells'. Salvation was pagan. Scotch towns were 'tortured by visitations of professional and amateur agents', and when Renton's Andrew Hannah returned from his 'visit' to Albion they hailed a disenchantment: 'the gall and wormwood must be drank when the hallucination is dissipated.'

How infuriating too that when the best English clubs, with their many Scotch imports, won in Scotland they wallowed in their superiority. Fortunately, in the annual internationals until 1888, the Scots held sway without using any of the professionals, like North End's Jack Ross and Villa's Archie Hunter, who made English clubs so good.

Scotch anxiety in the summer of 1888 was heightened not by the new League (which attracted little attention), but by Scotland losing to England, at home, badly, 0-5.

The prelude to The International was a Scotch inquiry into professionalism, continuing the argument about the social status and appropriate reward for football participants. Inquiry members trailed their findings as exposing the 'very loose' morals of the proudly amateur clubs: 'they have not hesitated to remunerate their players, often lavishly ... they have faked their books ... careless, but not criminal, actions are numerous ... paid players who are injured, provided football outfits ... Even Turkish baths have been paid for.' Clubs maintained cash-books recording actual moneys, and fictitious accounts for nefarious purposes, for example to fool opponents who were sharing half the gate. Individuals were given presents. A Dundee player (perhaps Billy Dickson) received a £50 testimonial and, most embarrassingly, Queen's Park's Walter Arnott made £150 from a Frank Sinatra-style 'retirement' match (he returned to play international football until 1893). Scotland's captain, Donald Gow of Rangers, 'distributed money presents to his players, and it was well known Arnott did ditto to the Queen's Park many times.' Jack Forbes received a testimonial from Vale of Leven, 'a handsome gold chronometer' with a massive and inscribed gold chain. By comparison Jack Milne, *en route* from Dundee Harp to Bolton Wanderers, was only presented with a pipe and pouch. Money was commonly given on a player's marriage, as 'half-a-dozen clocks or cake baskets are very inconvenient'. After all, 'to many a man [of lower social position] a money present was more acceptable than a present of plate.' Money also signified status. £50 was given the Scottish Association's Treasurer on his retirement, but Glasgow's honorary secretary returned his marriage offering as insultingly insufficient.

However, the Inquiry failed to substantiate what it had trailed, and was mocked by the Association: 'I had formed the impression that we were about to receive a revelation that would freeze our very blood, and make each particular stand on end like quills upon the fretful porcupine [laughter]'. Their rising figurehead Charles Campbell of Queen's Park, recently retired after thirteen years an international, denied 'veiled professionalism' and disdained the sub-committee's recommendation for regular oversight of club accounts.

Class behaviour also distinguished spectators at the Scotland v England International. Young 'Masher' went along: 'why, a fellow has no choice to show off his belongings … As it was my intention to do the Pavilion Stand, I got 'em all on and hansomed it to Hampden … It is fashionable you know for the best people to be late … and so we were late. But oh, my, I think it is quite too stupid, deuced stupid in fact, that these lower people blocked up the whole way to the stand. My collar, you know, was all creased and my cuffs dirty, and my hat was quite off balance by the time we reached the entrance to the covered stand. We paid our money. The best people always do. They dont slip under the elbow of some old player or official of the club … every seat seemed filled. My old friend Major McLeod of the Royal Garden Highlanders … "Hi, hi, old boy, we'll make room for you here".'

The 0-5 defeat occasioned 'qualms of deep humiliation and regret to every Scotchman'. The English, 'aided by no less than six professionals,' were overpowering. They had a temporary advantage in footwear: 'the Englishmen … were much troubled in the last half by the bars coming off their boots, and one or two rolled about the field afterwards like bags of sawdust'.

The English overcame their own social stresses. Centre-forward and Cambridge graduate Tinsley Lindley arrived with Corinthian 'Pa' Jackson (fresh from railing against professionalism as a Frankenstein monster) and kept their distance from the pros. That itself led to reaction: Accrington's George Howarth demonstrated 'a fine and large contempt for the Jackson clique of English footballers … [a] decidedly strong-minded young fellow and he does not think twice before speaking'.

The Scots had different problems. The disgrace was blamed on 38 selectors with a tendency to back-scratching 'intrigues'. Some had feared the worst of the 'arrant duffer' and 'pair of incapables'. It was said that the four-man Renton contingent played hard but were all heartily 'sick of the company they were in'. An impressive 15,000 saw the match and the committee took two hours to count the £750 gate, with another £80 going to Queen's Park, who took the proceeds of the grandstand in which Masher sat with Major McLeod.

That English raids continued after a 5-0 win was confusing. Did they still represent acceptance of Scotch superiority? If so, why were so many players treated badly when they got to England? Undoubtedly, many Scotch importations were short-lived: being amateurs, the men had no comeback to injury or lack of form. Successful imports were liable to be poached again. Scotch amateurs were in practice the only viable way of strengthening a professional team with competent players. The current rules were akin to dancing on a pin, especially where qualification mattered most, the English Cup.

This was the answer to Scotch puzzlement that the English gave more importance to their club's 'local prominence' than the patriotic one of 'national independence', of rearing their own players. This was always a Scotch concern (very sensitive about their national identity) rather than an English one (confident about their right to absorb the fruits of Empire). It exposed a short-term attitude to the capital of football players, of drawing upon 'Scotch preserves' as 'the happy nursery of clubs in want of amateurs'. Buying ready-made Scotchmen undermined English investment in their own. The Scots hypocritically urged the English Association to protect the 'honest professional' from the 'spurious amateur', who avoided the 'prescribed conditions and restrictions' relating to the pro qualifications. The latter was indeed the point. The 'army' of Scotchmen did not always stay amateur because they wanted to (although doing so kept open the option of a return). They responded to the 'urgent and tempting overtures from English club managers' to retain their 'amateur ticket'. This was the only option available to clubs with ambition to contest cups.

Different clubs adopted different methods. Sunderland waited for players to come to their Glasgow hotel. A Scotch paper printed a specimen letter used by the English, offering a job or apprenticeship leading to an eventual £3 or £4 per week: 'of course in the first place, I would require to see you playing.' In short they would come on trial. The trade grew. Emboldened by the success of the 'agent from Bolton', a whole army 'have like so many vultures pounced upon Dundee, and by a liberal expedition of bank notes, and the utterance of many fair promises, spirited away quite a number of covetous and easily gulled ones'. Footballers 'yielded to promises as brittle and uncertain as pie-crust'.

The oddest agent? 'Buffalo Bill' – the 'Burnley Yankee, disguised as a native of the Wild West has had some strange experiences … on the Kidnapping Path'. Another, EP Gordon, was scalped – his assailants retained a 'lock of his hair'.

The English press saw the Scots looking after their own: 'the modus operandi is that one player gets into a team, and then he arranges for situations for his friends.' So Burnley only 'worked the oracle' when player Fred Poland, formerly of Dundee Harp, reinforced 'Buffalo Bill'. Dundee felt 'threatened with desolation'. Dundee Strathmore, Billy Dickson's team, lost a whole forward line, and Wanderers, Harp and Old Boys many others. Elsewhere Burnley agents in the Vale district were making extravagant offers: 'Fancy, £60 down and £1 for each match played, and constant employment guaranteed.' 'Secessions' and 'rumours of waverers … set tongues a wagging:' 'a great blow has been struck at Association football in Dundee and it will be a long time before it recovers. A feeling of distrust … on all sides the question asked: "Who next"?' Retaliation was near. The town was 'highly incensed'. 'Threats, not loud but deep, are heard on all hands. "The agent" may look out for squalls when the opportunity offers.'

Kilmarnock, one of 1887-88's better senior clubs, had all but one of their forwards 'kidnapped' and the sole remainder was 'sorely tried'. When Arbroath lost two men, they feared the worst: 'now the ice is broken.' Their current international, Teddy Doig, remained: his later career with Sunderland and Liverpool would include winning English League championships well into the next century.

Scotch wolves, doing the Saxon's bidding, could come in sheep's clothing. Renton were 'severely hurt' by an act of 'contemptible meanness'. Bob McDiarmid had been induced to earn his living by the 'coaly Tyne' in 1887-88, first at Newcastle West End, then at Sunderland. The Scotch description is redolent of heavy irony: 'McDiarmid of Renton, had from October to June, been a horny-handed son of toil at Newcastle. Hard, honest labour had been his position, and for glory, and not for filthy lucre, had he laid his skill as a football player at the feet of the canny colliers.' That summer, he wrote expressing his willingness to return 'for ever', asking for his expenses from Sunderland and help in finding work. All was done but once home McDiarmid offered an injured finger as reason for not starting work. Nevertheless he took possession of 'a complete football outfit at Renton's expense'. Then suddenly he was gone, back to Sunderland with three promising reserves: 'his return was only a feint; and done for the purpose of drafting players.' McDiarmid would never again be recognised in the 'heroic village'.

Bootle player Campbell was busy on his 'holidays'. First he snaffled Scotland's most promising defender Bob McFarlane from under the noses of Third Lanark Rifle Volunteers, and of course all the League clubs. But Campbell went too far when he enticed inside-forward Wood from his home village, Moffat. 'Another good man gone wrong!' Campbell had arranged to turn out for his old club but after the Wood news leaked out, Moffat retaliated: 'when making for the field [Campbell] was told his services were not required. He felt small.'

The Scots took a jaundiced view of their prodigal sons. Dundee Strathmore's fortunes were at 'the lowest possible ebb' following Billy Dickson's departure and they were reduced to 'hoping something will turn up'. Strangely Dickson did, only weeks later, following his disgrace in a betting coup (see Chapter 8). There were therefore mixed feelings: Dickson, now Sunderland's 'pet and joy', was suspected of 'a poaching expedition'. His unexpected appearance prompted Arbroath's captain to remember how he 'sat on' Dickson in the Forfarshire final. 'He straightaway proceeded to repeat the dose,' which was greatly relished by the crowd. Dickson retired early. Dundee Strathie were not the Strathie of old, and lost 1-9. A final insult to the 'great man' was that 'his absence did not make any material difference, and if anything, the Strathmore played better without him than with him'.

Sunderland Albion was the most predatory of English clubs, so when their captain visited Dumfries, he was very suspiciously received: 'Sanny is like the proverbial rolling stone and there is little faith to be put in him.' The Scots insulted renegades whenever they could. As Sunderland Albion went unbeaten until Christmas, 2,500 Edinburghers were attracted to watch them, and were 'cruelly mistaken: 99% would have given double the money to be saved from watching … a worse collection of Scotchmen would be difficult to find'. They were third-rate, 'bandy-legged, too slow, ill dressed and one red-haired half-back delighted in exposing bare legs.' Were the Albion a top club? 'Yes, if the others stop playing.' A letter from another ex-pat described Sunderland's 27 players as 'only cast-offs from some of our Glasgow clubs'.

Luring the Scots away might just be the start. Some 'repented of their folly and returned to the fold. They had been sorely tempted, and succumbed to the wiles of the charmer in an evil hour.' Bolton clubs in particular found that promises of Scotchmen are 'so slippery nowadays'. Clyde committeemen outwitted Halliwell's recruiting sergeant, 'mighty' Jim Lucas and brought back 'deserter' Sawers. They also brought news of McGuinness's dissatisfaction. The Halliwell centre 'says another fortnight of Bolton life and he would be ready for the cemetery'. He was duly 'rescued' but not for long: 'we naturally did not expect McGuinness to again seek the flesh pots of Bolton, but he has. He shall be allowed to wallow.'

Similarly Kilmarnock's Alex Higgins had been 'kidnapped' to 'booming big' Derby County, who would have to improve to compete in the new League. Higgins escaped, and 'bolted' north, with 'three gents from the slipped club after him'. Once in Scotland, the Derbymen's attention drifted, and they saw the Glasgow Exhibition final between Cowlairs and upstarts Celtic. Cowlairs' McPherson brothers caught Derby's eye. They were a class act throughout the season and one played in Scotland's 1889 victory over England. But League clubs could not get them. When the Derby contingent 'desired to interview the brothers McPherson, Cowlairs did not appreciate and they beat a hasty retreat,' not forgetting to take Higgins with them.

Renton, World Champions, were increasingly presenting a 'most dilapidated appearance'. They suffered depredations at the hands of the English, and of the new 'Irish-Catholic combination' Celtic, but not the League. Renton's extras, which included a training diet of 'chicken bree' and port wine (£60 spent in 1887-88), were not holding their men. Their greatest loss was James Kelly, who played for Scotland from 1886 to 1896. The era's dominant half-back became Celtic's dominant chairman for many eras afterwards. Renton also lost McKechnie and Kelso to ambitious Newcastle clubs. But no one could get their forward stars John McNee and James McColl. League clubs tried: Burnley offered £60, Bolton wanted them and they had guested for Accrington. Albion offered 'Scotland's finest inside left' (McColl) a 'bunch of notes'. He was urged to 'retain the respect of all Scotland' by refusing the tempting bait, even though it was 'a fabulous sum', otherwise his 'reputation would be forever dimmed by desertion'.

So on the eve of the new League, in Dundee, 'quite a crowd at the station saw Dickson off on Friday evening. As the train steamed off, the great man amidst much laughter, doffed his usual headgear and donned his international cap.' But Scotland's centre did not join the Twelve Apostles. Outsiders like Sunderland were if anything more likely to secure top Scotchmen. The pressure to develop teams and clubs was independent of the League.

The League imported Scots, but rarely the best ones. Billy Dickson's rival William Paul remained with Partick: 'despite constantly being besieged from England, his fidelity is unshakeable.' Top Scotch back Jack Forbes orchestrated a prolonged courtship. He was coming to Lancashire, then not. First, he had been confused with his brother; then the suggestion 'was conceived when he was out of work. He won't go but if he did it would be Blackburn Rovers'. Preston's press dismissed the rumour as 'entirely without foundation, as the famous Vale player has never had the slightest intention' of moving. If he did come, the *Evening Post* swore on the 'highest authority' he would play for North End.

Why would North End need Forbes? Because the big summer signing was of a Scot, and by a League club. The news was received 'with great gusto' in Liverpool: 'Jack Ross has packed up his traps and left the Proud town.' When Ross played his first practice game for Everton on Wednesday night, fully 4,000 turned up to see the 'champion back of the world'. The most famous footballer: captain of the team that had dominated football since he joined from Edinburgh. His 'peppering' for leaving Preston was 'quite a repetition of the slating I got when I left Hearts'. Ross was laid back: 'of course, I've knocked about a good deal. I travelled over 12,000 miles in one season playing football.'

The Liverpool press reported his grievance. Ross had not been set up in business as promised, as Villa had given the Hunter brothers £200 to establish a draper's business and as League clubs would soon do for Jack Forbes and Frank Sugg. Ross also complained his 'right good wage' had not been paid regularly. Not so, said Sudell: he only lost one month, for using 'strong language'. Everton promised £100, plus £17 10s for his seven weeks summer wages. 'Boss' Sudell echoed the sourness of local journalists: 'Ross had made his name at Preston, and would bury it at Everton.' Preston's press continued to take cheap shots. They said he had second thoughts, asked whether he had got his £100 yet and observed that Ross's 'better half did not relish the idea of going to reside in Liverpool'. They affected scepticism that his press interview had carried the authentic Ross voice, and resented the comment that he found life in Preston 'too slow'. What else did he have to do, except train and go home? The sniping was reassuring: when 'officials sling ink about, and start blessing and blasting each other in the newspapers, you know the season of the bounding leather approacheth'.

Derby could not bear to acknowledge the fact that centre-half Harry Wharmby joined Everton: they said he 'left the neighbourhood'. County suffered for lack of a centre-half all season. Everton also gained from the 1887-88 quarrel between Blackburn forwards, eighteen-years-old Edgar Chadwick and schoolmaster Bill Townley. One of them had to go, so Rovers were 'sorry to lose' Chadwick, who won the League championship, appeared in two Cup finals and won seven England caps with Everton.

Preston and Everton had another tug of war over Bob Smalley. Preston's success had been based on Scotch teamwork, but there was a growing leavening of local talent in backs Howarth and Holmes and reserve goalkeeper Smalley. Even then, and even there, it was said that if you want to win something, you need committed players: 'the more local talent there is engaged in pot-hunting, the greater likelihood there is of success.' Smalley initially rejected Everton's overtures, preferring 'to increase his reputation' with Preston. Like Blackburn's Townley, Smalley was an amateur who both declined to play as a pro and yet turned down North End's offer on monetary grounds: 'Quite amateur, you know,' was the sceptical press comment. After 'swearing he would ne'er consent', Bob Smalley eventually accepted Everton's gold. As with Ross, the Preston press commented Smalley would be the sufferer. They also questioned, perhaps enviously, how Everton could pay all its players. Last year, 'when football fever was at its height,' Everton lost money.

Frank Sugg's heroic aura was formidable. The great Victorian sportsman gained lustre when his England cricket team twice inflicted innings defeats upon Australia in August 1888. But for whom would he play football in 1888-89? One offer was to captain an ambitious new outfit, Southport Central. But there was no shortage of League interest: Derby had been a past home; he played league cricket for Burnley. He would be hard to get: he thought it was time to start a sports outfitting business. Notts says he is 'sure to play for them', but readers were advised to take this with a 'grain of salt'. Bolton were interested, of course: Jack Bentley 'looks up from his auditing business, and, with a pigeon in one hand and a letter in the other, says "wait and see if he does not play for the Wanderers".' Frank Sugg of Everton opened his emporium at 27, Whitechapel, Liverpool. These moves to mine the sources for players cranked up public interest. In Liverpool particularly, 'you can't walk down the street without overhearing conversations in which fresh "finds" were reported or old diggings being worked immensely.'

All things being equal, North End survived largely intact for the coming season. However they had signed no new player and their fringe men were coveted. No sooner had their reserves 'swore allegiance' at their pre-season dinner than one was poached by 'mighty Jim' Lucas for Halliwell.

Could Preston win the league? Were they now vulnerable to Cup winners Albion; vengeful Villa, fuelled by last season's injustices; moneybags Everton; their fierce Lancastrian rivals Wanderers and Rovers, Burnley and Accrington; and the other Midlanders? North End were not sure they cared. Now they were off the hook with the Association, they thought the League a mixed blessing: perhaps only one lucrative game with the Corinthians in London; fewer trips to Scotland or to the new North East challengers; less choice all round. Was it worth it?

Few fared well in the week before the League started. The arrival of any new Scot was accompanied by the critical question: 'how long will they retain their capital reputation?' So, when Bolton Wanderers lost to Newton Heath on September 1st it provided 'an unpleasant reminder that imported Scotchmen are not always on form'.

Newton Heath won because Englishman Tom Hay was a 'perfect host in himself'. Ironically goalkeeper Hay had been the star of Bolton's legendary cup run in 1884: 'many and audible regrets that the Wanderers were foolish enough to part' with Lancashire's goalkeeper, who had 'few, if any superiors'. He was a real hero. Hay once broke his arm for Wanderers and dislocated a knee for Newton Heath, and each time the 'plucky custodian' played on: 'like the old hero of Cressy when his legs were knocked from under him, Tom fought upon his knees.' He also practiced the goalkeeper's black arts – he was said to be the first to pull down a crossbar (or before 1883, rope) to ensure the ball passed over.

Instead, Wanderers secured Halliwell's Oliver Fairclough until 'I got kicked on the breastbone of the stomach.' Without Hay or Fairclough, Wanderers played the League without a goalkeeper until Christmas.

Newton Heath's 'entirely imported' pros then knocked about 'like nine-pins' another League member, Blackburn Rovers. Rovers started badly, generally criticised as unprepared and unwilling to train. After three straight losses to 'outsiders' (clubs outside the Apostles), Rovers were grateful to get into the shelter of the League where they were the last, bar North End, to be beaten. Their celebrated, multi-Cup winning goalkeeper Herbie 'King' Arthur was so unconvincing at Sunderland (where Billy Dickson scored twice) he might as well have not played. Sunderland's win was no friendly – it was celebrated in the local music halls. Another 'outsider', Bootle, beat three League clubs, Blackburn, Accrington and Burnley in the run up. Or rather, beat up. As the first League Saturday approached three Burnley players were off work or under doctor's orders, having suffered from Bootle's tender mercies. Burnley had another setback. Goalkeeper Jim McConnell had had an accident at his School of Arms and was out.

These results prompted obvious comparisons: shouldn't Newton Heath, Sunderland and Bootle be Apostles, rather than Bolton, Blackburn, Accrington or Burnley?

Ross was no immediate panacea. Everton advertised his appearance, but the Association refused his registration, policing the restriction that professionals could only contract with one club a season. North End's permission came through just minutes before Everton's opening match. Everton's sensitivity about providing advertised attractions was well-founded, as the roar from 7,000 that greeted Ross's appearance was 'heard in Bootle'. Even this ordinary fixture against little Padiham made an 'astounding' £99.

However if the crowd turned up, Everton's goalie did not. Negotiations continued with Smalley and Welshman Sam Gillam. Both were 'coy', so Mike Higgins, longstanding half-back and 'licensed victualler', played goal – with a pipe. Surely 'champion' Ross would protect him – at least by 'ordering the pipe out'. 'The committee have noted the delinquency.' Higgins 'had only one shot to stop; he didn't stop it. Many spectators said Ross to blame.'

Then began a theme that would bedevil the club: who was running the team, choosing the players, deciding tactics – the 'champion back of the world', or his meddling committee? Jack Ross had argued persuasively for interventionist captaincy regarding the complexity of play and players, and the need for 'prompt measures adopted to frustrate every move of opponents'. He surveyed the Everton he was to shepherd through League football, and made changes to his committee's team: 'I moved several men last Monday night to different positions, because I saw that the game wanted forcing.'

League status was not predictive of the number of registered professionals: outsiders Blackburn Park Road (another in Blackburn's hierarchy) had 27, and Blackpool's South Shore twenty: League clubs Burnley and Accrington had respectively 25 and seventeen, Everton 29 professionals going on 36.

Smaller clubs struggled to keep their existing players, and to get them to play. Fred Geary would become a famous England player of the 1890s. In 1888-89 Geary was with a club destined to become a victim of the League. Notts Rangers had a side full of coming players, who would all find fame elsewhere, and Rangers would fold. Having received £1 a week throughout the summer Geary was acting in a 'high-handed manner', refusing to play football because he was running as 'an amateur at the various sports up and down the country. This is hard lines for the purely and strictly amateurs that compete at athletics sports, to have to compete against a professional. We have heard several competitors grumble at his receiving prizes at different meetings … and now the cat is out of the bag.'

For the time being, Notts Rangers had put Geary and other cats in the bag of a season's contract, to keep Notts County at bay. Derby County too preyed on local clubs. They chose wisely in Scotland – Ferguson from Hearts and Kilmarnock's international Higgins were 'sterling' – but sparingly: all summer there was talk and 'mysterious whispers about the composition of the team. We almost expected an invasion from Scotland, a sort of Preston North End combination, but it did not come to that. The team, and we are glad of it, continues mainly local.'

With Fred Geary's no-show, Wolves' pre-League fixture opposed ten-man Notts Rangers. When a hastily arranged replacement made it onto the pitch he caused considerable laughter: short 'nicks' and an absence of shin-guards on his thin, bare, unathletic legs. The Wanderers by contrast impressed in their 'white jerseys with black "necks" and white stripes'. Wolves had made every effort to improve their limited ground at Dudley Road. It was now partitioned from its neighbourhood by 'very substantial iron tubing. A new refreshment tent, made of corrugated iron sheets, has also been enclosed near the entrance gates.'

The League hardly featured in prospects for the coming season. Newspapers thought three developments promised to make 1888-89 more interesting than any previous. First, papers had opposed the drift towards all-year football, and felt vindicated by efforts to enforce limits (although the 1887-88 season had again lasted into June). This brought a satisfyingly Victorian reward: renewed zest after greater abstinence. Second, the English Cup would be compressed excitingly into next February and March. Third, the sharing of gate receipts between the semi-finalists and finalists of the Lancashire and Birmingham Cups – the extra income would induce the bigger clubs to try harder. The Associations' concessions came too late to head off the League.

Try harder meant putting out strong sides. The first test of club attitudes would come on September 29th, the fourth week of League fixtures and the Lancashire Cup's first round. There was no clash for Everton, who had insufficient eligible players, or North End, who had resigned from the Lancashire Association. So clubs like Blackburn now fancied winning this prestigious prize, unless the League 'spoils this'. Which competition would receive Rovers' strongest side, League or Cup?

Newspapers viewed the League – now presented as a series of home and away matches for the 'championship' – as a comparatively minor source of promise. It would 'further increase interest' during the fallow period between September and January, before the English Cup, the real event, took over.

The Scots inadvertently handed the League its final validation. Aston Villa beat Ayr 10-0 in their preparatory match. It did not feel right. There was a reason for Ayr's weakness. They would not have wanted to perform so badly: Villa would not arrange another fixture and their poor performance would put off other English clubs. Ayr had little choice. The Scottish Cup started the same day, Ayr's most important competition, promising fame and big gates in the later stages. Scotch clubs commonly still negotiated ordinary club matches, hoping that they would draw small fry. They could then divide their strength: enough to win through to the next round, and also enough to perform creditably in prestige games against important opposition like Villa. But Ayr drew a strong side in the Cup, so sent a weak team to Birmingham. Everyone lost out.

Preston suffered too. Glasgow Rangers had also gambled on securing an easy Cup draw, and a club of their fragile stature could not risk early departure from the Cup. But their stakes were higher, for they arranged to play the great North End. Rangers not only lost financially, but 'lost caste' with Preston and would 'be lucky to get another fixture'. They had assured North End the cup-tie would not interfere, but it did. The crowd was only 1,500, a fraction of the 20,000 a year before, and 'the smallest to see the North End in Scotland'. The gate was only £40. Rangers 'dropped a bit' on their guarantee, and North End did not appreciate getting the blame for the small attendance.

The real reason lay elsewhere. Rangers' solution to their double commitment was to play two separate matches at Ibrox on the same afternoon (three Rangers played both matches). This meant 'a double payment upon the supporters'. The great question was, 'would the immense crowd at the cup-tie retire peaceably at the conclusion, and allow the North End gate to be taken.' Or would it mean riot, batons, bloodshed, mounted police? The worry was unfounded: in fact they retired like 'factory hands at meal time'.

North End provided a 'really brilliant exposition of skilful manipulation … charmingly fresh and delightfully clever as ever'. Nevertheless, the relative lack of interest reflected a status-change. Defeats in the English Cup final and afterwards had delivered 'a rude shock' to their reputation, and then they lost Old Nick. On the eve of the League they did not seem so strong. Maybe in decline. Definitely not invincible.

Chapter Seven

Nazareth Suffers Cowardly Terrorism

First Coming

September 8th, 1888 – Preston 5, Burnley 2 – (6,000)

One thing distinguished the first Saturday of league football: 'summer has come at last.' The fine weather made it easier to cope with what had not changed: the visitors 'were late in arriving – shall we say as usual?' Sarcasm was rampant: 'a reward is offered to the first East Lancashire club who turns up within thirty minutes of the advertised start.'

The performance of the Lancashire & Yorkshire Railway Company was important. Half the Apostles lay within the jungle of sulphurous, satanic mills that the railway served. 570,000 people worked in cotton mills and another 240,000 in other woollen trades. The railway made regular, organised football possible, but its reliability always disappointed. The network was a dense complex of 590 miles and 309 stations or halts, no two being more than five miles apart. It was 'muck-and-brass': brass because it boasted the highest revenue-per-mile of any railway company. Muck because 'it communed with gaunt mills and gloomy terraces, lurked in damp cuttings and smoky tunnels, crossed murky rivers and congealed canals' [Blakemore, 1984 p.5]. Unlike other companies, their locos bore no fancy names and were uncompromisingly black. What was best remembered by travelling footballers out for horseplay was 'the carriage upholstery in indestructible horsehair fabric'.

North End's first home match since April, against old rivals 'and the match a "League" match', meant 'the excitement was intensified', and 'a big gate thronged the ropes'. North End were already 'going too far too fast' to last. On September 1st they had responded 'like giants refreshed' (beating Rangers 4-0) to 'the disgrace North End brought on themselves at the close of the season', when they lost three successive matches in Scotland. They returned to bet on breaking their 26-0 record, opening Lytham's ground (8-2). Next Monday, 208 miles to Birmingham to beat St George's, then 180 miles for a prestigious Wednesday afternoon fixture (10,000 spectators) at the Glasgow Exhibition against a strong Glasgow XI. North End would play 70 fixtures in 1888-89, only 22 in the League.

So the League was 'not a big occasion'. This result was a 'foregone conclusion' although Burnley were 'by no means to be despised [and] will not be at the bottom … with the prospect of a handsome reward, they tried hard to win.' Burnley were 'as active as bees … frisky as colts'. 'As is usual, when these teams meet, the game was anything but gentle.' Although Geordie Drummond was 'larking about', other 'hot' Scots, 'went for their opponents with a vim.' Combative Jack Gordon 'never played better', but showed 'exceedingly bad taste by kicking the ball out of an opponent's hand when about to throw in'. As English observers wryly observed, 'a little roughness was imported into the game.' Burnley's amateur goalie entered fully into the professional spirit: when charged, Mr Smith struck back like world boxing champion John L Sullivan: 'quite amateur, you know.' Burnley's notoriously aggressive 'small band of enthusiasts', advising 'kick in an opponent's soul case', were 'more at home in a low class gambling hell than in a respectable football enclosure.' Proud Preston had shown they 'are no deid yet'.

BOLTON 3, DERBY 6 – (5,000)

Who'd a thought it? There was no brave new world at Bolton either, a town where seven tons of soot fell on each square mile every year. Followers 'trudged the old familiar track to Pike's lane' past the 'purveyor' of 'Wanderers' Eccles Cakes', exhorting them not to 'forget the little fav'rite'. Derby's lateness compared unfavourably with other performers: 'if we go to church we expect the organist to be in tune with the voluntary; at the theatre the "goose" is early abroad as the overture tootles punctually; then why should we wait until tomorrow – or nearly so – for eleven men who are equally well paid with the sky pilot and the cat-gut torturer to put in an appearance.'

Then it all kicked off. 'By a colossal stroke of luck [Wanderers] forged three ahead in the first few minutes … the Derby County men were wobbling around in a sixpenny-Blackpool-steamer-in-a-gale sort of way.' County goalkeeper Joe Marshall came straight from Manchester Zoo: 'dodging about between the posts like a Belle Vue bear picking up nuts.'

Bolton's Kenny Davenport's first ever League goal was the prelude to a turnaround never equalled since! Their lead had been overtaken by half-time and the joke was on Wanderers' goalie: 'Bakewell threaded his way through the home backs, and Harrison, endeavouring to save, kicked the ball through his own goal.' The League had its first hero: 'the way he ran through the Trotters was a caution … Bakewell is a flyer and no mistake.' As for Wanderers, far from 'justify[ing] their inclusion in the League', they were exposed as 'about the laziest and most incompetent lot of blunderers it has ever been my unhappy lot to be compelled to witness acting the fool on the football field … no one can explain away their collapse … their backs couldn't play worth a cent. … [their] new men belong to the noble army of good-old-has-beens.'

Critics could not foresee 5,000 attending another League game 'unless something different is provided in the shape of excitement'.

STOKE 0, WEST BROMWICH 2 – (5,000)

If Bolton's journalistic style was over-blown, the Potteries reporter was commendably succinct: 'changing ends, Wilson sent in a beauty. Rowley threw out, and Sayer ran down. The ball went out. Woodhall failed twice, and should have scored.' Eventually, reporting clichés won out. When Stoke's heroic goalkeeper Billy Rowley was 'compelled to clear his goal by hurriedly throwing the ball away, Wilson, as quick as lightning, seized upon it and shot past the goalkeeper.'

Albion histories claim that this win means they topped the first ever League table [Willmore, 1980, p.25]. Except that there was no such thing. Other than wins, merit order was undecided. Derby scored six. Were they not top? The question was unasked. The Cup holders' form disappointed all but an admirer: 'I'll tell you what it is, chaps; if you win this match I'll stand cigars, and good ones, too, all round.'

'Being members of the league [Stoke] have had to strengthen their team to enable them to maintain their reputation … several other Scotch amateurs are daily expected.' The rewards were also evident: despite counter attractions – a cricket County Cup final and Burslem Port Vale beating Gainsborough 6-1 (perhaps in the Combination – no one knew), the gate was good. Was the attraction the Cup holders, or the League?

WOLVERHAMPTON 1, ASTON VILLA 1 – (3,000)

The League's first draw ended a typical 'scene of warfare': 'a slight scrimmage immediately took place around the Villa's goal … [then] a scrimmage occurred in front of the Wanderers' goal … Play became more exciting, and the home pets seemed determined to get a goal … White headed the ball through in an easy manner … The Villa men now showed up a little, and Green put in a shot which struck the home posts and turned inside.'

EVERTON 2, ACCRINGTON 1 – (10,000)

Anfield attracted the biggest crowd, by a long way. It was Everton's 'deucedly expensive' staff against a threadbare squad of part-timers. Accrington's sponsor was desperately scouring Scotland, 1888's equivalent of *Yellow Pages*: 'can you get your new forwards down in time, Mr JP Hartley?'

Accrington had just lost three first-team forwards, Bob Conway, Herby Fecitt and Jack Yates (who ended the season scoring an England hat-trick). The Scotch cavalry was slow to arrive, and their intended centre-forward, Boston's amateur captain Allin, 'telegraphed his inability to play in the morning.' Even the reserve-strewn Reds remained attractive visitors in Liverpool because Bootle beat Accrington the week before. Could Everton do better?

Accrington were late, but thought they did well getting there in two hours, and thanked the railway: ''ere's one for the Lancashire and Yorkshire.' 'Liverpool is not an easy place to reach, and as nearly all the team are working up to Saturday noon, they are unable to leave Accrington before one or two o'clock.' It was an express to Blackburn, 'snail-gallop' to Preston Junction, a 30-minute wait, another change at Burscough, before a long drive from Sandhills station.

Those waiting were at an 'utmost pitch of excitement' on a beautiful day. Some didn't pay: one 'hulking fellow tore down a portion of hoarding', and 50 followed him through 'the breach'. 'A little urchin trespassed upon the grass' and got a 'free kick' from an elderly steward. A 'lithe young fellow went for the official without ceremony, leaving him prostrate with the blood streaming from his face'. This 'viciousness as it was unwarrantable' yielded its own retribution as, in a 'general hustle' the 'young assailant fell prostrate in a fit', surrounded by a cordon of accusers – 'serves him right', 'hit him again'. 'The old man, half unconscious and bleeding, was also assisted.' A policeman asked 'what the row was about. It was about stepping on the grass.'

The grass was already a focus of conflict between Jack Ross and his committee, who forbade his team to practise, *Fast Show*-style: 'You, Everton team, keep off the grass!'

The Reds were 'simply astonished at the vast concourse of spectators, and no wonder, for gates of ten or twelve thousand are never seen at Accrington'. At 4.25, Ross 'planted his men with their backs to the sun'. A thousand ladies enjoyed the furious action around their new hero, lately snitched goalkeeper Smalley: 'Bob was knocked about like snuff at a wake, but for all that he managed to get the ball round the posts. Be me sowkins, ye'd have tho't there was a cup-tie on to see the pace they started at, so like flies playing "tig" and with about as much result as all the dribbling, passing, charging, heading, etc came to nought up at half-time.'

Everton scored 'amidst tremendous cheering and waving of hats'. Then Accrington's goalkeeping secretary Dick Horne came out, cleared the ball, collided with Edgar Chadwick's knee and 'fell like a hero, in the thickest of the fight'. Fractured rib. Accrington's 'particularly brilliant passing … being most unselfish' still outperformed Everton, who 'would do themselves and their club no harm if they practised a little'. After George Fleming obtained both goals, Everton's new secretary Barclay toasted his health in the Sandon Hotel: 'Call him back again … They did so and kissed him.'

Ten-man Accrington dominated the last half-hour as Everton were 'run off their feet'. George Howarth ruled midfield, 'Artful Dodger' Bonar dribbled and passed, and 'Smalley repelled some real stingers': 'five or six shots in rapid succession were hurled straight at his citadel … the fusillade terminating by Holden heading against the bar.' Holden pulled a goal back, then came again with 'a regular hot 'un'. Smalley saved wonderfully but was he already through the posts? Ref Jack Bentley said no.

Accrington were unimpressed with Everton: 'whenever they meet, I shall …. stake my small stake on the non-leaguers', Bootle.

SEPTEMBER 15TH – BOLTON 3, BURNLEY 4 – (4,000)

Bolton's renaissance had gone wrong: 'Mr Bentley's prognostications do not seem like being realised.' Jack Bentley changed his cast – only two players retained their positions – but the play was repeated. Wanderers gained a three-goal lead which they lost – Tait scored Burnley's winner. Burnley arrived – 'later than usual' – wearing the same jerseys. 'Here's a how d'ye do', said Councillor Horrocks, and the Bolton players disappeared, to 're-emerge in indigo blue'. The crowd were less phlegmatic: 'part of the waiting brigade … return in a body to the gate, and demand a return of their money.' Mr Bentley was advised to penalise his Apostles for late arrival. Bolton's correspondent was a little kinder about this second extraordinary defeat, for rather delicate reasons: 'having put a trifle on Burnley, "just for the sake of the odds," this was a bit awkward for me.'

EVERTON 2, NOTTS COUNTY 1 – (8,000)

Another confusing start. Notts waited in vain for cricketers Daft and Gunn, but they were both playing against the Australians at the Oval: 'begorra, to my stupid way of thinking it was a daft way of humbugging the public.'

Jack Ross showed his old devil: 'if it means doubling a man up, converting him inside a corkscrew, spinning him round within a six-yard radius and finally depositing him all of a heap outside …' Everton's wins were matching North End's but their teamwork was fragile: as Alec Dick's 'dreadful little leg was raised to clear the corner-kick Ross shouted 'let it go", and Notts scored.

Everton had forward trouble. Their first centre was a notable figure in Welsh if not Everton football history. Bangor's Bill Lewis had been playing for Wales for three years, and finished (in 1898) with 30 caps. Everton had no such patience, quickly labelling him as moving as slowly as a 'mourning coach'. Last week's hero, 'Black Prince' Fleming, was now yesterday's news: 'appears to dread a collision, and little wonder, he has had his shoulder put out three or four times. It is about time he made way for someone else.'

WOLVERHAMPTON 0, PRESTON 4 – (3/5,000)

This week saw the first League test of a football truism: 'we all know the evil effect upon football players of a hundred miles railway journey.' North End travelled first class, and then kept possession of the ball before scoring three quick goals. When an opponent broke into 'a free field', 'Safety Valve' Graham 'tripped him up' – the Wolfpack howled.

Birmingham, its founding city, described the fixture as 'a friendly match under the auspices of the recently created League'.

DERBY 1, WEST BROMWICH 2 – (3,000)

At first Derby felt losing to 'one of the two most formidable clubs in the world' was 'no disgrace'. Then they reflected that but for their goalkeeper's bad shoulder, they 'did not deserve to lose at all, for had Joe Marshall really been well he would have stopped at least one of the goals. In fact he admitted as much after the game. All the same however, we do not regard the Staveley man as a first-class custodian, nor as yet such a good man as he was a few years ago. He is not to be compared with Harry Bestwick, who, take him all round, was one of the best goalkeepers in the country, and whose disinclination to play this season has been a great disappointment … The goal is a fatal spot to be weak in.' Others were stronger: Arthur Latham's 'back play was about as fine as any we ever saw', and half-backs Albert Williamson (a 'knowing old hand') and Walter Roulstone ('takes the cake') upset Albion's stars Bassett and Woodhall. But Derby's forwards were literally 'ragged': Lol Plackett 'played with his head tied in a handkerchief, and even then sustained some nasty jars that compelled him to play chary'.

BLACKBURN 5, ACCRINGTON 5 – (5,000)

There was little novel about Rovers' first League match: they had met their 'rivals from the Cemetery Kingdom' 35 times since 1878, leading 21-10. Joe Lofthouse, who had moved to Accrington from Blackburn, 'catched it warm,' attracting 'whoops' from the 'gods' behind the goal.

Accrington 'twitted' their former player, Herby Fecitt: 'Good lad Fecitt, tha'rt playing at stan-off ageon.' Fecitt's reputation was: 'Herby never will shine until he has more nerve.'

Accrington still waited for Scots: their 'executive have had more trouble with this team than all the previous ones together'. Joe Hartley's new forwards from Oswaldthistle Rovers, Jimmy Holden and Jack Kirkham, both scored. Accrington led 5-4 near time, when a scrimmage bore down on their goal. Keeper Jack Horne, replacing his injured brother Dick, 'boasted he had not touched a ball since the charity cup-tie in June.' Now he 'hesitated with the usual result'. Fecitt.

ASTON VILLA 5, STOKE 1 – (4,000)

Stoke sent McSkimming (their summer capture from Kilmarnock) home to 'angle for salmon', and got him roughed up: he would 'remember his journey to Scotland in search of players for some time to come'. People were 'wondering when the team will be properly fixed. Several Scotchmen have been advertised as players, but up to the present have not turned up'. McPherson was the latest. The forward had just played for Scotland against Canada, and had a situation found, but decided to finish his apprenticeship. Stoke had another problem. They led at half-time thanks to keeper Rowley, but 'went to pieces' in the second half: 'want of condition is very apparent.'

SEPTEMBER 22ND – ASTON VILLA 2, EVERTON 1 – (5,000)

Everton's 'jolly little party' of 25 took the 12.15 out of Lime Street Station, enjoying the 'gigantic sandwiches' available in its fine saloon carriage. They set in train events that threatened their very existence, a threat prefigured by the reappearance of John Weir, who had provoked their suspension by the Association ten months earlier.

Everton also offered a symbolic challenge to Villa. Despite founding the League, Birmingham remained ambivalent about professionalism, particularly the opportunistic Scotch imports. Villa's eminence was based on the different model of Scottish integration. Their figureheads McGregor and Ramsay were both Scots and Archie Hunter was their captain, but his teammates were locals.

Aston Villa's steady rise had been overtaken by Preston's more aggressive importation policy. Now Everton offered a variant. Like Villa, they had a city's potential support. Everton were Johnny-come-latelys: 'a lot of players scraped together from the four quarters of the football world and sat down in a suburb of Liverpool where there was no Association football before worth talking about.' Unlike Villa they practiced 'football forcing', 'the most expensive, the dearest lot of players that has ever been got together,' on the back of ten thousand gates that Villa could only match on big occasions.

The biggest had come only eight months earlier, when 27,000 saw Villa cheated out of the English Cup. North End's chicanery that day was fronted by their captain ... now Everton's captain. At the end of their 'jolly' journey Jack Ross was 'jeered at and hooted' before suffering a football crowd's wit: Villains 'loudly asked if this was a cup-tie or friendly game'.

Everton's 'looseness in the eleven shows that it has been hastily flung together ... it is ragged, ragged in play and decidedly ragged in temper'. The Birmingham press thought referee 'Fitzroy the Fleet' Norris 'seemed to favour the visitors. "Seemed" scarcely expresses the action ... Higgins had his arm around Brown's neck and yet a free kick was given to Everton.' The Liverpool press saw a deeper truth: 'Brown held Mike by the jersey. Higgins then threw his arms around Brown. Of course everyone saw the latter action and the hoots of the crowd was something.'

Everton 'were a shady lot, but sadly addicted to tricks decidedly shady. In the first half they were out-paced, out-generaled and out-classed at all points.' Shadiest was Alec Dick who 'most savagely' kneed Dennis Hodgetts in the stomach. Hodgetts 'let him have one ... full in the face.' Norris missed the retaliation, giving the lie to his reputation: 'spider's eyes for everything against the Villa, and mole's eyes for everything against Everton.'

Birmingham and Preston newspapers continued Jack Ross's character assassination, claiming he was 'uttering dire threats' amidst the hullabaloo. The players fought back. The North End team 'publically [sic] dissociated' themselves from the campaign, and when Ross threatened to sue for libel papers apologised.

In the game, Everton were inspired by the devil: 'they worked like demons, with "old Nick" behind, coaching and advising.' Afterwards Villa's crowd assailed Dick in a 'shameful manner' and pelted the team with stones.

BLACKBURN 6, WEST BROMWICH 2 – (7,000)

'A surprise to the visitors, who never expected to be beaten; a surprise to the Rovers who hardly imagined they would win.' Bill Townley was 'magnificently unselfish'.

PRESTON 3, BOLTON 1 – (5,000)

Who'da thow't it? Bolton, unrecognisably better, were 'continually pressing' Trainer, Prince of Goalkeepers, who saved North End. Yet Wanderers had no new Scots: in fact Coupar played centre with his 'arm in a sling'; and Davy Weir's further 'angling' adventures had not produced any Scotch 'salmon'. Instead, their competitive new backs were both 'noted amateur' – Bethel Robinson, one-time North End secretary, and Dai Jones, the 'Prince of Wales'. Both were promiscuous with their favours during 1888-89, including games for North End. 'Eawr' Bethel annoyed Wanderers by playing three times a week – he was so 'willing to play for anybody, according to the secretaries of a dozen different clubs [that] Bethel has promised with all of them in the English ties'. Jones the back once told Jack Bentley that although he won Welsh caps over thirteen seasons, he was born in England. He eventually died of tetanus after a game.

Deepdale got into it. When Jack Gordon's knee-in-the-back sent Jones sprawling painfully into the touchline rail it was 'great fun'; but Bob Roberts was a veritable 'Goth' when he charged Gordon. Davie 'Croppy' Russell played, interrupting his comedy engagement in Blackpool, but his evident unfitness invited 'pointed and witty comments'. Geordie Drummond just exasperated. When he complained loudly about a disallowed goal – 'did it no go faur enough through for ye' – it 'fairly convulsed the spectators'. But otherwise, they protested: 'why, I could kick as well as that with my gammy leg.'

Wanderers still had hopes until, four or five minutes from time, the referee blew a shrill whistle, and on a bad day, 'the players, in no way loth, rushed towards the dressing tent.' Back in the pavilion the mistake was realised. Major Sudell called for a return, but both sides had had enough and even the galloping major had to mumble his apologies to those few remaining who expected a full 90 minutes for their threepence.

WOLVERHAMPTON 4, BURNLEY 1 – (3,000)

Trouble 't mill. Strikes stopped Burnley looms running and, 'counsel and advice having failed,' three footballers were suspended for going on an unauthorised Blackpool holiday – Tait was not back until Friday. When two goals were disallowed, Burnley 'fell to pieces' and remained 'totally at sea'. Wolves, who 'could beat them all ends up' anytime, objected to Burnley's equaliser: 'not liking this, [Wolves] determinedly attacked their opponents' citadel, and two or three players were knocked down … as Smith attempted to stop, White took the goalkeeper and sent the ball flying through the posts.' Burnley had a goalkeeping problem. Former secretary Jim McConnell was not recovering, and Mr Smith was not the answer.

DERBY 1, ACCRINGTON 1 – (2,000)

'Derby were in grand form and quite deserved to win.' Accrington's goalkeeper gave a world champion performance: 'Horne was a veritable John L Sullivan for punching.' Once a charge knocked 'all the stuffing out of him, but he lay on the ground and still punched'. Derby thought the attendance excellent. Accrington enviously noted County could charge sixpence plus enjoy £200-worth of season tickets, and more in the stand.

The Reds had 'their best pick of bone and muscle' as 'the good thing has come to pass'. Joe Hartley's 'hamper' of Scotch goodies had come early for Christmas: Rob Brand and Bill Barbour. When the Scottish Association banned Queen of the South Wanderers for professionalism a year later, Brand and Barbour featured in the evidence: 'Barbour, when thrown out of work ... received for himself and his family provision at a grocer's shop.' Mrs Barbour was offered £1 to 'induce' her husband to remain in Dumfries; and, once he went to Accrington, Wanderers funded a £2 10s expedition to persuade his return. Brand, who 'asked straight' for what he wanted, once received a suit of clothes for playing.

Together they met Accrington's 'long-felt want', and stood on no ceremony: Brand's 'shot passes Marshall, without stopping to shake hands'. County scored 'and the crowd yell – "One all!" But no. It was the classic offside scenario: '[Lewis] Cooper ran past the backs whilst the ball was in mid-air.' After Alex Higgins equalised, the match 'ran to dripping in the second half', although Derby's Scotch back 'Ferguson was as cool and collected as a receipted ice bill'. Always prone to overdo the cool, Ferguson later admitted deliberately handling a goal-bound shot. His 'excuse' – 'such a little fault' – was adjudged 'pathetic': 'like the girl with an accidental baby ... it is not honest play.' Still, a free-kick 'is better than a goal any way'.

STOKE 3, NOTTS COUNTY 0 – (3,000)

Jack Bentley missed his Bolton's improved showing as he refereed 'the most important match in the Potteries'. The large crowd was disgruntled that 29-year-old cricketer William Gunn did not show, and a disappointed Notts committeeman lectured recent Scotch amateur Bob Jardine on his shortcomings. When Jardine 'showed a somewhat rebellious spirit', he was dropped, until further defeats required a rethink. Stoke's win prompted second thoughts about their unsuccessful trips to Scotland: 'besides, look at the expense of these outings.'

SEPTEMBER 29TH – BOLTON 6, EVERTON 2 – (5,000)

Everton 'caught a Tartar with a vengeance', whilst themselves 'shaped like schoolboys'. Their riches were no proof against injuries, and newspapers received a 'very private wire': 'owing to so many men being lame, no team will be decided upon for Saturday until Friday night.' Bentley had continued to tinker with team selection – only goalie Harrison and Alec Barbour kept their positions. In miserable weather, Bolton got two each from long-standing star Kenny Davenport; from Scotch import Jack Milne; and local Harry Tyrer. Everton slunk home to 'miles of sackcloths and cartload of ashes' but all Trotterdom drank in celebration: 'there was a sound of revelry by night.'

WEST BROMWICH 4, BURNLEY 3 – (1,500)

Public support for the League was most grudging at West Bromwich, after 'the champions' lost 2-6 the previous week. Joey Law, who had trained Albion to the Cup, inspired his new charges to a 'strong and pretty passing game' and a two-goal lead. Burnley's Pat Gallocher was the best player on the field: 'his passing and runs were very beautiful' and his 'hot shot burst the ball'. Then Albion's Billy Bassett dodged, stumbled and, recovering instantly, 'banged in the ball.' Excitement continued, 'each team appearing warm.' Just before time, Burnley's new goalie Kay 'fisted back a shot' that Albion claimed, successfully, 'had gone under the bar … [Burnley] hotly disputed.'

WOLVERHAMPTON 2, BLACKBURN 2 – (3,000)

One of King Arthur's great games set up a Rovers 'equalisation'.

STOKE 2, ACCRINGTON 4 – (3,000)

Goals from Accrington's Scotch imports Brand and Barbour confirmed their new prosperity: 'the outside-left is of the best Brand.'

ASTON VILLA 9, NOTTS COUNTY 1 – (5,000)

'This match needs little description.' Birmingham found a match of unequal class of no interest. Nottingham took the 'catastrophe' more personally. Goalkeeper Jack Holland was 'simply execrable', whilst there was 'not a trace of enthusiasm among the forwards … Gunn has not yet thrown off his cricketer's legs'. The contrast between 6ft 4in William Gunn and Villa's 5ft 4in Dixon suggested a tragi-comic epic worthy of *Gulliver's Travels*: 'the leviathan's awkward advances … like a Lilliputian cat watching a Brobdignagian mouse. On many occasions it looked as if [Dixon] was going to be trodden on.' In the second half Gunn 'stalked off like an ostrich running away from a Shetland pony', but ran into the sand.

Derby 2, Preston 3 – (5,000)

As North End's train 'left the metals' they were an hour late, and rightly feared their reception: 'the crowd kicked their toes, cursed and chewed cigar ends till the train steamed in and the Preston men waved clean white handkerchiefs.'

The surrender imagery was briefly reinforced. Playing within six minutes of a five-hour-plus journey, North End 'were of course stiff' so Harry Plackett gave County a first-minute lead: 'to say a deafening roar rent the clouds would not touch the case.' 'The next half hour was ding, dong, but the Derby boys were having their share of the fun.' As usual for North End's opponents, County had spent the week trying to strengthen their side. Their weakness was at centre-half since Wharmby joined Everton. They offered Teddy Brayshaw, Sheffield Wednesday's England international, 'the tenancy of a public house!' But Brayshaw had 'taken a new love at Derby before being off with the old at Sheffield'. Wednesday refused to release him, so County used another Derbyshire cricketer – Levi Wright, the Derby Midland skipper, good enough to play football for North v South. 'Trainer now got hemmed in, and after he had returned shots from Cooper, Higgins and Bakewell', Wright's shot 'just went under the crossbar … the players could not be seen for applause; men rushed madly to the bar to allay the excitement with lemonade only; and Preston – well I must say they looked as though they were having teeth drawn'.

Or knocking teeth out. Archie Goodall reacted when a teammate was on the floor with the ball underneath. 'The Placketts were endeavouring to kick the ball away from under him, and Archie evidently thought they were kicking his man, and up went his bunch of fives.' Lol Plackett was knocked over, got up, and kicked and struck at the giant Goodall. Jamie Ross's hat-trick won the game: Joe Marshall 'looked at it, yes, even smiled at it, as much as to say "Call that one of Ross' shots" … but alas, too late. The leather wobbled past him … that would have caused a boiled pet rabbit to turn in the pot with envy for its tameness.'

So North End had won all four, but Villa had scored more goals. Villa and Albion had three wins each. Everton, Blackburn, Wolves and Accrington were a middle group. Stoke, Bolton, Derby and Burnley were already competing over who would have to retire, along with three-time losers Notts.

September 29th 1888, League versus Cup, Round One

This fourth Saturday posed the first challenge. Blackburn glimpsed a better chance of winning the coveted Lancashire Cup now that Preston had defected from the Association. But would the 'league requirement spoil their chances?' Rovers stayed pretty fair. True, they diverted two first-teamers to their Reserve, also bolstered by buccaneering Fergy Suter, who won through. Bolton were ambivalent. Their neighbours Halliwell 'don't relish their exclusion from the league in which their great rivals have a place'. Wanderers' poor start made Jack Bentley reluctant to give Halliwell further opportunity to mock their new status, and imported an entire side, Astley Bridge, as their Cup team. Halliwell had fun, knocking 'Wanderers' out – 8-1! Bentley's League had the last laugh – they had already 'shut out' the best teams from the cups.

THE TRAVAILS OF NORTH END'S RIVALS IN OCTOBER AND NOVEMBER

ASTON VILLA

OCTOBER 6TH – EVERTON 2, ASTON VILLA 0 – (12,000 *'if not [12,000], how was £170 raised from a 3d gate'*)

Revenge was in the air. The locals remembered Birmingham's abuse of their folk hero Alec Dick, so Villa were 'attacked individually and collectively by a lot of brutal and anonymous bullies, who seem to find a fitting home around Everton way – so much so that even small boys offered to throw a brick at the Villa for a penny'. Officially Everton, sensitive also to their vulnerable reputation, stage-managed a preliminary handshake between Dick and Hodgetts. When seconds were out, Dick was duly cautioned and referee McIntyre denied he was 'so cowed that he dare not order Dick off'. Everton's was a 'wondrous victory', a 'glorious event'. Villa's first defeat was attributed to an illness called 'Funk'. The club's response was a reaction called panic, and caused William McGregor's resignation. The League's founder lost his club.

McGregor objected to the hypocrisy of Villa signing Archie Goodall as an amateur, but as a professional could he play? Goodall embodied the contradictions of football's player rules. They were supposed to assert the English attachment to locality that the clubs themselves epitomised: to play, a professional had to be born, or have lived locally for two years. This discouraged immigration.

However, the reality of Victorian life made immigration inevitable: men moved to work, so why not play? Scotch amateurs provided quick-fix solutions to professional clubs. Another aspect of Victorian social life – rule-making by the Association's Committee – tried to square the circle, and proved its 'utter ineffectiveness'. Their outcomes conflicted with other Victorian values, like the appearance of honest, straightforward dealing. The failure invited conspiracy thoughts: 'some supremely clever individual, apparently to suit their own constituents, or to help them out of difficulty, induced the Association last year to interpret a man "found" a situation because of his football was still a full-blown amateur'.

Archie Goodall was an established player before the professional rules were framed, so was it even fair to apply them retrospectively? He was a 'well-known Scotchman' but 'accidentally born in Belfast' (his equally Scottish brother John Goodall was similarly accidentally born in London, so played fourteen England internationals between 1888 and 1898). The Scottish Association would not allow Archie Goodall to play there because he was a 'pro'. In 1887-88 he played for five clubs and accepted a Derby County 'present' for 1888-89, only to rejoin North End.

McGregor had urged Villa 'not have anything to do with [Goodall] as an amateur'. He wanted to maintain moral superiority over West Bromwich. Albion, under stress from their revolting players, had driven a 'waggon and horses' through Birmingham's restrained approach to professionalism and importation. Everyone saw that Albion's imports were all full-blown professionals: 'not one Scotchman is a true amateur.' Albion had suffered – their reputation, club harmony and performances.

OCTOBER 13TH – ASTON VILLA 6, BLACKBURN 1 – (5,000)

Villa initially found Archie work and played him as an amateur. With 'unexpected effect'. 'Whew!' As Rovers had routed Albion 6-2, Villa's win was all the sweeter.

OCTOBER 20TH – BOLTON 2, ASTON VILLA 3 – (10,000)

Villa's reputation impressed Bolton folk who nevertheless remained 'staunch for Wanderers in "their darkest hour".' It looked a proverbial '£1,000 to a hayseed' on Villa, but Boltonians were still on for a bet. 'Merry Trotters snapped up all the 6 to 4s they could get.' They 'lobbed up' to Pike's Lane in relays of horse-drawn buses: 'there wasn't a cab to be had for love or money.' It was 'like Manchester Cup day on a small scale' – clearly the 'league' had added value. Wanderers started 'buzzing' and centre Barbour, 'dashing past the backs finished with a splendid shot.' Obvious errors restrained Pike's Lane's 'referee baiting': 'it was a goalkeepers match. Warner won it for the Villa, and Harrison lost it for the Wanderers.' Bolton seemed set to stay on 'Queer-street' for want of a goalkeeper.

Newspapers were now uneasily tabulating the League results, usually in some form of merit order. North End were leading, Villa second; but after that it was unclear. Where fewest defeats mattered most, Accrington and Blackburn competed for third, with one loss each; ahead of Albion (more wins but two losses) and Everton (three of each). Derby, arguably top at first, now seemed bottom, although everyone saw it their own way. The following apocryphal conversation was reported occurring at 'The Green Man', Derby on Saturday night:

McBoosey to Tom Canttouchwater

'Shay, Tom, do you notish Derby Cantish topst of League lisht?'

Tom – 'So tish, Mac, whensh you holsh paper likshe that.' [hic]

NOVEMBER 10TH – PRESTON 1, ASTON VILLA 1 – (10,000)

Given Albion's decline, these were 'undoubtedly the best'. But between the goals, 'nothing was done on either side for about an hour and twenty-five minutes'. Somehow Villa had squared with the Association the problem of Archie Goodall's registration, so he came out and was initially flash: 'capital if he sticks to the legitimate, but he is prone to play to the gods.' Thereafter he 'bottled' Jamie Ross, the only North End forward who was not 'lame'. Villa 'profited a great deal' from 'special preparation' (a week without a Monday game). Preston dropped Geordie Drummond and decided upon the profile of a new crack left-winger: 'a total abstainer, and one not so confoundedly conceited.'

OCTOBER 27TH – ASTON VILLA 4, ACCRINGTON 3 – (7,000)

Earlier, second had played third, at least in some versions. Accrington set off at 7.30am to their admirers' cry 'Remember North End' (they had just drawn) and fancied themselves the 'famous Reds'. During a five-hour journey, they sang Scot Bill Barbour's newly composed song 'The Accrington fuitba' team'.

'Interest in the game never flagged for a single moment.' 'Albert Brown planted the leather nicely in the centre and in the twinkling of an eye Tom Green popped his cranium in the way and, hey presto, there was another yell more vociferous than the first, and the scores were equal.' Accrington scored again, only for Dennis Hodgetts to shoot under the bar. Jack Horne knocked it out: 'a goal was claimed, but after protracted discussion, no goal,' 'much to the chagrin and disgust of the Villans, who did not by any means relish the decision.' The Reds looked certain winners, 3-1 up with fifteen minutes to go. If the 'pace had been terribly fast' so far, when a strong breeze got behind Villa, 'goals crashed through quickly … amidst an almost indescribable yell of excitement. This was however as nothing compared with the din that arose a few minutes later when out of the surging mass of human frames Tom Green slid the ball through the Accrington posts.' 'What was that shout like?' 'Ask somebody who was able to hear it,' says my friend 'it deafened me'. No draw for unlucky Accrington although they challenged the wind one last time – 'an apparently equalising shot was just blown outside'.

With resignation, William McGregor realised his capital was out of his control. He embarked on a season-long battle to persuade Villa to become a limited liability company, and was not above threatening to withdraw his guarantee of Villa's losses. He sort-of won the following spring, and rejoined the board. But even as he threw his toy out of the Villa pram, McGregor knew his League baby was thriving: 'Villa had won one of the finest games witnessed at Perry Barr.'

WEST BROMWICH ALBION

At first the Cup-holders cut a fine dash, languidly arriving half an hour after advertised starts: 'the handsome Albion drove to the ground in style … nobody could grumble, although a few bare patches were to be noticed on the turf where an old cuss or two had fallen.'

It was all good fun: Albion's new centre 'Hendry did the needful with his beetle crusher … the pie was opened and the birds began to sing'. Albion seemed not to take the League seriously until they lost, and lost badly. They disdained their membership. Neither their AGM nor the pre-season briefing to the local *Free Press* mentioned it: fifteen fixtures were listed, 'with the leading English and Scottish combinations,' including Oxford and Cambridge Universities. Then Albion's veneer of confidence evaporated as they lost 2-6 and felt a lack of Scots for the very 'English emergencies' that were becoming commonplace.

The *Free Press* woke up to what was happening: 'as the weeks pass by the interest in the Football League Matches is becoming greater and greater … more than cup matches in the eyes of the football fraternity.' This was serious: Albion were Cup-holders and the real cup-ties did not start until February. Sadly the West Bromwich public took their cue from the club and few watched their exciting first home fixture. Newcomer Hendry's 'beautiful passing … was greatly admired', but their old heroes were disappointing expectations: 'Roberts stood as if stupefied and allowed the ball to pass under the bar … he must certainly be more careful.' Initially Albion were 'completely beaten at every point' but somehow won 4-3. The *Free Press* took grudging comfort: 'if they can give a whopping like this with four men away, what will they do with a full team.'

OCTOBER 6TH – WEST BROMWICH 5, DERBY 0 – (1,500)

County's Lewis Cooper was so slight that he was 'all angles when you run into him'. On this bitterly cold afternoon, Albion managed to break his collarbone. It set the scene for 'cowardly terrorism'.

OCTOBER 13TH – PRESTON 3, WEST BROMWICH 0 – (10,000)

'Whenever they tumble across each other it is a certainty of a big gate and a great game.' Albion seemed ready for the 'Cup Final reprise' as, despite winning all five games, North End were said to be 'fast deteriorating' and rather anxious: 'as this game was dangerous but without going in for any systematic course of training, [North End] took rather more than usual care of themselves, as to be in the best of humours.' The big crowd disproved another view that 'interest in the game is said to be on the decline in the proud town'.

This was 'one in a thousand, from beginning to end, teeming with interest … as an exposition of scientific football it was an educational treat'. North End felt vindicated that Albion had abandoned their principle of local recruits and gone the 'way of all flesh': Jack Hendry was their 'needy Scot'. Albion's mojo over North End disappeared with the moral superiority. Geordie Drummond (now 'first reserve') played 'a perfect game' at full-back, confounding his critics: 'tha must have been drinking vinegar for a week, and become sour'd to th' core.'

Albion's Scotch adventures continued to cause embarrassment. The agent from Dundee came to town to 'make the club stump up' his fee. Otherwise he threatened to take Hendry to Everton. As journalists conjured up Old Testament images of corruption, Liverpool was the 'Jericho' to Albion's previously chaste image. The agent boasted he had earned £50 from English clubs this season, and still had 'a large order in hand'. But he also suffered setbacks. He had hooked a goalkeeper for Bolton's urgent need and gave him a ticket to Lancashire and 'some loose cash'. Bolton's goalie never arrived.

OCTOBER 20TH – WEST BROMWICH 4, NOTTS COUNTY 2 – (2,000)

Albion were pursuing their own grievances: the 'Press chapel' was 'surrounded by a gang of angry and expostulatory players'. Captain Bayliss led the wish to 'visit their resentment' upon 'Nazareth', the Birmingham reporter who had criticised Darky Timmins' 'violent charge' breaking the collarbone of Derby's Cooper. Back in March, Albion's Cup final 'never-say-die' performance was applauded as quintessentially English. Now their 'cowardly terrorism' threatened another fundamental value, that of press freedom from intimidation. If the crowd followed the players' lead, reporters might need the 'back up' of a 'revolver or stout walking stick'. Fortunately supporters' comments 'were not the least flattering to the "lads", and no wonder why'. 'Nazareth' himself, mercifully absent from the siege, defiantly promised to 'nail the Albion or any other club's brutality to the mast come what, come may'.

Albion were still a 'long chalk from being in best trim'. Bayliss was advised to keep his 'unruly member' back a little and not shout so much at his men, and 'spectators as a counterblast heartily applauded' the victim. Opponents made tactical adjustment for dangerous forwards like Billy Bassett, giving 'very close attention … no matter whether they went or what they attempted, the Nottingham men seemed to be hanging on them like a dead weight'.

NOVEMBER 3RD – WEST BROMWICH 2, ACCRINGTON 2 – (1,000)

Their bravado had now gone. Albion feared a 'licking'. It 'meant the "lads" straining every nerve to stave off defeat'. They were intimidated. It was 'notorious fast how [Accrington] and the Wolverhampton Wanderers added to their fame in the League fixtures'. Albion had lost fame. Despite a reduced charge, attendance was derisory. For once Accrington were 'punctually to time', and 'ten minutes after, the Albion followed' – they had threatened not to play at all. Bassett set up Albion's opener when his beautiful centre gave goalie Horne no chance 'as Wilson and Pearson were on top of him and the ball was through the goal in the twinkling of an eye'. But Roberts mixed 'blunders' and 'brilliant saves': back John Horton made 'bad mistakes' and half-back Ezra 'Old Ironsides' Horton 'needs a little practice on the ball'. Following another reshuffle, 'Bayliss cannot play forward one half so well as he used to' and Hendry was 'out of place'.

Accrington's England pair, Howarth and Lofthouse, proved 'exceedingly fine', Joe Lofthouse crossing for both goals. 'Scorcher' Bassett had the last laugh by taking a back-heeled return, shooting 'a beautiful goal'.

Accrington centre Bill Barbour was unlucky. He hit the woodwork four times and then an opponent 'ducked' his ribs into his knee. Spectators rushed onto the ground and demanded his sending off. Barbour said the 'hostile demonstration … knocked all the football out of him'. They also 'hustled', 'loudly hissed and hooted' referee Armitt. Albion's players remonstrated – 'now you fellows, keep quiet: do you want to give us a bad name'. *Free Press* correspondent 'Half-Back' took a lofty view about a 'lot of unnecessary and ill-mannered hooting' and noted wisely that good decisions were 'groaned at as heartily as if … from the prince of cheats'.

NOVEMBER 5TH – WEST BROMWICH 1, BOLTON 5 – (6,000)

ALBION'S STORY

'The Throstles Heavily Defeated – Disgraceful Scenes.' The edgy Cup holders at last drew a crowd, for their traditional Wake Monday afternoon fixture, and went over the edge. They would not come back from a 'simply wretched exhibition'.

This time Albion took half an hour to decide to play, and then faced barracking by visiting Villa and Wolves 'shouters'. 'A Wanderer, not well versed in Scripture, was heard to say "How these Midland footballers love one another".' Goalkeeper Roberts was still suffering from Saturday's bruises: 'I should think the others were all over bruises, too, for I have never seen them play a weaker game.' Albion's Englishmen showed no stomach for a fight. Davy Weir scored three times and Bolton's tough-guys ruled: 'Roberts got on [Hendry's] track and spilled his lordship into the mud.' Wanderers had also borrowed Siddons from Albion's other rivals, Birmingham St George's. He was famously prone to 'paroxysms of rage' and near time 'deliberately struck [Hendry] under the chin with his clenched fist ... [Hendry] at once jumped up to retaliate, but the crowd, with angry cries, rushed into the enclosure with the intention of inflicting summary chastisement'. Albion protected Siddons and shepherded the 'roaring bull of basham' into their 'headquarters'. Game over.

Reporters followed the players off. Bolton blamed Hendry: he had shown a 'vicious tendency' even before 'cutting [Siddons'] lip clean through'. Journalists wanted Albion's view, but the club worried that this 'discreditable incident' 'will be borne in mind much longer ... especially by outsiders' than the defeat, and represented a 'bad stain on their reputation'. This 'very strong desire manifested to shut the mouths of the Albion players' required pre-emptive action: 'a gentleman who declared himself "a member of the committee", not only peremptorily ordered the players to say nothing but requested, as a member of the committee, that the reporter leave the dressing room.'

From bad to worse. Secretary Tom Smith resigned after a conflict that caused Albion's near strikes in recent games. When Cup final hero Harry Green announced his unfitness (rheumatic fever), Smith refused his request for full pay of £1 a week, and proposed only half. 'Captain Bayliss went to him and unpleasantness resulted.' The press turned against uppity players. Smith was right – players had been 'practically allowed to be "cock of the walk".' Again their admired quality of 'never-say-die' Englishness was turned against the Albion: 'no official with a spark of English courage can put up with constant badgering and ... gross insults.'

NOVEMBER 10TH – BURNLEY 2, WEST BROMWICH 0 – (4,000)

Albion were in disarray. Treasurer Louis Ford threatened resignation, they 'have a split in the camp, while their team is to be reconstituted'. Albion hit rock bottom against Burnley, who had conceded 38 goals in nine League games and 21 in their last three fixtures (1-6 by Notts County, 1-7 to Blackburn and 4-8 to Halliwell), and expected to be 'defeated at least by six-nothing'. When their latest Scotch centre was injured, Burnley soon had only ten men. The Cup holders must win and must score buckets. They lost. 'The split' cost Albion three players, so Bayliss played full-back with Oliver, a recent Small Heath player who 'thinks he is only second to Ross himself. He is the only one who thinks the same'. This was a far cry from those backs who won the Cup final – like England's Albert Aldridge – or Scotland's Andrew Hannah, whom they let go in September. Now they were beneath contempt: 'it is useless to criticise the play of the Albion in its present state. To play the rejected of Small Heath alongside Bayliss at back was simply courting defeat. Neither has a right to be in such a position, and it could only have been pure 'cussedness' that made Bayliss play there. Till the Albion's internal economy is revolutionised ... they will always be subject to the evil which is covering them with disaster just now.'

THE RISING CLUBS

EVERTON

OCTOBER 13TH – NOTTS COUNTY 3, EVERTON 1 – (4,000)

It was no part of Everton's ambitious script to give best to the league's 'worst' club. Notts was the last Apostle to win – 'the most deserved and least expected' – and defeat signalled Everton's growing crisis.

Against Villa, Bob Smalley 'was worth going to Birmingham to see ... as safe as a proverbial church'. Now he had a 'bilious attack'. The first goal should not have beaten him, and he carried the third 'through his own goal by leaning back and dropping it'. Daft goal. 'World champion' Jack Ross knew this should not be happening. He 'worked wonders' by going centre-forward and hitting a shot that 'would have gone through a brick wall'.

Notts' goalkeeper survived an 'extraordinary scrimmage': Holland caught the ball, Everton dashed in, knocked down and fell on him, but he heroically struggled out of the crush. Meanwhile the 'Nottingham Lambs' accepted as Gospel Alec Dick's 'dirty' reputation. He had as much consideration for County's 'manliness and their limbs as an Irish hurley player' (where every game included 'half-a-dozen maimings'). The 'much bitter ill-feeling' provoked insults – 'Dog' 'Pig' 'Sod' – even before he fought with England international, 'stiff-built little Albert' Moore: 'Dick fouled Moore, and as the latter was appealing for the foul Dick put his knee into Moore's back, and Moore retaliated by striking Dick a vigorous blow in the face.'

The English crowd had history. Nottingham's reputation for strong-armed intimidation of opponents and referees stemmed back to the days of Bendigo, Champion Prizefighter of All-England. His championship fights in the 1830s and 1840s attracted up to 10,000. His opponent Ben Caunt smashed a ring stake against Bendigo's back and fastened his neck between the ropes. When Bendigo was disqualified, pandemonium broke out as the 'Nottingham Lambs' attacked Caunt with sticks and stakes; fought with his ruffians; and dragged him out of his coach before he escaped bare-back on a stolen horse.

Political parties later engaged Bendigo and the Lambs to rough up the opposition at election times. Defeated candidates commented, 'what must the Nottingham wolves be like?' After twenty years of drunkenness, in and out of prison, Bendigo found religion and there followed a famous exchange with one of his former aristocratic backers. 'What's your game now, Bendy?' 'I'm fighting Satan now, your lordship, and Scripture saith that victory will be mine.' 'Hope so, Bendy, but if you don't fight Beelzebub fairer than you did Ben Caunt, then I'll change sides.' Bendigo's own change of allegiance led to an epic encounter when his 'Nottingham Lambs' – 'full of beer and impudence, ripe for anything' – heckled a revivalist meeting. 'He vaulted from the pulpit like a tiger from the den … Til the Ebenezer Chapel looked more like a knacker's yard.' After which:

Five repentant fighting men a-sitting in a row,
Listening to words of grace from Mr. Bendigo,
Listening to his reverence, all as good as gold,
Pretty little baa lambs all gathered to the fold.

Bendigo's Lamb successors were still ripe for anything. Dick had been hit by spectators during the game, and 'when time was called a rush was made for the visitors … and sticks were freely used. Dick was immediately singled out, and after he had defended himself for some time', received a severe head wound from a cudgel. Frank Sugg briefly grabbed the 'cowardly fellow'. Players and a policeman fought 'through the excited crowd' to escort Dick to the pavilion. Asked on Merseyside why they lost, George Farmer said they were all bruised and sore, and that was why.

Everton added more players. They had won the tug-of-war for heroic cricketer Sugg by staking him to a sports emporium, whilst local players were rejecting their terms as not good enough. Everton's 36 players cost over £100 per week. Thirty-five appeared in the League, and only Edgar Chadwick played all 22 fixtures.

Meanwhile there were deeper meanings to be pondered. Three results in successive weeks: Villa 9, Notts County 1; Everton 2, Villa 0; Notts County 3, Everton 1. Now these contradictory outcomes were contained ... within the League.

OCTOBER 20TH – DERBY 2, EVERTON 4 – (3,000)

Everton took a mixture of defiance and discretion back to the Midlands, a week after their misadventures in Nottingham. Frank Sugg braved his own history: some said, following his insults of Derbyshire CCC, that he 'dared not play at Derby owing to the cricket bother'.

Notts had apologised for Dick's mobbing, but said he brought it on himself by 'striking Hodder, for kicking Moore, for butting a spectator and special reference has been made to his language on the field'. Everton's new secretary William Barclay declined the apology, thereby grabbing defeat from the jaws of victory. Notts complained to the authorities. The League were not interested, attributing its own success to being 'burdened by no rules', but the Association 'took up the fight', convening a 'Misconduct Commission'. Everton, 'singularly disliked in official quarters', were vulnerable – 'it will be a death blow to Anfield football if they get another month's holiday. After their last suspension, they tried appeasement – 'gain the good graces of the Association by appointing a new secretary' – by dumping the provocative Alec Nisbet. Everton's commercial image epitomised the pro challenge to the ideal of pure sport, and now their Scotch indiscipline went beyond the pale.

The committee left Dick at home with a cover story: 'he was somewhat dickey, and had not quite got over having his hair combed by a baulk of timber by a Nottingham lamb.' Derby expected to see their former player 'Arry Warmby as Dick's replacement but he only 'came on the field ... at half time as waiter with throat gargles for Everton'.

The attendance tested the League's strategy of encouraging only one club per town as all four major Derby clubs had home games the same Saturday, and Everton's 'notoriety' was a real crowd-puller. A forward forgot they were on best behaviour. When Derby's Latham 'shook his anatomy somewhat suddenly,' the Evertonian responded angrily, 'where the elephant [code for swearing] are you coming to.' This recalled absent friends: the crowd 'wanted to know if that was Dick'. He was elsewhere, being blamed for the Reserve's first defeat: 'Dick wandered all over the shop and many gave him credit for losing the match.'

Derby goalkeeper Harry Bestwick, whose absence had been bemoaned earlier, was 'bothered by a blazing sun dead in his blinkers'. Then Everton bothered him: 'Bestwick was charged and fell with the ball

... right on the goalline outside the post; Everton bringing it in and putting through.'

OCTOBER 27TH – EVERTON 6, DERBY 2 – (4/5,000)

Jack Ross's defensive kicks were already legendary, clearing 'Kemlyn-road's chimney pots in the direction of Garstang': and when he 'gets a fair lift at the leather, one pictures a projectile from a hundred-ton gun waltzing down the enclosure'. But increasingly he had to be hero. The 'Anfield Roadsters' looked down on poor Derby, who were advised they would stay bottom if they could not leave home with more than ten men. But County scored first, so Ross swapped places with centre Frank Sugg and promptly equalised.

Ross had sensed choppier seas lay ahead at Everton, so went home to 'Fish' – the Edinburghers sounded the depth of the pond in which they would dump Ross if they caught him. He brought back Angus McKinnon who 'carries as much ballast as a fishing lugger, and tears through the wind like a cutter in a sou' wester'. Although McKinnon scored four times, critics sniped at Everton's reliance on their 'boss' changing positions to change a game – this might work against Derby, but not against crack teams.

There were inquests on every Everton team: 'why was Billy Briscoe played on the left' instead of his usual right; why play James Costley, the famous Cup-winning left-winger, 'in the centre, where he is absolutely useless;' why Keys, 'a very fine outside-right,' was 'put centre against Villa ... completely at sea'; why is Frank Sugg all over the place?

Frank Sugg was already restless about being moved around, but his days were too full to complain. Sugg's match day began with the 8.15am train from Southport to his sports shop in Liverpool. After a few hours work, at 11am he left for Anfield, played (in varying positions) against Derby then back to business at 6.45pm. He took the 9.30 train back to Southport, where his day was only just beginning. At midnight he left on a bicycle ride, arriving at Blackburn at 4.50am. After a snack and a rest, at two o'clock it was back to Southport in time for evening service. On Monday afternoon Everton had another match.

NOVEMBER 3RD – EVERTON 2, BOLTON 1 – (6,000)

Everton remembered being 'Trottered' 2-6 in Bolton's September mud. Liverpool imported 'real Bolton weather': 'a dull, leaden sky, a thick mist ... a constant downpour' – which halved the expected attendance. Bolton's keeper did not turn up. Wanderers had replaced Harrison with 'top sawyer' Dr Mills-Roberts, North End's Cup goalie. He kept goal the week before when Bolton beat Bootle 4-0 in an ordinary club match, which made Everton even keener to upstage their neighbours by beating Wanderers.

Mills-Roberts couldn't leave his Birmingham hospital and sent Sam Gillam, Wales' third top goalkeeper. This completed a certain symmetry – Gillam had failed to turn up for Everton's first game of the season. Behind the scenes Everton's power struggle over selection and tactics continued. Costley was announced as centre, Sugg let be known his objection to mid-game changes, so at the last moment Jack Ross decided to play centre. To Bolton's fury, Everton cast their covetous eyes on Alec Barbour, the best centre seen at Anfield this year. Whilst about-to-be-suspended Alec Dick got a special reception, a recently suspended local player, Brown, was chosen 'in face of serious objections by members'. Everton hoped that 'all his past delinquencies will soon sink into oblivion, if he honestly tries to play the game in a fair and manly spirit'.

The 'dispiriting conditions' caused hesitation: 'a little preliminary kicking among the surface water, which splashed up here and there.' Journalists were particularly needy: 'the ground swampy, the seats and desk for the unfortunate Press men so wet that but for the kind action of a gentleman in the stand, who supplied us with a number of old newspapers and a waterproof sheet, our lot would have been of the damp swampy.'

When they started, Farmer, 'fearing his unmentionables', took evasive action. Whatever their misgivings, the players warmed everyone up: no 'gradual simmering or sparring' but 'a full head of steam put on at once, every man working like a nigger. It was a regular scorcher,' a 'hot shop' ending with triumphant acclamation of Everton's winner: 'such a yell rent the air as must have been heard a mile away.' For the rest of the season, Wanderers swore to anyone who would listen that it 'never went through'. Enough: by the end spectators were calling out 'Time'.

By any reckoning Everton stood third, with six wins and three losses, but there was no official reckoning. They got little credit for this League high point. The factionalism was too obvious. John Houlding bankrolled the club but he was rarely hands-on. Last year's secretary was Nisbet, this year's was Barclay and next year's would be Molyneux. Another behind-the-scenes figure, Tom Howarth, was the man who signed Jack Ross. Everton's inconsistency was now being headlined 'Everton's Football Fiascoes'. Columnist 'Looker On' felt Ross's 'hands are tied' but did not endorse untying them; instead he wanted 'a practical committee of experienced footballists'. One problem was that the Committee had 'too many players to select from when picking the men'. But whether the power lay with Moneybags; secretaries and middle men; committeemen; captain or players, it did not lie with 'the great mass of members ... practically nonentities ... sunk into oblivion'.

NOVEMBER 10TH – BLACKBURN 3, EVERTON 0 – (6,000)
EVERTON'S STORY

Everton's rollercoaster rolled into Blackburn, Town of Smoke, or some did. Just as Blackburn were celebrating the capture of their Scotch saviour, Everton were bemoaning their loss *en route*. Four-goal McKinnon, who only played 'as the spirit moved him', simply got off at Preston Junction. Everton had 'a screw loose in the managing machine'. Fortunately, they took a spare, so seventeen-year-old Alf Milward, future England international, played centre. 'McKinnon's refusal to play' weakened Jack Ross's position in political infighting, as the Edinburgh man was his boy. Liverpool's press rehearsed the old grievances – Ross is not allowed to pick his own team: committeemen were 'mere talkers and theorists ... dissatisfied Evertonians went home swearing all sorts of vengeance against their committee'.

NOVEMBER 24TH – EVERTON 3, BURNLEY 2 – (8,000)

It was all about Scots. Jack Ross's honeymoon was ending as Everton lost momentum. Their 'truly astonishing' changes of personnel meant another poor display before the 'usual mammoth gate', not helped by new Scots Coyne (via Gainsborough) and Davie (Renton's centre in those epic cup-ties with North End in 1887).

BLACKBURN ROVERS
OCTOBER 13TH – ASTON VILLA 6, BLACKBURN 1 – (5,000)

Rovers started slowly. Unbeaten at first, they allowed lowly Notts to avoid defeat for the first time (it was premature to talk about gaining a point), then lost 1-6. Rovers were rebuilding: despite their Cup heroics in the mid-1880s, they entered the League after two moderate seasons. They had scoured Blackburn for younger men, like 22-years-old Bill Almond and Bob Haresnape of Witton, Bill Townley and the Southworth brothers from Blackburn Olympic. But they would have to go further afield for a leader to replace the inspirational Fergy Suter, Original Scotch Pro.

They wanted Jack Forbes, but as a shamateur, to play in the Cup. When Forbes strengthened an ordinary Glasgow Rangers team in the 1887 National Cup semi-final, Birmingham regarded Villa's opponents transformed into 'Scotland'. Rovers conceded eighteen goals in five matches. They needed a defence. Forbes came with 'a friend', who attracted little attention but was in fact Scotland's current goalkeeper James Wilson. Forbes and Wilson went home, negotiations incomplete: Forbes was an unemployed designer for calico printers, and needed a job, or something more.

OCTOBER 20TH – BLACKBURN 2, WOLVERHAMPTON 2 – (4,000)

Meanwhile, the old heroes pulled Rovers around. Wolves went two up, but eight-stone Jimmy Forrest (five Cup wins between 1884 and 1891) 'played one of his old games' and Townley 'ran rings' round Albert Fletcher, soon England's half-back.

NOVEMBER 3RD – BURNLEY 1, BLACKBURN 7 – (3,000)
ROVERS' STORY

If Blackburn patiently stalked their prey and waited until Forbes came to bay, Lancashire rivals Burnley were all hit and miss: their newest Scotch centre was 'dreadfully slow'. The match carried a wider lesson: 'when Blackburn Rovers passed, they played to perfection: when they played every man for themselves 'the Burnley backs robbed them'. Advice to budding forwards: 'go in for the passing game, for there is nothing to beat it.' Centre-forward Jack Southworth scored a hat-trick as Rovers totalled 31 goals in eight games.

NOVEMBER 10TH – BLACKBURN 3, EVERTON 0 – (6,000)
ROVERS' STORY

Jack Forbes' courtship had been as extended as his reputation deserved – 'undoubtedly the greatest back Scotland has ever produced'. He settled for good in Blackburn as his outfitting shop (his price for coming) flourished, so that Mr Forbes became a prosperous and long-standing member of the Rovers board into the 1920s. For the moment 700 Everton supporters arrived to find the town swamped with placards carrying a simple, but strangely unsettling message – 'Forbes Will Play'. He produced the goods alright – making 'ducks and drakes of the feeble efforts of the Everton right wing'.

NOVEMBER 17TH – BLACKBURN 5, ASTON VILLA 1 – (8/9,000)

Rovers reckoned it 'quits'. The grandstand wanted 'to atone for the thrashing' at Villa and they got a 'genuine', albeit disallowed sixth. Jack Southworth scored another hat-trick and Fecitt was 'never better – and again and again his brilliant play drew the cheers of the immense crowd'. Impressive, without Townley. Billy Dickson was contracted for, but did not come, so 'once famous Jimmy Brown' – Rovers' thrice Cup-winning captain and five-times England international – put on the 'war paint' again. Only 25, 5ft 5in, weighing less than ten stone, Brown proved 'as good a man as ever'. The League was giving Rovers a 'fresh lease of life'.

The cumulative results were now being commonly represented in a confused variety of tables: 'how the championship will ultimately be decided goodness only knows.' If points were the answer, they were either minimalist (one for winning, half for drawing – so that after nine games North End had 8½) or expansive (22 points for winning, and a debit of 22 for losing, so that North End had 187 points, and Derby minus 121). At the top it was academic: 'no doubt … [North End] is the boss of the league, reckon how you may.' But who was second? Villa had won more games and conceded fewer goals, but Rovers had lost fewer games and scored more goals:

Rovers – 10 matches: 5 wins, 4 draws, 1 loss; 39 goals for, 24 against.

Villa – 11 matches: 6 wins, 3 draws, 2 losses; 33 goals for, 19 against.

WOLVERHAMPTON WANDERERS

OCTOBER 6TH – ACCRINGTON 4, WOLVERHAMPTON 4 – (4,000)

The Reds, who normally wore white, sported dark blue serge knickers for their opening home match in this, their fifth fixture: 'what a savage lot the Reds looked in their new breeks.' Promising Accrington half-back Luther Pemberton was missing, injured at work that morning. Wolves were 'pretty near their wits' end' that referee Fitzroy Norris did not show, because it meant an extra three hours on their return journey: 'the usual preliminary practice was indulged in, but this business was very prolonged … nothing to do but wait … By and by a loud shouting mingled with laughter … [Norris] was doing a gentle sprint down the meadow from Burnley Road. The pace was kept up right to the field, and the rails being taken in great style, the referee ultimately landed in the field of play in what was considered good time from Bolton. He was not long in unearthing his whistle.'

It was a 'tough and pretty even struggle, neither side having any decided pull' until 'Horne was again beaten out of a rush'. The Reds were 'two goals to the bad', and 'who but the prejudiced could fail to appreciate [Wolves'] most brilliant play'. Cruel laughter helped as Bill Barbour earned his reputation as the 'goalkeeper getter', and fellow Scot Brand's magnificent 'real gem' brought 'plucky, hard-working' Accrington level at 3-3. But their real star was captain George Howarth, 'a host in himself', and compensating for Peter Chippendale being 'the proverbial bull in the crockery shop. He had one of those fits on Saturday'. Barbour converted Howarth's 'huge throw' and Accrington began 30 minutes of grand defence. Pressmen were standing at the gate to dispatch their messengers when a miskick gave Wolves a 4-4 draw. Accrington were philosophical: ''Tis not in mortals to commit success ... the fates decreed otherwise.'

OCTOBER 13TH – BURNLEY 0, WOLVERHAMPTON 4 – (4,000)

Fitzroy Norris was centre stage again, disallowing Burnley goals and allowing a Wolves shot that failed to go through the posts. Burnley's big crowd dispersed, puzzled by Wolves' 'unexpected form' (they were previously rare visitors to Lancashire) and 'in a very disappointed mood'.

OCTOBER 27TH – PRESTON 5, WOLVERHAMPTON 2 – (6,000)

Wolves' series of four successive Saturdays in Lancashire (no fixture computer yet) ended at Deepdale. Geordie Drummond was in Scotland attending a sick wife (she died a year later). He was not missed: replacement Jack Edwards was as 'good as the rest', so football agents were 'on his track'. Stoke offered to transfer his work from Preston's General Post Office to Hanley's.

Wolves took man and ball, but Preston's right wing quickly set up Goodall's headed goal, and Gordon scored with a characteristic screw shot. Wolves fought on, exhibiting a 'very cantankerous spirit' that did not wash with referee McIntyre. 'Anything but gentlemanly,' there was 'friction between several players and Mr Sudell the North End umpire'. It was close until Goodall and Ross hit late goals. The expectations on North End were high. Failure to win more easily against strong Wolves was attributed to 'very selfish tactics': 'unless some alteration is made it will not be long before they suffer their first league defeat.' The forwards were faulted for a circus act: 'the three inside players would selfishly monopolise the ball, and pass and repass until they were eventually robbed. With a few square yards in the middle of a sawdust ring it would have looked very pretty, but on a football pitch ... the spectators vented their displeasure in no uncertain way.'

NOVEMBER 3RD – WOLVERHAMPTON 4, DERBY 1 – (1,000)

The 'local men, playing down the hill, pressed and again scored, and after the visitors had broken their egg, the Wanderers scored again'. Everyone finished covered with 'mud and slush'.

NOVEMBER 24TH – ASTON VILLA 2, WOLVERHAMPTON 1 – (4,000)

The strong wind was 'a trouble and a puzzle'. Villa's Archie Hunter cried 'Keep the ball down ... [but] Goodall could not manage it'. Archie

Goodall, replacing the suspended Denny Hodgetts, nevertheless managed both goals, his winner being a 'flying' shot following 'strategic movements'. In between, Wolves equalised: 'a sudden dash right ... a brilliant run and centre by Knight, a straight swift shot by Brodie, and the trick was done.' 'Brodie and his mates' were just falling short of tricks.

ACCRINGTON

Accrington's contribution to the League, and competitive football, was to show the importance of the draw – six out of their first ten. As the League gripped public attention, arguments raged about value: should a win count more than a defeat cost? Was Everton's three wins and three losses really better than Accrington's two wins, three draws and one loss? The Reds gave draws a good name. They were not the dull 1-1s of later generations. Accrington drew big: 5-5, 4-4, 3-3.

OCTOBER 20TH – ACCRINGTON 0, PRESTON 0 – (8,000)

Their most famous draw, still mentioned in football footnotes. 'A BIG DAY AT ACCRINGTON.' North End were coming. They had rarely played at Accrington lately, and their withdrawal from that spring's Lancashire Cup final still smarted. The locals were confident: Accrington 'can always give North End a tight game'. Scots Brand and Barbour (ten goals in four games) were rapidly being 'canonised', 'two of the best forwards ever seen at Accrington.' North End were at full strength for the first time. Beautiful weather attracted Accrington's record gate of £173, 'a fine gathering of the classes and the masses.' One gentleman, refused entry to the stand, protested: 'but I have come 30 miles, and must see the match.'

The first 45 was 'as hard a fought half as I have seen for a long time'. Accrington, quicker on the ball, challenged a perfect defence, with Trainer busy and impregnable Bob Holmes a 'Champion' successor to Jack Ross. Preston's forwards were heavily criticised: 'undoubtedly Geordie [Drummond] has shaped but indifferently so far this season; but the support he generally receives from his partner is nil, and this absence of combination renders the wing useless.' Accrington pulled off the tactical master-stroke: veteran Jonathan Wilkinson 'stuck to Goodall like a leech'. The 'ancient' rendered 'the best centre forward in the world ... almost useless'. Only Gordon and Ross were 'worthy of the name of the club'.

'Defence killed the forward play' and Brand missed Accrington's best chance. A Barbour shot was going in, 'but the sphere twisted, and [Brand] had not time to recover.' A 'certain goal' lost – 0-0 was a 'peculiar result' but 'satisfactory and correct'. Close beside the press stand was a 'youth whose fingers were fairly itching to discharge a pop-gun … when the Reds scored.' 'Free Critic' thought 'it was worth going miles to see', and since he was paid twice (as reporter, and as Jack Bentley, referee) he did not share the colloquial view: 'once nowt is nowt, and twice nowt is nowt.'

The gist of the criticism was that North End might lose. Preston's press showed more spunk, sneering that the Reds only dented the League's last perfect record through 'special preparation'. The response was a paean in support of the footballer worker: 'Accrington's players, with one exception, are all hardy sons of toil … any man jack as happy working … as if he were lounging about all week, with nothing but football for a business.' The team all worked 54 hours the week before playing Preston: 'no big wages' and the club 'economically managed … We can tackle any club without "special preparation" my friend.'

OCTOBER 13TH – ACCRINGTON 6, DERBY 2 – (3,000)

From the start League football has been regarded as the paradigm of seriousness. Accrington's 'Artful Dodger' attracted censure for 'flash' rather than productive play: 'Bonar had not done much up to now … so of course he must needs play to the gallery, but as football spectators are now too well-educated his efforts met with disapproval. In years gone by, a bit of gallery play was regarded as something smart and was cheered by the multitude, but at the present time kicking the leather has come to be regarded as a kind of business and all foolery is expressly forbidden. Perhaps Bonar will do what I did, viz. make a note of it.' The frustration of infuriated critics would ring through the ages: 'carelessness in shooting … How often do we see players who have nobody near them make wild shots at goal when, if they could only control themselves a little and not lose their heads quite so much, they would at least send the ball somewhere near the hole.'

Rob Brand got a hat-trick but 'our lad from Oswaldthistle', Jack Kirkham, 'fairly fetched the crowd' with his magnificent fourth goal: 'one of the neatest I have ever seen … enthusiastic cheering, again and again renewed.'

NOVEMBER 17TH – PRESTON 2, ACCRINGTON 0 – (7,000)

Could Accrington repeat their heroics? North End's determination to re-establish the natural order, 'added to the rumours which were rife that Mr Hartley's men were in training, infused still more interest in the return.'

Reporter 'Free Lance' awoke to find a Saturday morning of wind, rain and hail and decided 'No Preston for this boy'. The hail stopped although the strong westerly gale remained. The Lancashire & Yorkshire Railway Company took 80 minutes to carry Accrington and 700 supporters fifteen miles. Then hurry-up: 'What a rush from the station! ... vehicles in abundance, and soon loads ands loads of Accringtonians were being driven at breakneck pace along the streets of Preston for Deepdale.'

Sam Thomson's left wing tricky play impressed, 'again and again bringing down the house.' But Joe Lofthouse scored first until referee Fairhurst (the editor of Bolton's *Football Field*) rushed to umpire Sudell – 'rather unusual conduct for a referee' – and Sudell claimed offside: 'the Accrington contingent took the decision like taking a pill.' Lofthouse, reacting rather stronger, 'waxed mighty wrath when that goal was disallowed, and well he might.'

North End showed 'better combination than they have for some time' (they had scored sixteen goals in their previous four League games). 'Seldom has there been a finer exhibition of goalkeeping at Deepdale.' Jack Horne pulled out one plum of a save after another. 'At length the climax came, "hands" fell to North End close in, Thomson placed the ball well in front, and with a mighty rush, the whole Accrington team were carried through.' North End dominated the second half.

'Twas so dark at end.'

NOVEMBER 24TH – ACCRINGTON 2, WEST BROMWICH 1 – (2,000)

The Reds' return with the Cup holders was a 'complete fizzle to the exchequer'. A gale kept the crowd down but entertaining Fitzroy Norris 'my curly headed darling was the referee once more'. In line with renewed encouragement from the Association to address violence, Norris issued cautions for rough play. Jack Horne was the 'hero of the match' whereas Albion's Roberts let Kirkham's shot roll between his legs and watched Barbour's floating header go by him. West Bromwich thought Accrington won 'almost by mere accidents'.

The top seven had already proved themselves as England's true first-class clubs when the League finally decided, at the end of November 1888, how to compare their results: two points for a win, one for a draw.

Preston 13 games, 24 points; Aston Villa 12, 17; Blackburn 11, 16; Everton 12, 15; Wolves 12, 14; West Bromwich 12, 13; Accrington 12, 12.

There was then a five-point gap to those whose class was in doubt.

THE STRUGGLERS IN OCTOBER AND NOVEMBER 1888

What the League decided and what was left ambiguous is revealing. For McGregor, the important thing was that first-class clubs played each other. That would draw the public. Comparing results (by 'averages', which was left undefined) was secondary to maintaining quality. So identifying the laggards was more important than a champion. Four clubs, a third of the membership, were in jeopardy. Once the League captured the public imagination, it seemed vital to stay in. Nevertheless, the shame of the underlying class assumptions – that their team was not first-class – remained a more explicit motivation than losing League status. At first this was little help, as five clubs drifted away from the others.

BOLTON WANDERERS

The focus was on management. 'Why doesn't Mr Bentley take the men on the field during the week and give them a lesson.' Wanderers had weapons, especially their English-born Scot Davy Weir who would earn his England cap against Scotland in April 1889. But old heroes like Kenny Davenport felt the carping: 'aye, they think I'm on my last legs, and can't play neaw, but I'll show them on Saturday.' Even their Scottish international centre was lacking: 'Barbour's weakness [is] that he cannot settle the ball ... He should learn to stop it at once.' Goalkeeper Charlie Harrison, initially admired as 'a boxer and can fist out like a demon', was soon advised to stick to 'fist out instead of catching and dodging'. Home matches proved dramatic and compelling events. Humiliatingly, Bolton twice lost three-goal leads but, after practice, they ran North End close and gained a galvanising 6-2 win against Everton. Redemption?

OCTOBER 6TH – BURNLEY 4, BOLTON 1 – (5,000)

Not quite. Bolton were 'fairly done up' again. Burnley needed it more: 'the rumour was prevalent that the situations of some Burnley players depended upon the result.' Wanderers were mere 'lookers on'.

OCTOBER 13TH – BOLTON 2, STOKE 1 – (3,000)

Both clubs had now lost four of five. Wanderers made a modest six changes, Walter Flitcroft returning as captain, 'stout as ever,' to give more bottom to their effort. Intimidating Pike's Lane turned the game: 'the way the crowd bullied the referee was something outrageous ... [if he] had not allowed time for Ramsey's display of temper when he kicked the ball out of the ground.' 'Just on the call of time,' Jack Milne's 'hanging screw shot' forced an own goal.

NOVEMBER 5TH – WEST BROMWICH 1, BOLTON 5 – (6,000)
WANDERERS' STORY

Bolton had suffered six losses in eight when they travelled to the Cup holders for the League's first midweek – Wake Monday – fixture. Wanderers ran out of players so the resourceful Jack Bentley, in London for an Association meeting, set the telegraph wires humming. He secured Siddons, one of last season's Derby Junction Cup semi-final heroes, now with St George's. A more cynical age would query the motives of Harry Mitchell, leader of both St George's and the League's rival, the Combination. If mischief was hoped for, it happened double. Siddons attacked Hendry, and the crowd ended the game abruptly. Albion were shamed, and Hendry and Siddons, along with Alec Dick and Dennis Hodgetts, became the focus of the Association's campaign against rough play. Meanwhile Albion retaliated against Siddons. Was it all right to employ another club's professional in a League fixture? Bentley published the wishful-thinking telegram traffic: 'Mitchell – "Have asked Alcock to allow Siddons to play". My boy wired to Roberts – "Mitchell says Alcock allows Siddons to play".'

NOVEMBER 10TH – WOLVERHAMPTON 3, BOLTON 2 – (2,000)

Phlegmatic Jack Bentley took two more foreigners because his reserve were contesting the English Cup: Lytham's Mercer, who had no time to get boots that fitted, and McGuinness, Halliwell's rave Scotch centre. Crowd-pulling ex-Prime Minister Gladstone was in town. Wolves' 'great unwashed' behaved 'like semi-barbarians … wild play caused by highly excited and howling crowd, who trespass on the field with the slightest provocation'. Bolton's goalkeeper 'Harrison was charged through the posts', and the ball followed him. A foul? After time? Wolves' winner stood: otherwise 'I fancy unpleasant consequences might have followed'.

NOVEMBER 17TH – BOLTON 1, WEST BROMWICH 2 – (4,000)

'Marvellous Monday,' Bolton folk had called the day Wanderers knocked the 'gilt off the cup holders' gingerbread'. Albion's quick revenge evoked a sense of grievance, only made worse when Fitzroy Norris, their former secretary, made abject apology. The teams had agreed 40 minutes each way because of the fading light. However referee Norris gave Albion the benefit of the wind in a 48-minute first half: 'this I cannot account for unless the watch went suddenly out of order. In the second half just the 40 minutes were played, to the surprise and thorough dissatisfaction of the spectators. I regret the error, and feel most keenly that the Wanderers have had the worst of it.'

NOVEMBER 24TH – BOLTON 2, PRESTON 5 – (10,000)

As was traditional, Jack Bentley prepared for this standout fixture by importing three Scotch half-backs (all ex-Renton) for the day. But Bob McDiarmid and McKechnie, fresh from Sunderland, 'refused to strip' if played out of position. Send for Bob Roberts. The crowd had not liked to see the 'Big-un' lying idle, and applauded heartily when he stepped on the ground from the grandstand, into someone else's 'pants ... and trotted about the field quite gingerly, especially when tackling, for fear of the seams giving way'. Ironically, Bolton came apart in the second half, overwhelmed by the 'very sloppy' ground and the gale.

After that it could only get better. And it did. Once the League decided how to calculate results, Wanderers flourished: only six points in their first twelve matches, but sixteen came in their remaining ten. Bolton became first-class again.

BURNLEY

Burnley's early wins over Bolton, followed by a 3-0 Monday defeat of Everton, vindicated trainer Joey Law's 'evident useful work' and the committee's effective disciplinary action against 'incorrigible' Scots. But 'how long will this form last?' The town anticipated a 'wonderful falling off' and it duly happened. Before long, committeemen were fighting 'in the streets'.

OCTOBER 20TH – STOKE 4, BURNLEY 3 – (3,000)

Burnley and Stoke were competing for salvation by different methods. Burnley based an agent in Edinburgh; Stoke 'had to telegraph and solicit services' from men throughout Britain. Which would produce reinforcements in time? The scene that Thursday at the railway station as Stoke's deputation awaited arrivals was captured for posterity, largely because of the hilarity it provoked in would-be spoilers, Port Vale:

'Scene: Party of four belonging to a certain football club, anxiously awaiting arrival of train from the north. Enter another party of four, representing certain dear neighbours. General excitement and anxiety of first four to conceal business. Tips flying about freely. Arrival of train without Scotch amateurs; exit of anxious party, amid comical cheers from the dear neighbours.'

Next day, centre James Sloane, grandly claimed to be from Glasgow Rangers, but really Monkcastle, actually turned up. Burnley's did not: Tait spent the week in Manchester and played instead with Newton Heath, so Mr Midgeley their umpire had to play. Stoke went three goals up but Burnley's Scot Fred Poland inspired a comeback to 3-3. Stoke's winner was a 'beauty' and Burnley's last-minute equaliser was ruled offside. More bad luck.

OCTOBER 27TH – NOTTS COUNTY 6, BURNLEY 1 – (4,000)

Things got worse before they improved. Nottingham was confusing. Burnley arrived to find County already playing an English Cup-tie. Although it was County's Reserve, and the League game followed immediately after, understandably Burnley's reporter thought they took a 'miserable beating from Notts Forest'. Scotch back 'Lang did not hesitate to indicate his opinion … Kay had not done his duty', and the goalkeeper was 'consigned to oblivion'. Burnley were on 'their downward course, defeat after defeat following with monotonous regularity'.

NOVEMBER 3RD – BURNLEY 1, BLACKBURN 7 – (3,000)

BURNLEY'S STORY

Against Blackburn, Fred Poland, an 'old goalkeeper' turned centre, 'was put between the sticks, and a right good custodian he proved.' Poland never played again. The pressure was on. Burnley now carried an unenviable reputation: 'the worst first-class club in Lancashire.' Rumour promised several new Scots but 'rumour generally lies'.

NOVEMBER 17TH – BURNLEY 2, EVERTON 2 – (3,000)

At last Burnley found ways and means. Centre-half Dannie Friel was made trainer and the agent in Edinburgh came through. Centre Ross McMahon and goalkeeper Cox arrived Thursday evening and practised Friday, and when McMahon was injured another centre, Mudie, arrived at noon on Saturday, and did not practice at all.

Whoever played this day was a hero. One correspondent finished his journey to Turf Moor on horseback, 'by the aid of a broken-winded, shaky-kneed old hack.' The 22 players were challenged by a 'wind blowing almost from goal to goal, and the ground was as heavy as lead'. As always Jack Ross was the player most closely observed: 'open dancing legs to prevent his opposing wing from shooting.' The two teams fought nobly until Burnley drew level, ten minutes to go: 'rain and hail came down at an alarming pace, whilst the players looked miserable in the extreme.'

STOKE

'Stoke, still loyal to the League,' were its first victims. 'The club agents of course came in for heavy work during the week' attempting to strengthen their Reserve before an English Cup qualifying round. They offered Halliwell's highly rated Scotch centre McGuinness a £10 present to play and a good wage to stay. He failed to turn up, instead earning a new reputation: 'everyone thought [Halliwell] had secured a flyer in

McGuinness, but from recent exhibitions, it would almost appear the young gentleman has not been taking proper care of himself' (Victorian code for alcohol misuse).

Warwick County goalkeeper Billy Rose's 'magnificent fisting', and 'the mean action of one of the backs in fisting the ball out', knocked Stoke out of the English Cup.

OCTOBER 6TH – PRESTON 7, STOKE 0 – (3,000)

Another McGuinness 'no-show' left Stoke with only nine men – they later presented a 'beautiful tea service' each to Walter Smalley and Dempsey, the North End reserves who made up their eleven.

OCTOBER 27TH – BLACKBURN 5, STOKE 2 – (3,000)

Stoke took a wrong turning after their win against Burnley. They arrived late at Blackburn, as not even Harry Lockett, the League's secretary, knew his way around Manchester. Being champions of the Potteries was no longer enough reputation: they 'have hardly shown league form' so far in conceding 28 goals and six defeats in eight games. Townley and Nat Walton made it four for Rovers by half-time. Stoke were beaten all over the shop.

NOVEMBER 3RD – STOKE 1, ASTON VILLA 1 – (3,000)

At last Stoke got another Scot although the Glasgow press, obsessed with North East depredations, described Bob Milharvie's destination as … 'Stockton-on-Trent'. Aston Villa's late arrival produced another wet and slippery match played in semi-darkness, and their failure to win 'bears a dark complexion' i.e. suspicions of a betting coup. Yet they only drew when goalkeeper Billy Rowley 'did not exert himself in the least' for Villa's goal.

NOVEMBER 12TH – STOKE 0, PRESTON 3 – (5,000)

North End were the big attraction on Michaelmas Monday, a holiday to decide potters' wages for the coming year. Preston's half-back Sandy Robertson was 'immensely pleased with himself' after his two goals supplemented North End's injury-hit forwards. In Preston, Stoke had only nine men. Here they were permitted thirteen: 'it was rather hard on Stoke for North End to show their superiority by allowing first one man and another to exchange places.'

Stoke's latest imports gave a 'sorry show', James Sloane playing handbags at dawn with Davie Russell: they 'struck a pugilistic attitude, and did a fair amount of dancing around, but blows were not exchanged'.

NOVEMBER 17TH – 'STOKE NIL, WOLVERHAMPTON 1 GOAL [DOUBTFUL]' (2,000)

Wolves 'succeeded in getting the ball through, but the spectators were unanimously of opinion that it was offside … Stoke played up well against these hard lines'.

NOVEMBER 24TH – 'NOTTS 0, STOKE-ON-TRENT 3' – (3,000)

Nottingham got their geography right but overstated their opponents' name. McSkimming gave Stoke an early lead with the wind, and afterwards Milharvie first rushed through Notts' goalkeeper Holland and then beat him with a 'clean shot'. The League was a real struggle: their 'emergency' Scots kept Stoke afloat, but the expense was great.

THE COUNTY SET – DERBY AND NOTTS

OCTOBER 6TH – NOTTS COUNTY 3, BLACKBURN 3 – (5,000)

Every rail trip from Lancashire to the Midlands was a trial. It usually started with a 'dense fog' over Manchester. Don't worry, said King Arthur, 'with the air of someone who knows … we should have plenty of sun on emerging from the city.' Then 'the long journey through the tunnels … with much shaking … our international made several visits to the ante-room, complaining of sea-sickness … you get as much rolling between Manchester and Derby as you do on an old Blackpool tug boat'.

Having lost their first three League games, Notts County rang the changes for the Goose Fair match that started the Trent Bridge season (the ground was only available for football between October and February). England's old warrior Harry Cursham replaced Scotch back Tom McLean who had broken his collar bone. Scotch amateur Bob Jardine, 'irritated' by his earlier disciplining, offered his services to both Forest and Notts Rangers but County needed his 'cleverness in screwing the ball in with his left foot'. They did not have much else going for them. English amateur Allin – the very same who failed to appear for Accrington's opener – was their latest centre.

Herby Fecitt's 'beautiful overhead kick' put Rovers ahead but Albert Moore got a late, desperate equaliser. For some, the 'less said about the play the better'. For others, 'one of the finest exhibitions of football witnessed at Trent Bridge.'

Notts were still busy 'decoying away' their neighbours, including Forest's Clements, who was 'a terror to forwards who are in the least inclined to "funk".' When they renewed overtures for the whole Notts Rangers team, the disruption was palpable: Rangers, top of the Combination, lost 0-8 at Sheffield Wednesday.

NOVEMBER 24TH – DERBY 0, BLACKBURN 2 – (3,000)

Although 'how [King Arthur] stopped that last shot of Bakewell's will remain a mystery', the 'most idiotic abuse' was levelled at the hero of the League's first Saturday, amateur George Bakewell.

Derby County joined the other strugglers after a respectable start. From 2-0 up against North End, they lost their next eight games, conceding 35 goals. The stuff of protest.

Derby's Athenaeum Rooms hosted an 'indignation meeting'. The underlying grievance was the football section's failure to separate from the 'doomed' County Cricket Club. The protestors took 'dead set' with 'arrant nonsense' against the one committeeman 'who has ever played the game', and the players responded by unanimously electing him as their next umpire. But correspondent 'Ticket holder' complained 'the matter uppermost in every man's mind was barely referred to, viz. the present discreditable position of the team in the list of League clubs'.

The County set conspired to confound the Apostles' main purpose when they postponed their League fixture for a Cup-tie. Notts were determined to survive the English Cup's divisional rounds to qualify for the real event in February. They were not going to scratch, like Everton. Nor had they matched Bolton Wanderers' foresight in recruiting a separate team. At first, they played two senior competitive games on the same day, skating thin around their commitment to League fixtures taking precedence. It worked. They won a 'double-header' at Trent Bridge 10-3 (Beeston St John's 4-2 in the Cup and Burnley 6-1 in the League, with Jardine scoring five goals).

Then it got harder. Notts Reserve were unlikely to beat Derby Midland (who proved Derby's best by defeating Derby County twice over Christmas 1888) in the next qualifying round. Derby County, not averse to inconveniencing their neighbours, were 'commendably generous' in agreeing the postponement so that Midland would face Notts County's strongest team. But this broke the League's 'cardinal law'. North End marked their cards: Notts were 'one to be dropped next April'.

The League's Jack Bentley, refereeing the tie, played it cool – wryly noting that Notts kept the right side of the Association, by leaving out ineligibles like Bob Jardine. County beat Midland 2-1, then promptly suffered a slapped wrist: 'no League engagement should be broken on any account ... in future the League games will be played as sure as Saturdays come round.' County exploited other loopholes for their Division Six final on December 8th. They fielded a team of ineligibles and borrowed players (especially from Notts Rangers) in the League (against the Villa, of all clubs), whilst their first eleven played the Cup-tie in Staveley.

Nottingham regarded undefeated Staveley as an 'uncivilised and ostracised part of the United Kingdom', so aimed to be in and out. Notts stripped on their special train, then, in their football clothes, wended the half-mile to the 'colliers' ground by the time the church clock struck half past two' (when the Association required Cup-ties to start). The 'men strong i' th' arm' [Staveley] had knocked Sheffield Wednesday, Middlesbrough, Notts Rangers and Nottingham Forest out of recent Cups and had given County several scares. They did again, taking the lead before Notts won 3-1. Afterwards, the 'women strong i' th' arm' mobbed umpire Cecil Shelton, father of County's noted half-backs – he fled back to the station minus his hat and nursing bruises and facial scratches.

Notts' defiance of the League had succeeded, at an alleged cost of £100 – previous seasons' expenses had increased 'trebly' this year. Then, too late, the Association's secretary Charles Alcock forbad County using Notts Rangers' professionals. Only months earlier, the Nottinghamshire Association suspended Notts for withdrawing their players from an inter-county game. All three defied. 'Snobbish' County had problems with authority.

NOVEMBER 3RD – NOTTS COUNTY 0, PRESTON 7 – (8,000)

Even coming off their own combined 10-3 win, Notts were not ready for Preston in miserable, muddy weather. Goalkeeper Holland had suffered internal injuries against Burnley: a 'rather serious accident … very bad in hospital'. Victorian hospitals were not safe places in which to spend ten days. Hugh Owen played goal. The Essex cricketer, and master of Trent College, was duly 'antagonised': 'Owen was charged through when holding a shot from Gordon.' Initially, North End's Davie Russell fisted out a goal-bound shot, and Notts supporters chanted 'How many goalkeepers have you got?' Afterwards it was 'awful to see', as Notts jaws 'droop and droop' and 'irate ticket holders' objected.

Nottingham correspondent 'Julius Caesar' agreed that County's backs 'bungled' and made 'fatal miskicks'; their half-backs 'could do little'; and the centre was 'lamentably weak … bit worse than customary' – 'but why do the complainers so furiously rage?'

Across the city the Forest met to decide whether to turn professional. Both clubs were among the oldest in the country. Forest had declined from a top-three/four side in 1883 to barely top-twenty five years later. They struggled so badly for fixtures that after five Scotch clubs and four Lancashire clubs declined they were glad to feed off County's crumbs – playing Derby when the two Countys postponed their League match. Forest had stayed amateur and virtuous (give or take a few Scots imported for matches with County), whilst County were professional and League. Was professionalism a matter of morality or pragmatics? Forest had England's centre, Tinsley Lindley, but he rarely played for them and men like Clements (the bungler) and Guttridge (the fatal miskicker) had 'gone over to the enemy' (County). As soon as committeeman Sam Widdowson persuaded the Special General Meeting to reaffirm amateurism, his brother, their giant goalkeeper Tom Widdowson, joined County with his own aphorism: a 'guinea in hand is worth all the amateurism in the bush'. He replaced Jack Holland, who 'puts a higher value on his services than they do' – but soon retired: 'he has not forgotten his knocking about.'

NOVEMBER 10TH – NOTTS COUNTY 3, ACCRINGTON 3
('MUCH SMALLER THAN LAST WEEK')

The League was exerting authority. Derby County were told to switch their ordinary fixture at Nottingham Forest to Derby rather than compete for attendance with fellow Apostles.

Notts had now been completely overwhelmed twice, conceding sixteen goals to Villa and North End. They made four changes but six or seven Reds 'were so foolish as to miss their train at Derby'. The Robin Hood Prize Band filled in the time, 'discoursing such novel airs as "Rule Britannia".' Half an hour later Accrington's 'delinquents were seen bounding across the grounds towards the dressing-rooms'. The 'fearful delay' meant the match finishing in near-darkness, the many pipe-smokers creating a flittering will-'o-the-wisp scene as Notts hung on. 'Close on time, in a desperate struggle,' Accrington drew level. Back home, they faced complaint: 'fact is, Sir, these draws are becoming a little monotonous.'

When draws became accepted, and earned one point, the League strugglers were: Burnley 12 games 7 points; Stoke 12, 7; Bolton 12, 6; Notts 11, 5; Derby 10, 5.

Halfway through, the first 'official' table appeared. The League's perfect complement. Two points for a win, 'a draw counts half a win,' nothing for a loss. Simplicity. McGregor's real vision. Perfectly understandable. Better than the League itself, which journalists had misunderstood. Twelve clubs meant 24 games each, right? Wrong. But two, one, nothing. Everyone understood that. Right. On Saturday, November 24th the Apostles found their Holy Trinity.

The 'fixtures' were Structure;
'2-1-0' was Means;
the 'table' was Vision.

Chapter Eight

The League as a Class Act

Football, sir, is the thing to swear by if we don't wish to be written down as a ignoramus or a Hottentot.

When they met on March 23rd, 1888, the League's founders may have known of an overseas model. In February 1876 the National League of Professional Base Ball Clubs was inaugurated and, overcoming rivals and opposition, dominated American baseball for the rest of the century.

Goldstein describes baseball's social journey through professionalism to league. Baseball, initially embedded in the rich social life of male fraternal organisations in and around New York, encountered contradictions as it developed. The pursuit of excellence, the ambition for victory and the consequent occasional loss of self-control was in tension with gentlemanly behaviour and the relaxations and pleasures of sport.

The New York press advertised how public interest followed excellent play, but also its inherent dangers: 'recognizing the importance of attendance figures, sportswriters, who usually saw themselves as promoters of the game, rarely missed an opportunity to mention the "numerous assemblage," the "immense concourse," [but] when players and spectators got excited, they began to tread on dangerous ground', particularly gambling [Goldstein, 1989, p.32]. Money entered with admission charges (1858), prize matches (1859), and the first paid players (the early 1860s). But after the Civil War baseball expanded geographically and New York lost organisational control. Clubs violated the rule against paying players so routinely that it was 'a dead letter' by 1868, and the National Association a dead authority [Goldstein, 1989, p.88].

The relationship between 'revolving' professionals (i.e. those who moved from club to club) and regular members of these fraternal organisations became dense and tangled. Players, increasingly imported from distant parts, became 'exempt' members, having no vote, occupying no office, and paying no dues. How could these be *bona fide* members, and how did they reflect upon a club's integrity? Hypocrisy was inevitable. As their ties with clubs became looser, player movements became more understandable and acceptable, but incompatible with regulations based on enduring club membership: 'while clubs battled among themselves over the legality or legitimacy of their actions, players continued to play, be paid and move on.'

As players' relationship to membership changed, so did the relation of the others towards play: 'the club's members merged with the rest of the club's fans, spectators both of the competition on the field and of the struggles within over financial rewards.' The vocabulary of management entered baseball, as the clubs, increasingly businesses, struggled to constrain quality players whose scarcity gave them balance of power. Their sanctions changed from the world of leisure to work: 'from instruments of collective, fraternal, clubwide self-discipline, club rules became regulations for the players to follow and for the captains – backed up by the club – to enforce' [Goldstein, 1989, pp.99-100]. From being outstanding exponents, players were dismissed as hired assistants whose superiority was attributed to long practice: 'that's all there is to it.'

Baseball moved into the world of capital and labour, with separate classes of directors, managers-captains and player-workers. Gate receipts became baseball's life blood, yet there was no 'predictable, rationalized commodity'. Its English-born pioneer, Harry Wright, found that 90 per cent of his correspondence addressed the time-consuming process of fixtures-making, a process of redirecting sporting emotions into profit: 'I am trying to arrange our games to make them successful and make them pay, irrespective of my feelings.' [Goldstein, 1989, pp.137-38].

The first attempt to collectivise the process of arranging fixtures occurred in the early 1870s (although there was still no fixed schedule between the handful of competing clubs), but only in 1874 was a season completed: in others, clubs withdrew because of financial problems or those caused by 'revolving' players. The National League of 1876 was explicitly concerned to break player power. A few financially strong clubs, given territorial monopolies of larger towns and cities and with tough-minded leadership and wealthy owners, united to limit competition for players, reduce salaries and introduce discipline into baseball workplaces. Few clubs made money initially, but the reserve clause, effectively tying players to their clubs, helped turn a high-priced workforce into 'chattels' [Goldstein, 1989, pp.149-50].

English experience of football up to 1888 reflects some of this account. Certainly the medium between commercial football and the motivation to play was its paying public, and this relationship was made gross. There was the story of the 'footballist' going to heaven and being shocked there was no admission charge: 'a footballist's heaven used to be the gate money on earth ... no gate money meant no fight and the fellows wouldn't go.'

British football differed politically from American baseball because football's Associations did not lose central control, clubs did not become overt businesses and players did not gain commercial power. Also, in terms of the all-important fixtures, English football generated both its ideal model and its bane, the Cup competition.

In February 1889 a baseball world tour visited the towns making the League – Derby, Nottingham, Manchester and Liverpool (where all-round sportsman Frank Sugg pitched for England). It was led by a pioneer of professional league baseball, Arthur Spalding – as much a publicist as Jack Bentley. Spalding hired detectives to keep tabs on his own hard-living players. When the Pinkertons accused 'King' Kelly of 'drinking lemonade at 3am in Chicago's tenderloin district', the star informed Spalding: 'it was straight whiskey, I never drank a lemonade at that hour in my life' [Levine, 1985, p.30]. The Leagues shared experiences. 1888's summer baseball season included 67 games in Boston, watched by 265,015, a 4,000 average comparable to the Football League's first season. The total attendance in eight American cities was 1,600,000, but admission charges were higher, as each club made £20,000.

The first League season changed football's class structure. The contestants were the Southern 'amateur' sporting traditions born of public school origins, and the North, with its amalgam of small business interests and community values. As in the previous trauma of 1884-85, football's political relations bent but did not break.

The League had proved a severe challenge, but the Association perceived a vulnerability – discipline. How could this collection of competing clubs take a sporting approach to conflicts or players' violent behaviour? Highly publicised incidents in October, particularly involving Everton's Scotch back Alec Dick, provided an opportunity of reasserting the Association's authority.

The resulting 'Misconduct Commission' comprised Southerners – the usual suspects: Marindin, Betts and Jackson – plus sympathisers like Sheffield's Charles Clegg who were equally anti-professional. Few were in doubt the Association held a 'grudge', and their Commission was a 'quiet dig at the League'. They quickly expanded their 'covert thrust' to target the League's champion. North End secretary Fred Dewhurst and player Davie Russell had to travel to Birmingham in late November and wait from five in the afternoon until midnight. No complaint had been made by referee Earp, but 'untruthful reports' had been sent to London newspapers about Russell's spat with James Sloane of Stoke.

These charges were dropped for lack of proof, but Dick, having fought with both players and spectators against Notts and Villa, was effectively suspended for the League season. One of his combatants, England's Denny Hodgetts, was banned for a month, as were Hendry and

Siddons following their unseemly episode at the end of Albion's League fixture with Bolton.

If North End were indignant at their treatment, Everton felt 'infinite disgust', and retaliated. They had warned: 'if the Association, through their Commission, have a "go" for the League, that organisation should be extended to all good clubs.' Now Everton, allied to 'Jack the Rambler' Bentley, 'strove might and main ... to make the League declare war on the Association.'

Initially, the League had offered a limited challenge to the national Association. The Apostles only targeted the County Associations, their pretensions and their rules. The League had no rules. They left rules to the national Association until they suffered by them. Ironically, the Association had become overwhelmed by its own rules (especially the damaging English Cup protests in 1887-88), and had decentralised. As with American baseball, the centre had acknowledged the spread of the game. Where the States had states, the Association bypassed the Counties and created ten regional divisions to do the menial work. These divisions not only ran the qualifying English Cup competition, they dealt with the protests. So the national Association rarely needed to meet.

But decentralisation meant increased representation, and Jack Bentley, as a divisional representative, took the League into the Association's council chambers. He did not play by the rules and was soon called to account for disclosing the Council's confidential proceedings.

Then in December 1888, Bentley joined Everton to challenge the Association on its weak points: the narrow competitive base (already exposed by the League); and its rules governing professionalism.

Football's 1885 settlement had constrained professionalisation within the principle that the professional must be known. He must register and his eligibility to influence competitions must be restricted. The registration was with one club per season. He had to demonstrate longstanding commitment to a club (two years) and live nearby (within six miles) to play in important Cups. Amateurs had few restrictions. Professional rules were a triumph of old forms of (industrial) locality over the increasing reality of the itinerant-immigrant worker. Knowing and class identity also chimed with what the public needed. They needed to know who was playing in order to decide whether to pay to attend. Not knowing was unacceptable. The home club gained the subscription of its members and its season ticket holders, and could expect consistent attendance by some supporters and spectators. Its responsibility was to find players who could compete at a level, and find fixtures with other teams around that level. The name of the other club, its reputation, its past achievements and results, and its known players – especially its professionals – were the means of structuring those negotiations. Once fixtures began, the possibility of ongoing relationships, even tradition, arose. Being let down in this process was trouble, and with media attention potentially humiliating.

Bentley's vehicle was a conference at the Commercial Hotel, Liverpool on December 8th, 1888, chaired by 'King John' Houlding (smarting under Everton's second disciplinary humiliation by the Association). Strictly speaking, the League were slow to join the fray: only Burnley supported Bolton and Everton, and Stoke, Villa and Albion initially opposed reform. Instead their ally was Lancashire, and their 'guide' was County secretary Richard Gregson, the victor in the Association's acceptance of professionalism in 1885. Gregson attracted 80/100 participants, representing a wide range of clubs employing Lancashire's 800 registered players, all frustrated by the professional rules and empowered by the League's evident success.

Jack Bentley won this campaign, hands down. At the conference he held together the differing interests and objectives of his constituency. Financially struggling Halliwell thought it 'ridiculous that they should be compelled to register' men retained at 2s and 2s 6d 'in case of accident to the first team'; whereas Houlding wanted it acceptable to pay a day's wage plus hotel and travelling expenses for Everton's imported Scots.

Bentley cut through the abstract views of the moralists by appealing to John Bull, to a common-sense understanding of what was important to the 'lost wages' professional: 'is there anyone foolish to … assume that a working man – a mechanic, or labourer, or whatever he maybe – thinks so little of his family and so much of football as to give up part of his time, and consequently part of his wages, to assist his club?'

Yet he also pandered to the prejudices against imported Scots: 'drinking seemed to be the only qualification for professionals now-a-days … give our own lads a chance … [and] have as good clubs and better morality'. Bentley supported this moral argument and admitted 'clubs did not seem to care to encourage local talent'.

The imagery accorded the paid amateur indicated resentment that his class identity was hidden. He wants to play without reward, but hints he is unable to play without recompense, and so receives 'heavy' expenses. Other classes look down upon the paid amateur: 'avowed professionals regard him with all uncharitableness; amateurs of a better sort fight shy of him.' The shamateur is in short an 'amphibious sort of creature'.

Bentley straddled the space of championing the craftsman's class (the League), and reforming the amateurism of the leisured class (the Association). The common language was the morality of open-dealing and locality. This champion of imported professionals acknowledged dishonesty – there were 'many suspicious characters in Lancashire and the Midlands' – and hypocritically objected to 'amateurs who were amateurs simply because they dare not become professionals'.

Bentley proposed Free Trade as the way to avoid clubs having to make dishonourable bargains – 'they ought not be hampered by rules'. Free Trade, not the ending of class distinctions: Westhoughton FC's suggestion to strike out the separate classes of amateur and professional seemed 'too drastic for the conference'. Free Trade for clubs, not players.

The amateur establishment reacted. Corinthian 'Pa' Jackson (also the Association's London representative), condemned the Liverpool Conference as 'a small knot of agitators', but secretary Charles Alcock realised the underlying class implications: 'the link between amateurs and professionals should be distinct and unmistakable … no good can possibly be done by reducing the barriers which divides the classes.'

When Jack Bentley entered the Association's Council the League became a 'big … unruly boy in the house' [Pickford, Introduction, *The Football League*, 1938; Bentley, 1905, pp.11-14]. Clearly there was life after its Cup. The League gave the professional world a new competitive model. The Association's rules of player eligibility had been motivated to keep the Scottish Association on board by retarding importation, but the League only needed the Scots as player-workers. Bentley outflanked these convoluted definitions by changing the locus from player to club and competition. In essence, it was sufficient if a player was acceptable to the club and the competition. There were now only two competitions that mattered. The League needed to limit the chaos of poaching, and create a space for the orderly transfer of players. In February 1889 it ruled that a player's eligibility was limited to one club a season, unless the player and both clubs agreed to his 'migration'. By March the consultations resulting from the Liverpool conference were in. Bentley had built his alliance. For the Cup, the challenge was down: if the Association stuck to its restrictions on birth, residence and longevity, it would do without the League's best teams. On May 24th the Association caved in. Jack the Rambler had ripped the insides out of its monopoly.

This settlement strengthened the player's need to register, and registration became English football's 'reserve clause', tying players to their clubs. It was even more draconian. Baseball's reserve clause required clubs to specify their reserved players and restricted them to a few, initially three then five. Registration applied to every professional. Over the next few years Bentley made players commodities: by extending and strengthening the League cartel; through formalising the transfer system;

and eventually by imposing a maximum wage. As generations of British footballers and their successive unions expressed it, Jack the Rambler made them slaves.

As in America with baseball, newspapers promoted the League as an exemplar of sporting excellence. The League benefited from a generally slow period in news just when the medium was expanding rapidly. In politics, Prime Minister Lord Salisbury was a secondary figure to the grand old man William Gladstone. It felt like the end of an era, delayed. The 79-year-old Gladstone would become Prime Minister again and was still making the radical agenda. His adoption of a Home Rule solution for Ireland was slow-moving and complex to negotiate, whilst the Fenian outrages had abated and the worst excesses of absentee landlords on the people of Ireland were lessening. The most newsworthy of Irish personalities was Charles Parnell, but the sexual climax and moral tragedy of the Irish leader's downfall was yet to come. The Tories had lost their star performer Randolph Churchill when he tantrumed out of the Government. Imperialism was poised between the ambiguous adventures in Africa of Gladstone and Disraeli, and the overt Scramble for Africa of the 1890s. Only a search for explorer Henry Stanley, wandering the continent after he found fame for finding missionary David Livingstone, excited ongoing press interest. Otherwise there was unease about a greater threat of war on the European continent, as countries established bigger standing armies. Never before had so many men been in uniform, and yet there was no actual war. Two German Emperors died during 1888, and Kaiser William ascended a throne he would lose in 1918, after the Great War. The papers had no reason to note the birth, under another name, of Adolf Hitler, on April 20th 1889.

Of course, the real media star of 1888's autumn was Jack the Ripper: his murders dominated journalistic efforts, gripped the public imagination and sold newspapers throughout the country.

Inevitably football crowds were influenced by this dominant motif, initially in the guise of an East End character, 'Leather Apron,' who was an early suspect for the crimes. 'Go on, Leather Apron,' was the encouraging cry for home teams out to intimidate visitors. Conversely a newspaper correspondent mocked a match report 'drawing "leather apron" like atrocities in his imagination'. The report had described 'very bad' conduct by spectators who practiced 'dirt and gravel throwing' and encouraged their players to 'Jump on the b****rs'.

Referees were commonly called 'Leather Apron' and later 'Jack the Ripper', or both. Their imitators produced panic throughout the country. For example, a young girl named Duffy went to fetch cows home for the night, when a strange man, only partially dressed, 'leaped out of the fence and chased her through the field, saying he was "Leather Apron".' She ran home breathless, 'without waiting to bring the cows.' Jack the Ripper replaced Leather Apron partly because he wrote to the press naming himself as the murderer. Provincial imitators got in the act by explaining 'London is too hot for me, so I have shifted my place for a while to this shanty.' By December, Jack the Ripper was in a League town: 'Dear Boss, the tecs think they are kinder cute, but I've shifted 'em off this yer scut ... The super looks like a yard of sump water starched ... I'm now in Blackburn ... Jack the Ripper.'

Newspapers underwent a huge expansion during Victoria's reign, due to falling prices, increased advertising and technological advances. They provided working people with entertainment and information. Papers became not only 'dynamic and profitable' but provided a dominant form of 'social knowledge ... an essential reference point in the daily lives of millions of people' [Curtis, 2001, pp.55-64].

The New Journalism combined lurid stories of death and disaster with summaries of political and economic events through a style that 'evoked comment, invited speculation and engendered passions'. Detractors saw a new age of 'journalistic barbarism', and even practitioners dismissed their art as 'mental food given them in minces and snippets, not in chops and joints' [in Curtis, 2001, p.62]. Oscar Wilde declared that 'journalism justifies its own existence by the great Darwinian principle of the survival of the vulgarest' [in Curtis, 2001, pp.65-66].

Making 'run-of-the-mill sensationalism' from frequent occurrences like football matches was not easy. Results were themselves powerful, relayed to newspapers by the flourishing agencies and telegraph/wire services – the news factories akin to the ubiquitous manufacturing factories. Then there were the controversies and near things that produced results. Match reports, often detailed in the case of local or specialist sporting press, added immediacy.

But newspaper coverage was also moral. Newspapers 'continually reinscribed the boundary between normative and deviant behaviour' [Curtis, 2001, p.54]. Dominant values were restated in comments that followed match reports, or the weekly notes that appeared in many provincial newspapers. Whilst vociferous crowds acclaimed or condemned every dribble, pass and tackle, commentators made considered judgment. First of all, competence. Football as work, as productivity. Each home player's performance was assessed against a norm. Rarely was the judgment 'good enough'. Individuals were generally good or bad, successes or failures. They performed against time, against their history or potential.

They held or lost form; promised to improve or threatened future disaster. Judgment was routinely comparative. There was always a best man on the field, best back, best half-back, best forward. They were judged as a team, and as these units within a team.

Behind the team was the town. Behind new standards of competence and productivity were old traditions of pride and locality. A player's failure might be personal, and expressed directly, while criticism of his selectors was usually indirect and corporate. But when the players or crowd stepped outside the norms of acceptable physical engagement, the town's reputation suffered. The relationship between the club and the town counted.

Commercialisation also changed the class relations of sport. In cricket, the professional had been a servant of the leisured class, as teacher or practice coach. Moralistic commentators complained that football professionals did not teach.

This might be true of a football club's leisured class members, but the Scotch pro could inspire working men. For example Jack Madden: 'one of the smartest centres ... dodges and passes with puzzling effect, whilst his shooting is effective in the extreme, his shots going true and fast.' If the League wanted the best, its clubs would want Madden. Indeed their agents got roughed up in Dumbarton when they came after Madden, Alex Latta and George Dewar (both the latter beat England for Scotland in 1889 and then joined Everton and Rovers respectively). Madden earned lasting fame as a teacher. In fact his statue adorns a European capital city. Not London, despite a late-career season with Tottenham Hotspur. Nor Glasgow, where he helped Celtic win their first Scottish Cup and League titles. Nor Scotland, for whom he scored four goals in the British Championship in 1893. Madden's statue is in Prague. From 1905 Madden coached Slavia Prague to dominance, claiming the inaugural National League in 1925, and a further seven titles in thirteen seasons. He led Czechoslovakia in the 1924 Paris Olympics, and Slavia provided seven of the squad which lost the 1934 FIFA World Cup final against Mussolini's Italy in 1934. Finally, Slavia won the 1938 Mitropa Cup, then Europe's premier club competition. Jack Madden earned his statue.

In 1888 Madden was Gainsborough Trinity's professional, where he inspired a future English star. 'Flying' Fred Spiksley was Sheffield Wednesday's darling of the 1890s. England went unbeaten in seven games when 'Spiks' (five goals in his first three internationals) ran their left wing; he scored a memorable hat-trick for the Football League against the Scottish League; and two goals in the 1896 Cup final. At 5ft 6in and slightly built, he was fast, tough and skilful, but above all he 'read' a game. After retiring, Spiksley coached in Sweden, Germany, Mexico and Spain. In his memoirs Spiksley described the gospel. When eighteen, he was reduced to tears by Madden condemning his 'beautiful goal' as 'selfish play': 'through not being allowed to play selfish, my play and the team as a whole was improved.'

This was not the old class world in which the professional taught the club members: Spiksley was just a younger pro. Now that football was a show for spectators its class relations had changed: 'professional teams are looked upon as the servants of the public.'

The changes brought by the League went too far: 'the link, often a very slight one – which now exists between the player and the locality which he nominally represents will be broken.' They threatened a future without roots, of 'rival troupes' put together by 'enterprising speculators'. For the Nottingham columnist 'Julius Caesar' this would lead to the nightmare represented by American baseball's entrepreneurs. One word – 'unwholesomeness'.

Yet, supporter allegiance could develop with fascinating speed. What was the difference between 'Julius Caesar's' nightmare and what happened in Sunderland in 1888. Sunderland Albion was founded after a tiff in the running of Sunderland FC [Nannestad, 2002]. Was that a class conflict between the ship owners Marr and Tyzack and the Scotch schoolteacher David Allan? If so, which group was the greater entrepreneur? And, how did so many people develop such a sudden, fierce attachment to this new club two miles from the old, and such a profound rejection of the existing one? Within months, knowledgeable visitors felt Sunderland rivalries outweighed those in Liverpool and Bolton.

Somehow, spectators refused to allow players and officials to own a club. Supporter allegiance fused all these elements: ownership of officials' good moves and bad; players' success and failures; the local boy and the import. A chance of success was the most important thing, and the outside player could always come in.

Judgment of competence and productivity, and feelings of allegiance, were implicitly in conflict with a deeper but sometimes inconvenient value – sportsmanship. The former usually prevailed, but generally they were presented as compatible with fair play. Conflict between professional expediency and the niceties of amateur ideals was generally hidden or, when unavoidable, was presented as an aberration to be deplored.

Despite Jack the Ripper, newspaper coverage gave great momentum to the League: 'thanks to the individual, whoever he is, whose brain first hatched the idea.' Manchester's *Athletic News* even took credit, to William

McGregor's evident annoyance. *Athletic News* claimed five references in the previous two years. In August 1887 it suggested an 'interesting experiment': to vote the best sixteen clubs and 'then follow them up in a statistical sense, from week to week', particularly (but not exclusively) how they 'might do against each other'. This was not the League as it emerged, rather an elaboration of what had already appeared, particularly in Birmingham sports papers. Their selected best sixteen omitted a third of the later Apostles.

In turn, football fuelled newspaper expansion. On the League's first morning, September 8th, the *Liverpool Echo* sent out private posters to all newsagents announcing a special football edition at 7pm, printed on pink paper. Liverpool's *Express* learned of this 'exciting intelligence' in the forenoon, and promptly determined to issue an earlier edition, sent staff to football matches, and telegrammed 'for any amount of pink paper'. A few minutes before seven its *Pink Un* appeared, albeit the *Express* reported only half-times, whilst the *Echo* had full-times.

However, the League also rode a tide. No League club in the North East, but 'football is at its height of popularity in Sunderland ... the circulation of its Pink edition has increased seven-fold'. Newspapers themselves had increased four-fold in the previous 40 years, and the number of dailies had risen from fourteen in 1846 to 180. Everywhere 'it is quite the rage for the press to give a "true record" of the results of the Football League matches'. Some were snooty about others getting the results of five [sic] of the twelve clubs wrong.

There were specialist sports papers in Newcastle, Stoke, several in Glasgow and Birmingham (where *Saturday Night* sold 25,000 copies in 1887), and 'football mad' Lancashire sustained six specialist papers. Blackburn's *Northern Daily Telegraph* advertised itself as the 'LEADING FOOTBALL MEDIUM' [sic], publishing three editions on Saturday evenings: 'the First at Six, the Second at Seven, and the Last at Eight O'Clock.' Its own 'football h'a'penny' *Pink* edition was copied by Liverpool: 'imitation is sincerest form of flattery.'

Newspapers welcomed the League partly because they knew their fellow 'writers on football have favoured the scheme'. The *Burnley Gazette* overstated the League's challenge to cups, anticipating that League fixtures would have precedence over even the first three rounds of the English Cup: 'unless there is a prospect of a good gate these cup-ties will not be allowed to stand in the way.' This was wishful thinking – Burnley would have been delighted to reach the third round (i.e. the quarter-finals).

Newspapers had already established their role in conveying football information. Club 'Correct' cards (i.e. early programmes) were limited:

'owing to some blunder, the positions of the visitors had been entirely misplaced, and I fear that the great bulk of the spectators who relied upon the cards were awfully misled.'

The first series of five matches attracted 29,000 (£500-worth), 'vast crowds' from which newspapers immediately concluded the League would be a 'paying concern'. In reality only Everton attracted a noticeably large attendance. The League's rival, the Combination, neglected publicity, so 'no-one except those actually engaged in the matches seem to know anything about them'. The League quickly gained an advantage over the Combination because its scores established visual power and commercial value: 'Mr Editor, I must compliment you upon your *Athletic Journal* football result cards. It is well nigh impossible to get a look at them for the crowds of people who hover round the various shop windows in the town where they are exposed. No business should be without them.' Results exerted a powerful effect. Ordinary match admission charges were often fourpence, but punters were willing to pay two shillings, six times more, for a presentation card printed with match scores.

Initially, newspapers did not distinguish League from ordinary games, but soon grouped those results separately, although the title varied – e.g. the Football League Cup. Very quickly, 'the Figures for the League Championship are scanned every week with the greatest of interest … the positions of the various teams is getting to be looked for and discussed.' The table gave an added dimension, so that after just four weeks, 'chief interest … centred, as usual, in the contests arranged by the Football League … as well as of games of lesser importance.' The League was already pre-eminent.

The League missed a trick by refusing to indicate how to compute its results. Just before the League decided its mode of reckoning, the *Accrington Observer* published three different tables in eight pages: one applying the McGregor proposal that the League adopted; another simply alphabetical; and a third in which draws counted as half wins and half defeats. Under this arrangement leaders North End, with nine actual wins and two draws, had a record of ten wins and one loss; Accrington's two wins and losses and six draws became five wins and five losses. Preston's *Post* complained that the points system 'completely altered' their previous win-based tables, prepared 'on the ruling of a prominent member of the committee' (probably William Sudell).

Before the League, cups were the thing, and gave the lie to the Bard's famous saying: 'Shakespeare once saw a football match before cups were introduced, hence his famous words, "the play's the thing".' The Cup motivated players, as Blackburn's Cup-winning back Joe Beverley stated:

'if they have any play in them it brings it out.' Equally, when clubs like Sunderland scratched from the English Cup, probably fearing punishment for playing ineligible players, their name became mud: 'the very word bear[s] the stamp of cowardice! Beware. It is by such treatment that you lose the confidence of the public and the respect of the football community.'

Medals were so important that, when North End pulled out of the 1888 Lancashire Cup final, Darwen Old Wanderers and Witton played a match for the runners-up medals. By 1889, the League had broken the spell of the Lancashire Cup. Blackburn Rovers' did 'not want to waste Saturdays on unremunerative Cup ties when they can do much better with ordinary games'. Similarly Accrington (who took under £5 from a Lancashire Cup-tie in Halliwell) are 'not enamoured of the prospect of sacrificing another Saturday afternoon for the prospect of an inadequate return'.

The other problem of Cup competitions was moral. Defeat was so final that clubs resisted through protests. One columnist contrasted 'the glorious game of football' with inglorious cup protests. Cups 'exemplified' different aspects of Victorian life. The nobility of struggle, 'the rough-and-tumble incidents of life,' and 'the survival of the fittest' was negated by exploiting a rule-book: 'let no team take advantage of what the lawyers call a technical objection in order to carry out a trophy.' To protest that an opponents' pitch was three inches short 'sinks very, very low in the mire'. Any successful outcome was morally worthless: 'strictly speaking' players might be entitled to medals 'but what then? No honours in this stern race of life are long held on technical-objection grounds.' The League was a third way. Newspapers could exploit its tangible outcomes but clubs need not protest because they could recover.

The League also saw it through: it kept faith with the published weekly tables by completing its fixtures, even though, nearly four months after the outcome of the Championship had been decided, interest became slight. The League's success contrasted with the Combination's failure. When Bolton's Halliwell broke a Combination fixture, they received threats as well as moral condemnation: '[to] break faith in the most unwarrantable manner ... may be instructive reading for other clubs having fixtures with Halliwell ... very disgusting to find Halliwell absolutely refusing to keep their engagements.' Halliwell's sin was total: 'if the Football Combination has any RAISON D'ETRE for existence at all ... its engagements must [be] faithfully kept.' They suffered: when a second league was reconstituted for 1889-90 as the Alliance, Halliwell were rejected, and the club disbanded in 1892.

Initially it was difficult to understand comparative performance. The League necessarily meant as many defeats as wins, and for most clubs being 'mediocre' meant being … middlish. Newspapers mediated the fallacy that all clubs ought to be successful. For example, in early November, West Bromwich's *Free Press* appealed to fellow lookers-on: 'it must have occurred to many of the spectators that there was just one thing which was a little too common in both teams, viz erraticness in their weekly performance. One week they play the finest game almost, and the next they fall to the mediocre.' In fact Albion had disappointed in almost every match, win or lose, in comparison with the expectations arising from the previous season; whilst opponents Notts had managed one draw in six games and conceded 24 goals.

Football's impact increased, with the League in the vanguard: 'if we pick up a paper nowadays … we are greeted with several columns of football news.' This was tough both on the football reporter and those supplanted: 'First reporter: I'm just about dead. I've had to fill about six columns a day this season.' Second reporter: 'That's queer. I can never get a decent report into the paper, never any room; I have to cut everything down to the smallest possible space. What line of work are you in?' 'I'm the football man. What's your department?' 'I'm reporting sermons.'

As with later generations, the football reporter had to work out social distance. Many assumed they were writing for the knowing. One abandoned description because 'nearly all my readers I suppose were present at the match themselves'. Who were these readers? Reporters implied football was democratic. Social class divisions were apparent, but inoffensive: 'look round the ropes on a good football day … clergymen … medicals … clerks about town … sons of toil.'

Another columnist, faced with a sensitive explanation, took refuge in a shared community: 'for reasons well known to the Accrington football players …' Player movements in the North East were so frequent that even for Scottish internationals journalists delegated investigation to their readers: 'why McKechnie left West End. Well, you see it was through – Oh, find out for yourselves.'

Many journalists were close enough to the club to recognise the players well enough, but in the heat of struggle, mistakes were inevitable. One reporter called out to Accrington's captain and England international George Howarth: 'I say Fecitt, who scored that.'

As in later times, the public had a love-hate relationship with their footballers. There was appreciation of skill – professionals can 'put side on, or drag, or screw … as a billiard player' – and its effect on the watcher – an expert 'pass' through a crowd of opponents 'is astounding to the onlooker': it was 'equally pretty' to see the pass accepted.

Newspapers persuaded themselves that people tired of football, and were opposed to 'the interminable length of the season'. Arguments for a close season were based on 'the game is being greatly overdone'. They also feared that 'more and more each year' is expected of players. Being a pro was 'downright hard labour' and promising players who have 'overdone it' have become 'miserable failures'.

Both reporters and authorities were aware of significant change. The Association's secretary Charles Alcock realised that 'a wholesale system of passing' was 'placing dribbling at a discount'. Even the scrimmages were diminished. In an English Cup quarter-final in 1881 between Stafford Road (captained by Charles Crump, in 1888 the Birmingham Association's figurehead) against Old Etonians (with Arthur Kinnaird, in 1888 the Association's treasurer), Stafford's goalie fell on the ball. Everyone else piled on top and a 'regular Rugby scrimmage' developed. Minutes later Kinnaird wriggled out: 'I claim hands, somebody must have handled the ball.' Referee 'Pa' Jackson replied grimly 'I've not seen anyone handle it'. So Kinnaird buried himself again.

A player who straddled these eras risked mockery: '[Hoban] has played since the days of stage coaches and is about as fast as one now.'

Newcomers were closely observed. Scotch players came from economically depressed cities like Glasgow or mining villages like Renton, where footballers 'spring up like mushrooms … struggling home in their begrimed state, to turn out clean, tidy and full of life on the football field'. But the Lancashire centres to which they moved were rarely prosperous: 'work was sometimes provided for a football player in a town where he was a stranger, and where the natives were walking the streets for want of employment.' So the 'evils of importation' were personal. Scots like Barbour and Brand came to clubs like Accrington to replace local lads. Were they worth it? Those who saw them practice said 'they will turn out proper "trumps" but a 'prentice venturing too close to the Cemetery ground caught a heavy ball in the face: "What's ti want shootin like thad for, mon. Has ti no sense".'

Accrington's Scotch 'B's were successful, but failing professionals had a difficult social life. In the autumn of 1888 Newcastle's clubs, West End and East End, were losing out to Sunderland's clubs. Soon they were getting 'wolloped' every week. Yet annoyingly their players still fancied themselves too much: 'to see them you would imagine they had bought the town. It makes me ill.' Similarly, 'footballers are very proud men, too proud to carry their bags home.' Their failures were social, personal, political and sporting: 'as lazy as a fat alderman and as greedy when in possession.' In Glasgow, Rangers' decline meant captain Donald Gow received a parcel at Ibrox containing the 'carcases of eleven little mice'.

The process of securing a new player was always intriguing, and hardly reflected well on anyone. The potential import's motivation was rarely virtuous. Reports from the recruiting town were silent about the target's allegiance to his current club. He might be persuaded by the recruiters' persistence, ingenuity, even subterfuge. Alternatively it might involve using faraway agents to obtain a player on reputation or on trial. For the English, obtaining a Scottish import was a practical matter. Once he was signed, however, morality returned: 'a club angling in Scotch waters and fetching a big "bite" is applauded, but another [English] club "who bags the big bite" is poaching and execrable. These funny footballers.'

Fred Spiksley described how he was the only local survivor when Gainsborough Trinity recruited four Scots forwards in October 1888. Played at centre-forward he was 'entirely boycotted as they played in pairs the game through, and finally, disgusted, I obeyed [the spectators'] request to "come off the field" by doing so'. Spiksley was only persuaded to remain by being paid (five shillings away, half a crown at home). When Burnley (facing a relegation battle and North End in successive weeks) poached Angus, McKay and Brady, the news leaked out: 'the 12.30 train steamed into the station, and the directors with their prey came forth from their hiding place, they were met by several Trinitarians who each threw a flour bag, and they departed like millers.' The fourth, Coyne, disappeared to Everton on Friday night, so Gainsborough's nine men scratched to Grimsby in the English Cup.

Burnley then established a Detectives Committee 'to put a hedge about their men'. When Sunderland came after Alec Brady, 'the poachers were compelled to take refuge in a weaving shed near to the Burnley slaughter-houses.' Brady rejoined Sunderland. Years later, Spiksley and Brady were reunited at Sheffield Wednesday, but had only one verbal exchange in eight seasons, when Spiksley misplaced a pass: 'That was a bad 'un, Fred.' 'It wasn't a good 'un, Alec.'

Recruitment often arose out of the very process of competition: 'if an opponent impresses, the committee decide how much money or advantages they will give him. Then the player is hunted up at home by emissaries, but this is risky for the pirates ... If possible, the player is smuggled away and the pirates get him to skip. Then the desired acquisition is taken to a hotel, plied with his favourite "pizen" and good cigars, and his feelings worked on until he comes in.'

Everyone could benefit. In September 1888, a local footballer – 'being possessed of more money than most folks' – celebrated his promotion to the first team by determining 'his dearest pals should have a downright good dinner that very night'. The dinner 'was everything we wished for, and heaps more than we wanted, and as for drinks, well we had as many sorts in two hours as it is possible for a man to have in a lifetime. After dinner we had a game of football with the waiter, and next … threw coppers to the street lads … we were seeing double … our football pal declared we must not walk anywhere, so we had a cab across the street. We gave a bob to the policeman across the street – indeed I never saw so much money spent before. Our "lavish friend" astonished every policeman he saw by giving him a bob or two-shilling piece. Some thanked us, and with a look of incredulity as to our state of mind, some said wicked words, but we were utterly oblivious, and beyond picking quarrels with mere policemen.' Eventually a cabman propped the worse-for-wear footballer against his front door. His wife took the cabman's details in case he was needed for the inquest, and dealt with the immediate situation: 'Jane, bring the bucket and a floor cloth.' Domestics were unimpressed: 'Master William, I don't think so much of you as I used to, for I 'ear you're one of them confessionals what plays football for money.'

An amateur was a hypocrite, as in the old joke: 'I am an amateur. My wife is not. Send all cheques to her.' There was however an undoubted material basis for recompensing 'peripatetic amateurs', whether individuals or troupes like the Corinthians – 'the expenses of going about the country are heavy'.

The amateur champion 'Pa' Jackson knew he was in a fight with the League. One skirmish was the annual 'North versus South'. Annual, but for how long? In his journal, Pastime Jackson complained that the League wanted to kill the match, having 'already shown much antagonism'. Whilst the South chose a team of internationals (mostly former public schoolboys), the North (whose selectors included Jack Bentley) boasted no international, and only five League players. Jackson saw the slight, and felt the loss. The match cost £103, and made only £90.

As players, Jackson's class was being overwhelmed. The North-South match was held in a future breeding ground of English football, Sunderland. The local professionals were Scotchmen, but they were surrounded by a coming mass of locals. Outside the ropes of the professional grounds, the 'town moor and vicinity literally swarmed with [teams] displaying no hesitation to carry goal posts and other accessories of the game over long distances.' Sunderland was 'fairly on the job' for football – street youngsters were dribbling a 'penny ball, a piece of a brick or an old tomato tin', and dreaming of being a 'very great man – aye, perhaps even a professional football player'.

Jackson championed the English amateur, but he had no truck with Scotch attempts to contain professionalism. His amateurism was a matter of class identity; expenses maintained a class standard of living. Working-class reinforcements were an expense. James Lundie (then with Hibs) helped Corinthians beat Queen's Park. Afterwards he was 'called into the room' where the sixteen touring Corinthians each 'dropped a sovereign into his hand' [Lincoln, 1912 p.311].

The Scotch campaign refused to accept reality, pretending that its working-class corps of footballers lived according to the precepts of a leisured class. The Scottish Association did not try to define the abstract boundary between professionalism and amateurism. They trusted to the border, requiring the player to convince a Professionalism Committee of his amateurism before playing again in Scotland (see Chapter 9).

Jackson dismissed these efforts as interfering with labour mobility: it would not work, the Scots are as 'powerless to cope with the action of supply and demand as with the powers of nature'. 'On plain meaning' they contradicted English notions of sport and freedom. The Scotch rules interfered with every Scotch match in England, and preventing professionals returning as amateurs was 'contemptible'. For Jackson, 'professional' and 'amateur' were not enduring identities, just phases in a working-class Scotchman's career: 'the day comes at length to every professional when he can no longer find a Lancashire club to hire him,' but he would still be worth his 'wages lost' to a 'Scotch organisation'.

The local youngster, dependent on the generosity of an employer sympathetic to the local club, faced both stick and carrot: 'the prospects of a young dribbler would be materially increased [by joining a club], whereas a refusal might raise influential obstacles, which would make his bread scarce, and his butter scarcer.'

During September and October 1888 the hard world of professional football was contrasted with the innocence of a tour by Canadians. It is difficult to reconstruct in retrospect these tourists' purpose and motivation. The Canadians essentially earned fixtures by their performances. Early dates were in Belfast, then Scotland then England. Good performances earned them a match with Scotland (not subsequently recognised as an international) and a social highlight was against the Swifts at the Oval, at which royalty were expected (although did not turn up).

Canadians were entrepreneurs pitching for business through fixtures. They had an advantage of mixing familiarity (many were ex-pat Scots) with American exoticism. Their most famous mannerism – 'you bet' – gave them good publicity. Seven thousand watched them play Newton Heath in Manchester, which meant sharing £100 – 'Canadians still on the job – you bet'. Similarly they bemoaned their worst show: 'what's wrong with the boys? They're all wrong? O yes! Don't bet!' They did so well that they rejected Jack Bentley's overtures for a fixture with the League's Bolton: 'we came here to enjoy ourselves, not to knock ourselves up.'

Football matches were complex social events, which could be sufficient motivation – Hearts' goalkeeper said he only played against the Canadians to enjoy the after-match dinner. These events started when visiting teams arrived. The Canadians were not pleased by Queen Park's hospitality – they had to find their own way to Hampden Park, where they waited fifteen minutes for their opponents. Similarly, Sunderland felt badly treated on a visit to Grimsby: 'there was no one to meet them at the station when they arrived, and they had to find a hotel and also the field on which the match was to be played, and ... when it was all over, and Sunderland had gained a hard victory, they were not even entertained to tea, in fact they were taken no notice of whatsoever.'

These tour matches also celebrated new technology – there was a twenty-minute delay for taking photographs at one Canadians match. Against Notts County at Trent Bridge their lack of ruthlessness was also celebrated: 'a matter for comment and praise was the entire absence of roughness or paltry appeals.'

The League took organised football to a new level. It did it by accident, by extending what was already there, and by embodying Victorian concepts of class within a sporting structure.

Class assumptions underlay the League, and the League built upon the embryonic class relations within clubs as workplaces. Class was its overt imagery. First-class clubs should play one another. The public would watch first-class teams. Players were or were not of sufficient class. In Victorian society, outward form reflected moral status: the League gave professional football its outward form. It was open in its League Table, straightforward in its admission charge and disciplined in the relationships between its employees, employers and workplaces, and between local players and local clubs.

The League also expressed other aspects of Victorian morality. Towards Christmas 1888 the Association acted against the excesses of professionalism. Rough play, attacks on referees and other violent incidents were being regularly reported. One of many examples occurred in the North East, and featured George McKay, within weeks a League player with Burnley: 'a more disgusting scene has never been witnessed on a local field than that of last Saturday afternoon … Wardroper fell from a trip by Smith, McKay ultimately jumping upon Wardroper, and someone else kicking his ribs. Whilst down, Wardroper made savage hacks and struggles with McKay, until parted by the crowd, which rushed on to the field of play … Clarke wanted to write McKay's epitaph.'

Later, after the 1889 Cheshire Cup final, Northwich Victoria and Crewe Alexandra assembled on opposite platforms of Middlewick station. Their differences led players to leap onto the metals and fight desperately. Eventually, the Vics crossed the line and invaded Alex's platform. Passengers bolted left and right as outnumbered Crewe abandoned the station, but Sergeant Wynne and his policemen shepherded them onto the special.

A match between local Scotch sides was more thoroughgoing: 'the two teams knocked each other about, and attempted almost to turn one another inside out … the ball should be left dead until two or three players almost attempted to get down each other's throats … charging was the order of things and it began at the entrance gates … what a howling multitude to be sure, and the crowd had much to answer for the rows which followed … general display of fisticuffs ensued … A rougher display I have never seen, and although I am informed that the same thing occurs on every occasion when the two clubs meet, I cannot realise how this can possibly be, in the present day … if football is a science in Annandale then it is scientific brutality … when even committee men encourage the players to acts of violence, something surely is radically wrong.' The referee said that only fear of a riot 'prevented him from ordering the offending players from the field'.

Was this the behaviour of a Christian people?

Chapter Nine

'If it's Christmas, it must be Sunday'

Doesn't Christmas look 'sick' without a rattling good football match?

The Twelve Apostles of football went astray during December 1888, so that by Christmas itself, 'the League contests have been cast into the background, and almost forgotten.'

Initially they threw it away. Having established their identity and momentum based on five or six games each week, the League yielded both on December 1st. The reason was inter-Association matches: city against city, county against county. They were the nearest equivalent of the county-based cricket clubs, which survive into the 21st century, and the representative competition in rugby union, which failed with the 1990s' coming of professionalism. Club resistance had already restricted inter-Association matches to a date or two in the schedule, such as December 1st. The League chose discretion rather than confrontation, and avoided 'unpleasantness' by releasing players.

The League's principles were thus compromised. Whilst six held the League fort, the others took guarantees. For example, on official inter-city day, North End wittily beat Manchester District 4-0 (crowd 9,000).

LEAGUE POSITIONS: NOVEMBER 30TH

Preston 13 games, 24 points; Aston Villa 12, 17; Blackburn 11, 16; Everton 12, 15; Wolves 12, 14; West Bromwich 12, 13; Accrington 12, 12. Burnley 12, 7; Stoke 12, 7; Bolton 12, 6; Notts 11, 5; Derby 10, 5.

DECEMBER 1ST 1888 – ACCRINGTON 5, BURNLEY 1 – (5,000)

The League's boast of full-strength teams wasn't realised: each lacked three first-teamers, representing Lancashire in Edinburgh. Accrington played fair with their public and reduced admission to 4d. This was a match of local feeling, with 'too much of the scramble and skittle alley … rough play throughout'. Barbour and Brand each scored early goals, then it kicked off: 'Cox after being charged by Barbour, struck his opponent as he lay on the ground.' When Barbour retaliated, back Sandy Lang rushed in threateningly. All Scots. Soon after, Lang 'flagrantly' struck Barbour in the face. These 'petty strifes were so noticeable' that eventually 'everybody was called up' and cautioned. Burnley's 'hot-headed supporters' protested, particularly their equivalent of Villa's McGregor, Sydney McFarlane. This gentleman 'took the liberty of marching on ... as a sort of super referee'. The Cemetery Ground howled, 'Fetch him off,' but McFarlane 'would not be persuaded to retire by an ordinary constable ... needed a full-blown inspector of the blue coats'.

Burnley introduced three more outsiders and many hoped 'they will remain outsiders, for their play ... will [not] enable Burnley to get anywhere near the top of the tree'. Importation for 'one match only' was now the fashion: 'other consignments had been expected.' Scot against Scot: 'Brand played immensely ... McMahon received some gratuitous medical advice when his leg gave way' i.e. not to play any more that day. Accrington were 'something magnificent' in the last quarter. With Barbour, Brand and Kirkham 'playing like clockwork', they conjured three late goals. Never a 'more exuberating' game. 'It took the palm.'

WEST BROMWICH 4, EVERTON 1 – (1,500)

Everton were miserable. Jack Ross away with Lancashire, a 'wretched pudding' of a ball to start, and only nine men to finish. For Albion, 'Bassett's shot fairly staggered the goalkeeper'. Their crowd staggered no one.

STOKE 2, BLACKBURN 1 – (5,000)

The result 'beggars description'. Everyone 'bet almost any odds that Blackburn would beat Stoke' even without Jack Southworth (playing for Lancashire). In Stoke, 'so intense was the excitement that as the teams left the ground men were actually seen to hug and kiss each other, while the shaking of hands continued throughout the evening.'

Blackburn took an unexpected loss hard: 'weeping and wailing and gnashing of teeth when the [news]boys shouted 'The Rovers defeated'. The players lost a goose each, promised if they could get to Christmas unbeaten.

The League was working. Over the next two months, before the English Cup's first round on February 2nd, the stragglers responded to the challenge of competition. Even 'despised Notts County' beat Accrington, Wolves and Albion in succession. Bolton and Burnley had the third and fourth best records whilst Everton and Rovers the worst.

DECEMBER 8TH – BLACKBURN 4, BOLTON 4 – (7,000)

Their first League clash. Workers argued at lunchtime: 'I'll bet thee my knife to thy knife and teeth Rovers to win agen th' Wanderers.' Mr Hartley, Accrington's boss, refereed, acceptable to both.

Unacceptably, Rovers started with ten men, which caused 'ructions' and 'severe wiggings'. Local player Bob Stothert made up their eleven but got in the way, twice kicked wide, and was clearly a hindrance. Brogan gave Wanderers the lead, then went off injured so Jones the back 'took precious good care that nobody charged Harrison'. Townley equalised but Milne put ten-man Wanderers 4-3 ahead. Splendid passing by Rovers enabled Stothert, yes Stothert, to equalise. Loud, ironic cheers.

BURNLEY 2, STOKE 1 – (4,000)

The first ever relegation battle. This match contested the last of the four 'withdrawal' places. The 'retirees' would be thrown on a 'question of mercy' from the first-class clubs.

Stoke set off at 9.50am, and got home at midnight – 'not much time for sight-seeing'. It was 'continuous charging' on 'treacly' ground – they 'dropped like birds on "the 12th", mainly from trips'. A 'very old hand' said it was the roughest he had seen – 'the Burnley men had to win'. 'Hope never to visit Burnley again.'

WOLVERHAMPTON 4, ACCRINGTON 0 – (2,000)

The published League table made each position mean something extra. Both had fourteen points and were not far off second: it never, ever got better for Accrington. On a sludge skating rink, it was downhill from the third minute, when in-form Jack Brodie put Wolves ahead. Two more goals, 'one a good one and the other shady.' It felt bad:

'I was an eye-witness to a very tragic affair on Saturday – leastways I've had the idea since that it was something of the sort. Down in the Dark countries was a very unfortunate expedition for the Reds. The news of their fight for the fourth place in the list dropped down on the local tribe in the evening like bolts and thunder. Four to nothing – 'absolutely nuffink!'

In Accrington, everybody's question was 'What were they doing?' 'There wasn't such an eager demand for the football specials on Saturday night.' In Wolverhampton, however, 'I had speech with a merry "Hamptonian coming from the field". Well, you've got the nuggets today,' says I. "Yes, and we've played a goodish sort of game too." "You have and there's been a fair bit of luck about it." "Aye, you've been a bit unfortunate, but we all have a turn".' It was one thing to lose to North End, but this was something else: 'four to nothing is a flogger and no mistake.'

NOTTS COUNTY 2, ASTON VILLA 4 – (1,500)

County mugged the League. With their strongest eleven in Staveley for the Cup, this team had only three 'regular playing members' – others 'had never played together before under the chocolate and blue colours … a most motley crew'. Their latest centre was 'a bigger failure than ever'. In 'one continuous downpour', Notts lost respectably, so maybe got away with it.

PRESTON 5, DERBY 0 – (4/5,000)

Even North End played 'the Notts County trick' of a weakened team, in an ordinary fixture the previous Monday – 'there was some scrambling around to get an eleven together'. When Sheffield Wednesday's 'desperate energy' produced a winner – North End's first English defeat – their spectators 'burst with excitement'. Whilst Wednesday reckoned themselves now among the Apostles, 'very little importance was attached to the match or the defeat in Preston.'

'Some of the North Enders got a bit knocked about' in Sheffield, so even North End's resilience was failing. An old warhorse, Jack Inglis, played for Scotland before winning the National Cup with Blackburn in 1884. This blast from the past answered Sudell's call, and quickly scored. Then nothing, and Deepdale began to encourage Derby to equalise. County's Alex Higgins was hampered by 'a weak partner and a bad knee'. Some thought Will Cropper was on the County right wing but it was his friend, and County cricket captain, Will Chatterton, who found it tough going: 'evidently thinking of his cricketing days, [he] would never face a charge, preferring rather to lose the ball.' It was typical aggression just short of rule-breaking: 'a bit of temper … but there were no fouls according to the strict letter of the rules, and so far everything was fair and straight.'

'They ought to have won by ten goals,' said the spectators.

DECEMBER 15TH – WOLVERHAMPTON 2, WEST BROMWICH 1 – (3,000)

The fog came down, and stayed a month. The 'Wandering Wolves' started the season with a 'pretty heavy adverse balance' and still had had no large gate. Albion did not change that.

Albion equalised with a smart move: 'Bayliss walked leisurely to the spot with the ball, put it quietly down on the sawdust and immediately kicked it to Pearson, who banged it through before the Wanderers had time to move.' Wolves' winner came from their own quick thinking: '[Tom Hunter's] screw shot nearly off the line went bang through goal while Brodie was clearing away the custodian.'

STOKE 0, EVERTON 0 – (2,000)

Everton's organisation was coming apart: 'no one to act up as umpire. Rather warm this for a first-class club … at the solicitations of the worthy captain I pocketed my pencil and filled the unusual role of trotter along the touch-line.' The journalist umpire got too warm 'in a top coat, so during a pause I doffed it'. His big decision came when Jack Ross 'handled in front of his own goal, and many grumbled … it wouldn't have mattered in the least, as Bob [Smalley] was waiting behind, smiling in anticipation of a wet fistful'. But as Ross 'beautifully accounted' for the free kick, 'All's well that ends well.'

BLACKBURN 5, NOTTS COUNTY 2 – (5,000)

Old heroes and not new Scots made the difference. Notts led 2-0 in the second half until referee Norris got fooled by Jimmy Brown, Blackburn's Cup-winning captain: 'the ball went fully two feet over the bar, but owing to the mist, Mr Norris could not see it, and Jimmy Brown claimed vociferously. Good old Jimmy.'

Harry Cursham could not leave his business for such a long journey, so County 'cast for a centre in Dundee', and 'hooked a gudgeon … Galbraith will probably not be heard of again'. This was ungrateful. Galbraith reported to 'Mr Brown' at Rovers' ground: 'he had come to play centre for them, and wanted some togs.' Puzzlement: this week Rovers had eleven. 'The stranger realised he was talking to the wrong Mr Brown'. The right Mr Browne (County's secretary) had no togs for him, so first half Galbraith confusingly wore Rovers' 'blue and white' and in the second 'a red scarf across his breast'. By then he could neither be seen nor heard in 'the heavy fog', and afterwards he was left to 'shift for himself', back to Dundee.

Nor, from the stand, could the ball be seen 'for fully a quarter of an hour at a time. The roars of cheering gave notice of each goal by the Rovers'. Only one of seven goals was seen, with spectators 'questioning any stray player who came near'. County accepted enough goals were scored, but appealed to the League that the referee could not have seen them.

ACCRINGTON 1, ASTON VILLA 1 – (4,000)

Villa's early passing was worthy of the League's founders, and 'will long be remembered', with their goal a 'Brummagem Beauty' meriting the 'finest description': Green 'brought the house down, by catching the ball with his heel and landing it over his head into the goalmouth'. But Accrington always fancied themselves on the brink of League success –

'Yes sir, we were near it, jolly near it,' – so a disallowed goal caused a 'regular flareup from the gods'. Referee Jack Bentley might be popular most places, but 'somehow or other, Mr B does not hit it very well with the Accrington folks'. When the Reds thought the line was crossed, 'Warner was appealed to, on his honour, to say whether the leather was through or not, but the Villa keeper discreetly held his peace.'

Their latest Scotch import also upset folks. Accrington had been spoilt by Brand and Barbour's success, and Hope Robertson's failure after three matches was 'difficult to account for ... very good credentials, and a more likely fellow – well-built and strong – never stepped on the field'. But he was a 'complete failure': spectators 'jeered almost continually and when he did happen to kick the ball, indulged in ironical applause' (he later played in Everton's 1890-91 Championship side).

BURNLEY 2, PRESTON 2 – (8,000)

Burnley had 'fresh' Scots and fresh confidence, and started 'right merrily' – teenager Alec Brady (poached from Gainsborough) made North End look a 'bit slow'. Still, Sam Thomson's goal was the 'smartest ever got at Turf Moor' and Jamie Ross scored 'a gem' of an equaliser.

'The vigorous manner in which they took man and ball' showed Burnley 'had been specially prepared for the occasion'. Player-trainer Friel had 'done good', demonstrating that 'with a little practice ... the team would be one of the strongest'. A £114 gate was pleasing. President Massey gave captain Keenan £5 for the team, the rest of the committee another ten shillings each and Vice-President MacFarlane hosted a supper at the Bull Hotel. All for a draw.

In contrast, North End were 'fast going to the wall'.

DECEMBER 22ND – WEST BROMWICH 2, BLACKBURN 1 – (1,000)

The folk of West Bromwich cold-shouldered Albion again, missing 'another rattling good match' – a repeat of the 1886 National Cup final.

ASTON VILLA 4, BURNLEY 2 – (2,000)

Villa's crowd was little better. Burnley – fresh from drawing with North End – were small attraction.

PRESTON 3, EVERTON 0 – (8,000)

The prophet returned to Deepdale as an opponent. William Sudell greeted Jack Ross 'like a gentleman', and the healing public handshake invited a 'grand reception' and speculation about 1889-90. Ross had time at the interval to complain about his committee to reporters. They said

Billy Briscoe was too slow: 'let me have him for a month and I'll take that out of him.' No. Now the committee had to play him, and Ross said 'didn't little Briscoe bother Graham?'

WOLVERHAMPTON 4, STOKE 1 – (1,500)

'The locals played … with much dash.'

DERBY 3, NOTTS COUNTY 2 – (2,500)

Derby had lost their previous eight League fixtures, but recovered some confidence beating the club that most coveted their League place, Sheffield Wednesday, in an ordinary fixture. County versus County was 'exceedingly rough' – both ended 'lame'. Harry Cursham was the 'most conspicuous offender' – weeks later he retired, for fear of being killed. A 'wonderfully even' match but 'neither club can really be reckoned first-class just at present'.

BOLTON 4, ACCRINGTON 1 – (5,000)

Vindication. Wanderers had tried four different goalkeepers lately, but the players wanted Charlie Harrison, and three brilliant saves 'brought the house down'. His counterpart Jack Horne, being tipped for England honours, was the 'essence of cool'. But Davy Weir's hat-trick was 'simply irresistible', even when his screaming shot hit Horne and rebounded over the bar. That's what 'every scribe' thought, but goal given.

It was the season for wishes. Accrington had two, for goalkeeper Horne – 'JKH – an international cap' – he was made reserve; and their forward heroes Barbour and Brand – 'For the Scotch Bs – A long career with the Reds.' Within a fortnight Sunderland Albion had filched both. Here's to Accrington's League future.

THE CHRISTMAS LEAGUE TABLE

Preston 16 games, 29 points; Villa 15, 22; Wolves 15, 20; Blackburn 15, 19; West Bromwich 15, 17; Everton 15, 16; Accrington 16, 15; Burnley 16, 10; Stoke 16, 10; Bolton 14, 9; Notts 13, 6; Derby 12, 5.

North End and three other clubs had only six League matches left.

THE OLD FOOTBALL

Football at Christmas did not go unchallenged. Football as a public event was possible because it was a public holiday. It was also a religious festival. In 1888 the Chief Constable of Oldham knew there was something more powerful in Victorian England than Christmas. Sunday. And so he said Christmas Day was a Sunday (even though it wasn't), and football a 'horrible desecration' against the Lords Day Act. However 'his Magistrates were unable to say whether Christmas was Sunday or not'. 'Alas for constables! And alas for magistrates too!'

Football could lead people into sin and danger. At a rugby match at Manningham, Bradford, a youth died when the boundary fence collapsed, crushing the boys sitting below the boards. The coroner decided there was no culpable negligence but the match proceeds of £115 went to the parents of the deceased and seriously injured boys. A headline 'Footballer Killed' described a spectator 'returning from a match by rail without a ticket, and met his death in trying to avoid paying his fare [twopence] by jumping out before the train had stopped.'

Real footballers, Scottish internationals, were also in trouble. Robert Buchanan of Abercorn and Alex Lochhead of Third Lanark were found guilty at the Govan Police Court and fined £2 and 30 shillings respectively for their fight. Bailie Marr advised Lochhead it was a 'far manlier part if he had turned tail and ran'. 'The court were somewhat perplexed' that no witness was able to recognise the men. Onlookers think they know footballers, but this was an illusion. How come? We know players from their 'general form and semblance and position in the team, and they are content with that distant knowledge'.

The day itself was a shocker: 'Christmas Day 1888 will long be remembered as the dirtiest, most miserable and "darndest" apology for "the day that comes but once a year", that ever mortal was doomed to see.' At Accrington, visiting defenders sheltered in the dressing-tent until 'dashing out when the goal was threatened'; and at Burnley both teams refused to return after a break. Storm or no, 3,000 'shivering types of humanity assembled at Pike's Lane to witness the Wanderers in their fight with the famous Scotch team … After cramming myself with Christmas fare, I buckled on my armour in the shape of top-coat and leggings'.

Old football meant a pagan world of wild tribal battles and Scotch invaders. First choice was internecine warfare, where League status meant nothing; and where League crowds were dwarfed: Birmingham St George's 3, Aston Villa 0; Derby County 1, Derby Midland 4. For County this was simply 'Christmas calamity', following an earlier December defeat by Derby Junction. Villa were so intimidated by the loss, and exhausted by their League efforts that they cancelled a Scottish tour. Their reputation still suffered by association: St George's went instead, and lost 1-7 to Glasgow's parvenus, Celtic, although the gate was a compensatory £310.

Outside the League, East End and West End battled out the Newcastle derby before a big crowd, and in Manchester on Christmas

Day, 'disgraceful' scenes saw West Manchester's Lowe, who was nearly Accrington's League centre, fight with Newton Heath's Burke. Both were sent off.

'All Liverpool is agog' for Everton versus Bootle. After their vicious spat a year previously, on the pitch and in and out of Association Inquiries, this was the 'reconciliation game'. The crowd was the biggest of the season, 16,000, the gate was £350, the pitch was 'ankle deep in mud', and there were no goals. Of course they had to play again, in March, when, despite doubling prices, a record 10,000 crowd (£204) saw Bootle ahead 3-1 with minutes left. It was one of Jack Ross's last matches for Everton (see Chapter 11), driven back to Preston by 'threatening letters' and smashed windows in his Anfield house. However Ross's 'judgment at the crisis' in this Liverpool derby earned cries of 'Bravo Jack'. Everton's late recovery to 3-3 spelt disaster for talented Bootle goalkeeper Jackson. He had to retire: 'my reputation's ruined.' How had Everton escaped: 'Luck, pluck or what?' Bootle suspected the devil's work. In April, a 13,000 crowd saw Bootle finally win a decider, 2-1, but it was too late – Everton were moving out of Bootle's league for 1889-90.

Nottingham Forest's 3-0 win over County in December (thanks to Tinsley Lindley's shooting) made £172, so the Christmas return at Trent Bridge could finance Scotchmen. For Nottingham traditionalists like columnist 'Julius Caesar', these imports for a local conflict 'still seems an odd thing to do, to bring strangers into the team once or twice a year'. But the answer applied in Nottingham as in Lancashire – imports gave the clubs 'prestige and its supporters value for their money'.

Notts secured Queen's Park's Tom Robertson and expected William Sellar, who played for Scotland against England in four successive years, 1885/88. Sellar was a real amateur – he 'is none too anxious to work – gentlemen never are' – and he never arrived. Four Cowlairs came. William McLeod, known as 'the man with the wig', brought the McPherson brothers for Forest. Tom McInnes, a 'star of the first magnitude' and soon to play for Scotland, was contracted to County.

When he saw McInnes on the train at Carlisle, McLeod – Cowlairs' 'general boss' – improved the odds by frightening him off. 'This naturally made Notts a bit wild, and Mr Edwin Browne sent out "copy" for a poster, explaining what McLeod had done, and condemning his conduct as unsportsmanlike.' Forest 'construed' the secretary's action 'as an inducement for the Notts crowd to molest McLeod – though of course the Notts people would never think of such a thing – they thought it better to hint to Mr Browne that if the posters were circulated the Forest team would be conspicuous by their absence on Boxing Day'. If Mr

Browne had 'torn his hair' at McInnes' loss, he now ran 'the risk of having some of the Trent Bridge Ground pulled about one's ear ... The posters were not issued.' A swarm of 'pottering scribblers' made much of this football gossip, but everyone was assuaged by 'cutting up' the £247 gate.

Between 12/13,000 watched from all sorts of vantage points, including many vehicles that 'signalled goals by tooting horns'. Notts played 'brutally' and a Forest half-back was so seriously injured that it was 'rather uncertain if he will ever play again'. County beat ten-man Forest 4-1: 'Notts, I hate 'em.' Tom McInnes (who later played a decade of League football) watched the game, quietly, from the top of a private 'red omnibus'. Christmas was a time to hate your neighbour.

Christmas wouldn't be Christmas without the Scots: making or receiving visits. 'Pa' Jackson condescended to start the Corinthians' northern tour in the 'highly delightful suburb of Manchester called Newton Heath ... it is to be hoped that their eyes will not be dazzled with the glare of the sun'. Five thousand inner-city suburbanites did not see much of the stars (including England centre Tinsley Lindley). There was heavy fog and Corinthians only arrived at kick-off, and could not wait to leave. Jackson telegrammed Glasgow rubbishing Manchester and looking forward to your 'great city ... only a small guarantee here'. Already he had rejected Nottingham Forest for not guaranteeing Corinthians' 'heavy expenses'. Travelling was 'most costly'. Jackson was far from apologetic about their financial demands, and quite prepared to upset the Scotch amateur establishment by dealing with Celtic, the new Roman Catholic upstarts:

'We will leave your city with a hundred pounds and two swagger dinners. Am told Queen's Park angry at my fixing with the Celtic, but amateurs must live, my boy; yes, they must, even if the charge of professionalism is laid against their door.'

The Corinthians were late ('Excuse given – engine drunk') and got two 'simply enormous attendances'. They made £120 from Hampden Park, but took a 2-3 defeat badly. At the post-match 'swagger dinner', Jackson commented sourly that, of all the contributors to Queen's Park's victory, the 'referee most deserved being cheered'. When the Walters brothers complained their offside tactics had not been appreciated, the referee replied they were 'not quite smart enough, and this trick did not come off'. Their umpire constantly 'ran up to the referee with uplifted flag. Mr Jackson just claims a little too much. He eternally has that flag aloft.' Jackson was one of those umpires: 'certain people shout offside in their sleep.'

Then, augmented by three Queen's Parkers, the Corinthians lost 2-6 to Celtic with 15,000 present. The Corinthians' tour matches were watched by 60,000: £700 was taken in Glasgow alone. Plus Newton Heath, Durham, Edinburgh, Sunderland and North End. Over £300 in ten days. 'Everybody is now asking where the money goes.'

The tour ended at Deepdale on Monday afternoon, January 7th. Fittingly, the arch cricket shamateur WG Grace 'has been asked, and he will come if he possibly can' to referee. Notwithstanding, 'the stands were completely full', and despite 'all the mills and workshops in full employment', there was an attendance of fully 4,000. North End wore 'as ugly a garb as possible – a tight-fitting orange and black striped jersey, giving a wasp-like appearance.' The tourists had lost their sting: 'playing matches every day in the week, and throwing in some lengthy train journeys, mingled with several good dinners, is apt to make the form a bit mottled'. In their extremity, at last, the 'Epistle to the Corinthians' was heard. They saw that 'collective is better than personal play' and imitated North End's short passing. But seldom have 'Graham, Russell or Robertson done better in either tackling or feeding their forwards' – 3-0.

If Queen's Park and Celtic stayed at home, many others went south. It made financial sense. At home, over the holidays, not one match in Dundee yielded £10 in gate receipts. No one was quite sure whether the tours of the Scotch amateurs were holidays or a tough life. Some thought, 'about the hardest worked of her Majesty's subjects this past week or two have been Association footballers, who have been at it ding dong since Christmas Day.' Ironically, because the League would end these Scotch holidays, 1888 saw the biggest invasion ever. 'Rich pickings.' It depended whether the Scotch club negotiated a guarantee or a proportion of the gate. Either was good: 'half gates' in thousands 'are worth picking up' as 'the public have not shirked their part of the work.'

However some Scotchmen played harder off the field. The English achieved 'not creditable' victories: 'the slaughter was general, and the victims unresisting.' 'The majority simply look upon them as pleasant excursions [and] waste their strength and their substance in riotous living over the border.' So, whilst the League established a reputation for real competition, belief in tour games was waning: 'holiday football is no test of the merits of the combatants.' The charge of financial opportunism was contrasted with real football: 'between League matches and Cup-ties English clubs are compelled, so to speak, to aggrandise themselves.'

Nostalgia was uppermost in the mind of Scotch journalists among the big crowds at Glasgow's Central Station on Saturday night to see off the great 'stars' of Third Lanark and Cambuslang. 'Both teams were provided with splendid saloon carriages,' a reflection of how important players had become and how much clubs could afford in the way of expenses, or what was called 'etceteras' for accounting purposes. Only eight years ago, both 'etceteras' and 'big gates were unknown'.

Players' attitudes can be glimpsed in their messages home. Scottish Cup holders Renton made a customary Christmas tour, but to the North East, not Lancashire, for 'higher guarantees – a most important matter with Scotch clubs'. Posters advertising their status as 'champions of the world' were all over the Northern counties, but Renton's telegrams convey distress:

'Beds damp, blankets scarce, whiskey bad, atmosphere vile, coaldust triumphant. Will never visit Newcastle again, might as well take a trip to Hades ... McColl has been offered a public house, a preaching tent, a hot potato cart, and a blushing young maiden thrown in to make life a pleasure, if he remains here. McColl has been praying over the offer all day. The blushing young maiden squints, and that may settle him.'

James McColl was a star but he was not alone. All asked: 'the trains from the north on Saturday were all heavily laden with football teams, but how many will not return?' The *Newcastle Chronicle* had 'not the slightest doubt but that the secretaries will find employment for some visitors to stay'. Being a Victorian publication, they were discreet about other inducements, such as 'blushing young maidens', squinty or otherwise.

After entertaining 12,000 Novocastrians, Renton went off to friendlier climes: opponents Sunderland included four recent Renton teammates (McDiarmid, McKechnie, Davie and Coyne). The perfidious McDiarmid – who had twice returned to the village a prodigal son, only to run off with the family jewels – aimed to deprive the blushing, squinty young maiden of her prize catch: 'did McDiarmid polish off McColl? Not much.' In one of their collegiate 'swagger dinners', four touring teams and the Newcastle Scots heard George Phillips, the Association's man in the North East, toast 'Health to the Ladies connected to the Hotel ... [it] brought tears to many an eye'. Renton beat Sunderland 2-0 and Middlesbrough 5-1: 'their short passing and speedy runs kept the people yelling with delight.'

In Lancashire the top Scotch clubs, like in-form Cup semi-finalists Third Lanark, mixed confidence with suspicion of English repression: we 'will drive everything before us here, just as we have been doing at home. It has got round that we are a coarse lot, and the police authorities watch us like hawks. Coercion in Ireland is not in it with this.'

Telegrams traced Scotch adventures in Lancashire's fog: 'peculiar haze in the atmosphere – a bilious tint – Cambuslang scored a great victory –

North End never in it. Haze getting worse.' Notwithstanding, North End fielded five reserves on a ground as hard as Preston's famous cobble-stones. Cambuslang's 2-0 win was a notable scalp.

God-fearing Glasgow Northern FC feared the Good Lord more than Bootle: 'pubs being open on Sunday we visited many, but the liquids we despised. Could not desecrate the traditions of Sabbath as we hold it at home. President Martin does not let us beyond his reach; he is awfully straitlaced, but tonight we will dodge him. Just going to give Bootle a New Year's thrashing.'

Heart of Midlothian's 80-year-old touring President (also their Member of Parliament) used experience to manage his players – he 'used to be in the slave trade himself, and knows all about that sort of thing'. At Sheffield Wednesday they prompted an interesting query about inter-Association authority: 'can an English referee order a Scotch player playing in a Scotch club off the field?'

The original Scotch pro Fergie Suter told his old club: 'betting all in favour of Wanderers but we will show them what Partick can do.' Thistle lost 1-6 to Bolton – where their showman, Campbell, 'took the cake and the ladies DID admire his bare-headed performances' – and 0-10 to Accrington, for whom Oswaldthistle's Jack Kirkham scored six and whose own Scotch 'B's showed the 'most brilliant combination seen on the ground'. Glasgow Rangers knew they would get beaten, even though James Gossland, 'our advance agent' (a Scottish international from 1884) 'has made everything right … After our defeat by Rovers tomorrow we will go to Manchester Skittle Alley'. Ignominiously, Rangers were then beaten by North End Reserve. The Rangers would only recover when they follow 'what their best friends advised them long ago … the players must be sought … and placed when found' i.e. find them jobs.

In all there were 70 holiday games between English and Scotch clubs. The average gate was £50.

Could the Scots get their players home? They had a 'high old time' in Merrie England: 'the smiles of the maids and the gold of the men were very tempting … but all have returned to their wigwams.' Despite netting nearly £100, Third Lanark Royal Volunteers denounced the 'persistent and even impertinent attentions'. One agent's 'attempts to intercept and interview the players was most audacious' and all were 'tampered with' despite their minders. They hired a private bus to avoid seven football agents lying in wait at their hotel – 'land sharks … the team marched into it under careful survey and taken to the pantomime'. Everton offered Jimmy Oswald a handsome sum to stay and other Volunteers 30s for one match. The English 'disgust visitors by their detestable attentions'.

Partick Thistle's telegram reported fiendish diversions: whilst Fergy Suter 'showed us the monkeys at Belle Vue [Zoo]', William Paul was 'closeted with the football agent, who offered him tons of money'.

The League's Scotchmen went home for the holidays – the English dismissively said they went 'for their clothes' – and usually wanted to stay. Accrington's Scotch 'B's Rob Brand and Bill Barbour had proved themselves 'great favourites in the town'. But Barbour was sick of being an English 'amateur' – there would be no more Accrington for the 'demon centre, if he can find a job in the town'. Instead, Brand and Barbour cashed in on their fame by strengthening Sunderland Albion in their latest clash with Sunderland. They played for a 'silver cup given by local councillor' in front of an 'enormous attendance', led 2-0, but when Sunderland scored a disputed late winner, the Albion withdrew in protest. 'Mob law held sway'. A free fight ensued and Brand and Barbour on the Albion brake were pelted with stones, mud etc.

Their return to Dumfries had been disappointing. Initially 'a great delight ... seen the error of his ways', now they were once again 'renegades' who had left Accrington 'shabbily'. But the Saxons taught them 'crooked ways', so 'truly the sins of the wicked shall find them out'.

Barbour 'maintains he can easily prove his amateurism'. Easier said than done. The Scots welcomed 'penitents' from the 'land of their servitude' like rich men into the kingdom of heaven. They had to show the 'wisdom to repent, and the energy to atone'. A new Professionalism Committee sat in judgment. James Sloane received £2 a week during a handful of games for Stoke 'while doing nothing but playing football, the club not having been able to find a situation'. He was suspended. When two Hurlford youngsters played briefly in Newcastle, their 'chief' had to 'mount the stool of repentance ... to rent his garments ... atone for the wickedness of his thoughtless twins'.

Alex Higgins scored twice for struggling Derby on Boxing Day, then returned for the holidays. He 'unexpectedly applied for liberty', perhaps trying again for his cap against England. Sceptics cautioned he was on a 'missionary expedition' for 'some class specimens from the Rugby stud' (i.e. take Kilmarnock players back to Derby) – 'Keep a sharp look out, Killie'. Higgins claimed to be 'so unworldly as to lose wages' through football. He told the Professionalism Committee 'in all seriousness' that Derbyshire County Cricket Club had appointed him head groundsman: 'although he knew absolutely nothing about his duties, he had charge over practical groundsmen already there.' When the Committee suspended him, he returned to the League and scored six goals in eight games in County's improved finish. Higgins stayed in Derby for Christmas 1889, scored five goals against Villa, and lost 5-6. His son earned the family's next Scottish cap, 21 years later.

Meanwhile, the Professionalism Committee spent six weeks investigating Renton's Andrew Hannah. He agreed to find players when Gainsborough Trinity 'baited their hook with the promise of a poodle'. Poodle? 'Then a bright idea struck Hannah.' Watt and Coyne, 'whose inclination towards play was more pronounced than towards work,' were unattached and 'sma'' persuasion despatched them to the 'land of the bloated Saxon'. The poodle was unwell so Trinity sent Hannah a sovereign. The Committee exonerated him of being a 'veritable agent' but said, return the 'filthy lucre'.

The practice of playing three different elevens against Wales, Ireland and the cream against England, meant that the Scottish international trials, highlighting the top 50 prospects, marked the cards of the 'Football Supply Company'. Previously the 'round-mouthed Englishman with his bag of glittering gold' had been discouraged by 'warm receptions [that] terrified their cowards' hearts'. Rough handling was now substituted by more subtle humiliation. Neil Munro of Abercorn would score in Scotland's 3-2 win over England in April 1889. After the trial he was visited by 'one of these cringing, soulless Scotchmen'. The agent had 'slyly gone about' his work: he 'whispered to' Munro that he 'had something to say to him'. £2 10s for two years. 'With a merry twinkle in his eye' Munro encouraged the agent into the 'sacred precincts of the "Dive",' where, after "standing treat" to one and all with liberal hand, he was cruelly subjected to a perfect storm of abuse and raillery ... [He] can only be described as a traitor'.

The Scots were still reinventing football. A tidier English Cup and the routines of the League meant the English thought they had resolved the big questions: when was it too dark? When was a match a match? Was a player's intention to play relevant? One club alone, Third Lanark, experienced many of these debates.

In a benefit for an old Queen's Park captain, Third Lanark introduced Auld (captain of Sunderland's League championship sides 1891/93) as a substitute. Queen's Park did not want their loss to count as an ordinary match, Third Lanark did. The Association reasserted a fundamental principle: 'an official match can only be played with the eleven players who begin.' In contrast, the English Association discussions about 'substitutes' anticipated ordering an 'equivalent opposing player' to retire if an opponent was too injured to continue.

Meanwhile Third Lanark were on the wrong end of several protests. Glasgow's Association ruled the referee should decide if it was too dark to play; whereas the Scottish Association overruled the referee's judgment of light. In the Affair of Love's Labour's Lost, Love played for a club in a cup-tie later ordered to be replayed. He claimed eligibility to play for the Volunteers in the same competition, because the earlier match never really happened. The Association decided his intention was enough. Another referee disallowed a Third Lanark goal against Renton in the semi-final because the first half had elapsed, although he had not blown the whistle. 'No wonder the Volunteers hold indignation meetings and talk of football leagues.'

Nevertheless, Third Lanark reached the Cup final, against newcomers Celtic. In an officially amateur sport, to whom did a match belong? The final provided the same challenge for the Scottish Association as had tested the English Association: 'cup-tie or friendly?' 'Such a day! And such a crowd! … we must modify our ideas and enlarge our horizons.' That the crowd 'should hopelessly beat all previous Scotch records, in a day when blinding clouds of snow were falling almost continuously, did have a strong tendency to knock us speechless'. Seventeen thousand 'exposed to the heartless elements' for two hours beforehand.

Neither club was willing to take 'cup-tie risks' but remembering the way North End stitched up Villa a year earlier … 'mutually agreed, by means of a legally drawn-up document … to each table a protest.'

'Brown, on behalf of 3rd LRV FC, and Glass, on behalf of Celtic FC agree to play a friendly game instead of a cup tie, the ground and the weather being unsuitable. Both clubs concur in requesting the Association to fix a new date for the playing of the final tie. Signed William Brown, President, 3rd LRV, John Glass, President, CFC.

The players fought out an authentic final, on several inches of snow, without 'a pin-prick of difference between them'. Third Lanark won 3-0, the purity of their goals cutting through the complexities: 'neat, clean and unequivocal. They required no refereeing to establish them. Everybody saw them scored, and everybody admitted them as without a blemish.'

The Scottish Association rejected the clubs' agreement as unconstitutional but decided to re-play the final anyway. Suddenly the officially amateur game was overwhelmed by riches. The first gate had yielded £800 plus £120 to Queen's Park from the stands. What price the replay? A guilty sixpence, because the first crowd had been fooled? Queen's Park would not agree, because Hampden Park might be damaged again. They wanted 'quality rather than quantity' so, by a 10-8 vote, the Scottish Association decided upon a shilling admission.

There were 'thunderous' conflicts. Third Lanark players, led by star centre Jimmy Oswald, refused to replay. At the original final, 'when the team were dressing in the pavilion' their committee asked them to play a friendly. No way. 'We have come up to play a cup-tie, and a cup-tie it must be, or we don't turn out.' It was called 'the Match of the Misconception'.

They replayed. The gate was 'mere pin money', £710 plus another £120 for Queen's Park's stands. Third Lanark won, but it was a 'straggling' affair, and all three goals were disputed.

Christmas was a time for charity and pantomime. Charity matches were a part of big football, so when there was a mining disaster at Hyde, a benefit for the victims and dependents was quickly arranged. Trouble was, the precedents were very uncharitable. The last time North End played Hyde it was 26-0. For their brave rematch Hyde had Bolton Wanderers' Alec Barbour at centre and imported Petrie from Edinburgh. It made £150.

It was also brave of Everton to play a pantomime match with local theatrical artistes. Even beforehand Everton's record of 'maiming' their centre-forwards (so many suffered long-term injuries) led the local press to propose pantomime characters – Buttons, Cinders or Idle Jack – for the position. On a snowy Tuesday afternoon in January, 10/12,000 watched, bigger than all but one League crowd. The approaches to the ground were as usual: 'card tricksters, prick the garter men, thimble and pea manipulators, and others of the same class … with sweeteners or dupes.' So Everton's League side took on sixteen 'Theatricals turned out in grotesque dresses, make-ups and antics', and despite Jack Ross as driven serious-captain, the fun soon began: 'a sack of property lemons about the size of pumpkins, were brought on and after the players had bashed them about on each other's heads, they were exploded either by sitting on them or …' (more in similar vein). It was a last straw for Ross, who wailed: '[Everton] can't play football and I shall never be able to make them.'

Christmas was also a time for guarantees. The League enhanced the market position of the Twelve Apostles, both improving their status and increasing rarity value, whilst at the same time exploiting the new vulnerability of ambitious non-League clubs. For example, Sunderland and Newcastle had watched the League with frustration. Their four clubs could only play one another and they couldn't always only play one another. Other matches were usually one-sided.

Sunderland needed to play the Apostles to justify their pretensions to join them. But 'life was not worth living' when Bolton Wanderers, likely retirees as one of the League's 'last four', beat Sunderland, serious aspirants to replace them and fielding several Scottish internationals, 10-1!

The result cemented the League's reputation, and persuaded Sunderland Albion to guarantee Bolton £40. Albion felt sure to do better. Sunderland's supporters performed a successful spoiling operation: 'most of the wall posters announcing the arrival and performances of the Wanderers were destroyed, special care being taken to obliterate the record of Sunderland's defeat.' Sunderland Albion 'sadly over-reached' their guarantee, and lost, although only by 1-3.

THE END OF THE LEAGUE?

DECEMBER 26TH – DERBY 2, BOLTON 3 – (3,500)

Alex Higgins' 'marvellously good' shooting put County two up, but rampant Wanderers fought back, and their winning movement 'went zigzag' through the defence. Our intrepid reporter then fled: 'a terrific storm then broke over the ground and after successfully braving the elements for a few minutes your correspondent was obliged to beat a hasty retreat into the interior of the pavilion and saw no more of the game. The rest of the play, I am told, was of a rough and tumble character.'

WEST BROMWICH 0, PRESTON 5 – (10,000)

At last a crowd: 'the Albion were anxious to win this one.' The League had been so disappointing for the Cup holders. North End's only serious challengers for two years, Albion were now struggling to stay above halfway. And the crowds had reflected the disenchantment. Today it was different: a 'capital gate … and a capital struggle to get into the ground'.

North End had played Christmas Day and left Preston in a 'dilapidated' (i.e. drunken) state at 11pm, reaching Colonnade Hotel around 3am. They were 'glad to get a few hours' bed, then sightseeing, then a tram to the ground. 'Both sides meant their utmost.' Albion 'worked like demons'; North End strolled four first-half goals: 'Birmingham people confessed that they had never seen such a scientific game as that exhibited by the visitors who, time after time, went right through the Albion defence with some magnificent passing.' In Preston the wired news 'led to great rejoicing'.

DECEMBER 29TH – PRESTON 1, BLACKBURN 0 – (9,000)

After another all-night journey, in the middle of nine games in sixteen days, North End's humour was not improved by Rovers taking man and ball. Their 'reprisals' left an acrid taste. Actually, Reverend Akred of St Helens called North End's 'big heavy fellow' ('Safety Valve' Graham) 'atrocious' for frequently 'grassing' Bill Townley, who was 'about as substantial as two laths nailed together'. His sermon, to Baptist Church workers, initiated a press controversy, 'Is Football Demoralising?' (see Chapter 10).

Weakened Blackburn gave North End 'such a putting-up as they have not experienced for some time back'. Davie Russell, 'through having a stick thrust in his side during a piece of larking,' struggled and Sam Thomson was an 'utter failure, being too slow to be of use'. Despite the petty duels (particularly Townley 'potting' 'little demon' Ross), it was 'square fighting for the result': 'the fact that each side had two or three free kicks for fouls proves the desperate character of the encounter.' The only goal was a 'rattler'. Gordon escaped Rovers' 'saviour' (Jack Forbes) and middled for Goodall – 'impossible for any custodian to save'. 'Yell of the season.'

These days, Forbes was 'beating all competitors into a cocked hat in his hosiery shop and had to go to Manchester to replenish his stock in three days.' His shop was always crowded: 'popularity is a splendid impetus to business.' North End supporters wanted a new outside-left 'even if he has to be put in the stocking business'.

ACCRINGTON 3, EVERTON 1 – (4,000)

Everton were disintegrating: 'to leave home with eight men, with the odd chance of picking up others on route, was hardly good enough.' After Christmas excesses, a teetotaler seemed prudent, so Harry Parkinson of Bell's Temperance ('the Abstainers') became a 'pressed' man. Frank Sugg fortunately turned up, and Edgar Chadwick joined later. The Reds 'squeezed [three goals] out of the motley collection of shots which went wise or otherwise'. Twice Everton's 'shirt sleeves flew up and the ball was handed out' – with referee Norris 'much too wide awake,' the free-kicks proved fatal.

'Bravo Accrington. One degree higher in the scale is a feather in thy cap.' Brand and Barbour had taken the Poor Boys 'very near the top of the ladder', past moneybags Everton.

ASTON VILLA 4, DERBY 2 – (4,000)

Derby also had trouble. Lewis Cooper could not come, and George Bakewell managed to get left behind, so ten arrived. This is not what William McGregor envisaged for the League. Harry Plackett's injury left County with nine until Bakewell appeared.

BOLTON 2, WOLVERHAMPTON 1 – (5,000)

An unlikely result in the early days, but now Bolton took five successive wins into the Battle of the Wanderers. The League was closing up.

When Wolves led, Bolton 'brisked up considerably' and Davy Weir's grand shot equalised. The winner saddened the 'very demonstrative … small knot of visitors from the Midlands'. Then Charlie Harrison took over: 'this much abused goalkeeper seems to have plucked up heart, for he now plays a really dashing game, whereas he used to suffer from a distressing malady known as funk.' The 'cheering was almost continuous', and he was 'carried shoulder-high to the dressing tent'.

BURNLEY 1, NOTTS COUNTY 0 – ('GOOD GATE' 'LARGE CONCOURSE')

'Caution was the password' on the frozen ground and both goalkeepers were 'beyond praise'. When Yates shot over the bar, County's Tom Widdowson, nearly 6ft 5in, 'threw the leather towards the centre,' thinking it went through.

WEST BROMWICH 2, STOKE 0 – (1,000/1,500)

Whilst Jack Hendry was 'doing his time', Albion's latest Scotch back, 'unearthed from somewhere,' was not of the 'required class'. Rossendale v Rawtenstall in Lancashire attracted a bigger crowd.

JANUARY 5TH, 1889 – EVERTON 1, BLACKBURN 0
OR AN ARRANGED DRAW – PROVISIONAL RESULT(S) – (6,000)

The League ran out of steam. So many fixtures, so much bad weather, too few players. Frost and fog had been virtual ever-presents for a month. Grounds were 'hard as adamant and as slippery as ice … [but] it takes a lot of "weather" to stop the dribblers'.

These teams looked at the dangerous surface and a big crowd that had 'little chance of seeing much', and Jack Ross told the press box 'we are going to play a quiet game today' … the captains agreed a league draw, 'whatever result'.

There were immediate consequences. 'Grumbler' fled to the 'footwarmers' in his 'Hansom Cab' – 'I confess to a slight flutter of pleasure'. Then, once Everton scored, Rovers 'did not exert themselves in the least possible way'. So, 'as a league fixture, the game … will be counted a draw, but between club and club, Everton wins'. 'The crowd were much disgusted when it leaked out that they had been treated to an "exhibition", and that the victory was no victory at all.' And of course, 'the trouble this arrangement caused after the match was phenomenal and attributable entirely to the question of bets being off.'

But what seemed a sensible if 'curious agreement' was a serious challenge to League authority. Ross had gone back to the old days. Conditions prevented a true test of the clubs' respective class, so it was 'honours even'. But in the new currency of a League 'point' there were consequences for the other Apostles. At season's end this point might be the difference between Everton being in the 'last four' or not.

WEST BROMWICH 1, WOLVERHAMPTON 3 – (4,000)

Albion's popularity was waning, 'even at reduced prices,' and many supported Wolverhampton. 'Wanderers showed what good stuff they are made of by sending West Bromwich to the right about.' In dense fog, Albion's backs crouched down to see the ball and went walkabout: 'Brodie carrying the ball with a man on either side, and the Albion backs missing, Roberts and the ball were carried through together.'

BURNLEY 4, ASTON VILLA 0 – (6,000)

Without William McGregor, Villa's organisation was failing. Archie Goodall arrived in Birmingham on Saturday morning with a severe cold caught travelling from Scotland, 'so Allen had to be fetched from his work – all grimy and dirty. He was bundled into Archie's togs, sent off to Burnley.' Trouble was, Goodall was a giant, a circus strongman in later life, whilst Albert Allen was a little 'un. 'T'aint likely he could play with his boots stuffed with paper to make them fit.'

Secretary George Ramsay was also in Scotland, 'kicking old boots.' The press criticised the 'blundering mismanagement' of Villa's usual team selection on Thursday night – 'this was to INDUCE them to come to practice … not a single man KNEW FOR CERTAIN that he had to be at New St Station at 9am at Saturday morning, til the Friday post.' Too late for those already gone to work – it was only after selection that players finalised their arrangements.

Freddie Dawson was 'a late bird'. He got home near midnight Friday to learn he was 'wanted' and as a matter of fact he could not get leave. He did not know what to do and after pondering the dilemma decided to get up early next morning to see if something turned up. Sleeplessness took its toll, and he overslept.

Villa started with eight, including Denny Hodgetts, who had been suspended for five weeks. Two others arrived, 'in a bustle,' after fifteen minutes. Burnley 'maintained an almost incessant attack, and the Aston goal had miraculous escapes'. Such a 'thorough castigation … it was a shame to bring [Scottish goalkeeper Cox] back from holiday to practically watch the game'. Villa's Warner stopped it being 20-1: 'he never had so much work to do in a match before, and he never did it so well.'

The result was significant, because it decided the first League championship …

PRESTON 4, NOTTS COUNTY 1 – (4/5,000)

Because, of course, North End won, despite County fielding 'quite eleven captains' who were 'champion claimers'. After 30 minutes, Notts keeper Tom Widdowson 'threw the ball up to fist away, when Goodall rushing up, breasted it through'. The first League champions then disappeared: in the fog 'not one of the contestants was visible'.

North End had scored 68 goals and conceded thirteen: an average of 5.23 against the strongest of England. Yet even then their acclaim was not unanimous. A table published the following Monday of all clubs, based on goal average, had North End second: after 33 League and ordinary fixtures they had scored 3.74 goals to every one conceded. The Crusaders were better, after twelve games. Aston Villa were the second-placed League side – sixteenth.

North End's win was not only invisible: there was no fanfare, no celebration and no trophy. Not like that public acclaim for winning the Lancashire Cup in April 1887. That was the trouble with the League: you never knew when it was over. It began 118 days ago and would not finish for another 104 days. The League just faded away. It was done and the Cup was almost upon them.

League – Top Three: Preston 19 games, 35 points; Aston Villa 17, 24; Wolves 17, 22. (With only five League games left to play, Villa could only reach a total of 34 points. Preston already had 35. The first League title had been settled as early as January 5th.)

Chapter Ten

'Cropper was a stranger to me'

Dan Doyle

WILL CROPPER

Saturday 2.40pm, January 12th 1889, Clee Park, Grimsby. 'About as wretched, miserable and dreary-looking day ... However the chasers of the leather had the temerity to face it, I am at a loss to understand.' Only 400 were present, twenty times less than the record 8,000 who watched the Cup-tie with North End a month later. In that match Grimsby's Scotch back Dan Doyle would play 'skittles' with the famous North End forwards: once mowing down 'Gordon and Ross awkwardly in the same run'. On January 12th the 'mere handful' of 400 watched the ball clear twenty-years-old Chas Coulbeck's head, 30-odd yards from goal. Clee-thorpe's left-half, assisting Grimsby in this ordinary club fixture, realised the danger and turned quickly. But not quickly enough. His immediate opponent, Staveley's forward Will Cropper 'made one of his well-known runs'. He 'dodged round' Coulbeck at top speed to collect the ball and go for goal. But unseen to Cropper, the covering back Doyle was making for the ball from a different direction, also at top speed.

A typical 'Scotch amateur', Daniel Doyle had had a busy year. Earlier in 1888, clearly a coming man, he moved from Paisley to Broxburn, to East Stirlingshire and Hibernian, then briefly to Sunderland, stepping up in class each time. James Lundie eventually recruited Doyle to strengthen ambitious Grimsby for their needle local qualifying tie with Lincoln in the English Cup.

Will Cropper was a substantial sporting figure. Passing his 26th birth-day a fortnight earlier, he had been a regular Derbyshire county cricketer since he was nineteen. Cropper batted well and bowled a fastish left-arm, with a high delivery and the ability to 'get work on the ball'. When Derbyshire were not occupied, he had a 'roving commission and played with various clubs'. His County teammates had included League foot-ballers Frank Sugg and Will Chatterton. Once, both Cropper and Sugg scored 80s to save a match against Lancashire and then Cropper won it with four wickets in the last hour. He also took 7-43 for an All-England XI against the Australians at the Crystal Palace in 1886.

Although he played for Derby County in the 1886-87 National Cup, Cropper 'was just coming to the fore as a football player' and was a 'dash-ing – perhaps too dashing – centre-forward.' He had helped Staveley,

Chesterfield's most senior club, to recover from a 1887-88 season riven with strikes, and was 'largely responsible in achieving their remarkable success'. Staveley's only defeat in 22 games occurred when Notts County neglected their League responsibilities and brought their strongest men for the English Cup-tie. Cropper had just won his first football honour, being selected for Sheffield the following Saturday, and 'singular to relate [Cropper] did not wish to go to Grimsby', preferring to make 'every preparation for getting in trim for the contest' in Glasgow. The annual Sheffield v Glasgow battle was one of the oldest in the football calendar. It would be a victim of the League, just as Cropper was a victim of Doyle's committed professionalism. This Glasgow eleven, chosen by vote from 43 club nominations and with a cap as reward, 'was the worst abused team which ever left home.' Yet it included many internationals and four sometime captains of Scotland in Donald Gow, James McLaren, Jimmy Oswald, and Tom Robertson.

Staveley's leader was George Hay, part of the clan that included Tom Hay, the Newton Heath and former Bolton Wanderers goalkeeper. Hay, Staveley's cricket pro and himself an old Derbyshire bowler, understood sporting discipline and pressed Cropper to play. Staveley had a 'big reputation' to defend and were already missing two of 'their Cup team'. Grimsby, itching to get into the League and with an almost all-Scotch eleven, were increasingly selective in their fixtures. Having established local pre-eminence over Lincoln and Gainsborough Trinity, Grimsby bemoaned their lack of quality opponents. Further afield, they had twice held their own against Sunderland and beat Bolton Wanderers before Christmas, but played few Combination fixtures. Grimsby impatiently awaited the end of the League so they could arrange ordinary matches with that 'magic circle' of clubs and 'measure themselves against the best'. They also needed testing, to prepare for their English Cup-tie against unbeaten Sunderland Albion. So Grimsby represented an important fixture for Staveley who would have to be strong to earn another fixture. Will Cropper had to play.

The ball bounced up. Despite being played in pouring rain on a quagmire, both Doyle and Cropper jumped to 'breast the ball'. Doyle was fractionally quicker and, still in the air, took the ball on his upper thigh. Will Cropper 'received the full weight' of Doyle's raised knee in his abdomen. Two days later, Doyle, who gave his occupation as 'dock labourer', defensively assured the coroner's jury that there had been no prior provocation or intention: 'indeed it was the first time we had met.'

The suspicion was that football provided a context to settle scores. This assumption about sport's potential for revenge was expressed, in the

Nottingham Daily Express, regarding American Football: an aggrieved player 'never complains, but possesses his soul with patience, and awaits a moment for retaliation. When it comes, he squares accounts expeditiously and effectively'. The other defender Charles Coulbeck recalled his narrow escape: 'I was within a yard of it all. I just bobbed out of the road, or I should have been between them, and have caught the knock. I never saw him afterwards.'

Everyone thought Cropper was 'winded'. Sympathetic players and referee Robert Charles Hall (fish merchant and Grimsby's captain in 1886-87) gathered round and advised Cropper to sit in the grandstand for a while. Remarkably, he anticipated his eventual diagnosis by responding 'I think it has hurt my bowels'. In 'dreadful pain', Cropper was helped off by George Hay, who reported his remarkable prescience, saying 'they have killed me'. Dr Grimoldby, who had been in the ground, quickly attended and Cropper was moved to Topliss' Coffee-rooms, just fifteen yards outside the football field boundary, where Town had their dressing rooms.

He was very tender and suffering 'very severe shock.' There Cropper remained until 9pm when Dr Grimoldby arrived to take him to hospital two miles away, but saw 'at once … he was too sick, and somewhat worse', and could not be moved. Another doctor confirmed this opinion and they left his attendants, Hay and a Grimsby schoolteacher, Mr Patmore, to administer three doses of morphine suppositories. That was welcome as Cropper took a turn for the worse approaching midnight. Hay telegraphed home that he had had a bad night. Cropper said he was sorry he could not play in Glasgow, but otherwise was in too much pain to talk. At 8.30am he lapsed into unconsciousness and died around 11.30. The death was caused by acute peritonitis brought on by a rupture to his bowel. Dr Grimoldby reported Cropper 'was as strong a made man as Doyle, and one of fine physique'.

Victorians ritually said nice things about the dead. Cropper was that respected social figure, an all-round sportsman. As well as being an international cricketer and a footballer able to represent his city, Cropper ran sprints, was an excellent cyclist and good swimmer, one of Derbyshire's best hockey players, and was once one of three Croppers who won a football match on skates for his village, 11-2. He was also one of many active sportsmen who doubled 'in business as a newspaper [sporting] correspondent'. Cropper was described as in good spirits on the journey to Grimsby and in general 'quiet, unassuming, and above all abstemious'. The latter was usually code for avoiding alcohol misuse, but the coroner found another meaning when he concluded that Cropper had had a hand in his own death: 'it was an extremely foolish thing ... for a player at football to enter into a game just after a meal and full stomach.'

It was also common for victims to foresee their fate in some eerie way. Hereabouts, future England forward Fred Spiksley 'had a presentiment' that he would fracture his fibula against Sheffield Wednesday on his nineteenth birthday, and he did. It was with Wednesday that Spiksley later earned international fame.

So it was with 'poor Cropper'. One appreciation recalled that he 'ofttimes remarked to me what a foolish game' football was, because 'you can never depend on the fairness of your opponent's game.' That was 'why Cropper never really cared for the game'. In fact he was reported to have given up football after witnessing several serious accidents, and experiencing a scary near miss. Once chosen for Eckington (another victim of Notts County's run through the English Cup's qualifying rounds) he got within sight of Staveley station when he had a presentiment and pulled out of the match. His replacement was killed by an opponent's charge.

News of Cropper's death was relayed by telegraph and special messenger to his home, where he lived with his father in Brimington, a mining village. That night, at 10.30, there were 'batches of young people' outside and inside there were 'continuous rows of blinds being drawn as a token of esteem and respect'. Mining villages knew how to recognise fatal accidents at work.

Mr Cropper senior arrived in Grimsby the next day, just as the Inquest, also in Topliss' Coffee-rooms, finished. Grimsby Town Club Executive supplied a handsome oaken coffin, with brass mountings, and just before 5pm, the hearse, the mourning coach, and the Grimsby team on foot, sent him home by train. They started a public subscription to defray these expenses, whereas Staveley FC and Brimington Cricket Club started one to erect Will Cropper a memorial.

Grimsby also provided captain Bob Macbeth with a handsome circular wreath of white flowers, enclosed in a glass case: 'In Memoriam – In token of the great sorrow and sympathy of the Grimsby Town Football Club, Grimsby January 17, 1889.' It was a big funeral.

Consequences came quickly. There were fears that rough play accusations 'might work a serious injury to the Grimsby club, which has quite enough sins to answer for'. The latter was a criticism of Town importing so many Scotchmen. Mr Lammin, the secretary who had built Grimsby into 'a power in the land', resigned (his replacement was Cropper's attendant during that fateful night, schoolmaster Patmore). Despite the coroner's jury deciding it had been the 'purest accident', Sheffield Wednesday's committee called off their fixture with Grimsby for that Saturday.

There had been no appeal made to the referee when Cropper received his fatal injury, and therefore no foul. Hall only blew because Cropper had been 'hors de combat'. Afterwards reports varied. Some described a commonplace game, others one in which Staveley were the victims of their opponents and crowd: 'when they remonstrated with the Grimsby players for their unnecessary roughness, they were boohed.'

'Is Football Demoralising?'

The death precipitated a moral crisis, as papers and authorities contemplated football literally 'coming a cropper'. Footballists knew 'pessimists will again be up in arms condemning the game of football in no measured tones'. London papers blamed 'rough play', and football anticipated that 'the medical journals and other folk who know very little about the game will be agitating for an alteration in the rules of football, and decrying it as a brutal game'. The satirical magazine *Punch* produced a teasing London view of the violent world of League football in an imagined match between 'Midland Yahos' and 'North Country Savages'.

'Pa' Jackson's journal *Pastime* took up the controversy, 'Is football demoralising?', addressing the triple evils of rough play, gambling and drinking. It was a moralistic campaign that placed football continually on the defensive. It was a class attack: 'football, having become a democratic game, is not always played in the spirit which regulated the encounters of teams from public schools and universities.'

Football's defence was largely abstract: 'It is the essence of sport to contain a spice of risk … danger is the zest and honour of the game.' Or it embraced the new Victorian social co-option of Darwin's Origin of Species: 'no game extant … so admirably exemplifies the rough-and-tumble incidents of life, which better illustrate the theory of the survival of the fittest, as the glorious game of football.' Or it was frankly nationalistic: 'players aver … that not a little of the fascination of football lies in its personal risk-taking. This is a good John Bull feeling.'

The Association could see this crisis coming. Professionalism was already being blamed for both rough play and crowd violence, yet it was rare for offenders to be sent off. So the Association targeted the new high-profile exemplar of professionalism, the League, for disciplinary suspensions (Dick, Hodgetts, Hendry and Siddons – see Chapters 7 and 8) and issuing new dictats discouraging player and crowd violence.

Association President Marindin went public. Marindin would resign after the League coup removing the professionalism rules in May 1889, which he saw as a step too far. But in November 1888 he led their public response by giving a widely reported press interview.

The controversy had a class agenda. Was there a symbiosis between the working-class player and his working-class crowd that was destroying idealistic, muscular-Christian sport, and in a wider sense threatening public order and the social status quo? Was the player being paid too much and, in order to maintain this income, going too far in roughness and other chicanery? Was the crowd influencing play through their gambling and then, further fuelled by alcohol, responding violently to frustrations? In both cases, did the working class have too much money and freedom for their own good, and for the good of society?

The wider background was a serious law and order crisis. In February 1886, following a meeting in Trafalgar Square at which radical speakers accused employers of keeping working people in chronic poverty, there was disorder and looting of West End property. Then in November 1887, during another mass rally, a police charge left hundreds of people badly battered and bruised. The imagery of West End and East End made propertied London only too aware of their vulnerability, and it was a proximity echoed in other British towns [Jones, 1976]. It was fear of the mob: and every football crowd teetered on the edge of being a mob.

The physical engagement of football onlookers with the play was captured by one 1888-89 account: 'watching a certain match the other Saturday amongst an excited crowd, we received many a kick, both front and back, thinking we were among a particularly excitable lot, we shifted positions, but it was ever the same thing wherever we went; whenever there was an exceptionally interesting bit of play, or a good kick at a critical moment, a great many of the spectators had a good kick too, unconsciously of course, with the result, that their neighbours' shins and pants suffered, all round.'

Football crowds had a sense of their own power and of their ownership of space and time. In January 1889, 1,500 Notts County supporters left Trent Bridge 'according to custom' through the old pavilion exit gate and the inn yard. But a truncheon-wielding policeman challenged custom in a 'ridiculous and unpleasant scene'. The gate was forced and the policeman hounded to retreat into an adjacent lodge by a hooting crowd.

Marindin was careful. He explained he neither opposed professionals, nor advocated temperance at football matches although alcohol use was common: 'crowd hilarious and whisky bottles produced, whisky put where the flies could not get at it.'

Marindin's target was 'rough play' and his scapegoat umpires who lacked the 'moral courage' to confront the evil. It was not just in the League. In the Combination, Leek complained of Newton Heath's roughness and particularly their international centre Jack Doughty.

Centres were allowed to rough up keepers, but Leek called Doughty 'brutal'. Referee Ormerod, a senior figure in the Lancashire Association, responded in the press, rather equivocally: Doughty might have gone 'ten yards' out of his way, but still he 'accidentally came into contact with [the goalkeeper, although] I have not the least doubt that your reporter concluded that he had kicked him'. Ormerod instead thought the 'baby-like conduct of the Leek umpire … caused a little unpleasantness'.

Leek concluded this approach lacked 'moral courage', and engaged Fitzroy Norris for the return. When the Heathens complained that Norris was not on the Combination's list of referees, Leek said we 'must have someone with a firm hand.' Norris proved no better, confiding to Newton Heath after the match that the whole Leek team were babies, and their crowd tantruming toddlers: 'your team was heavier and, naturally the collisions on charging were mostly to your advantage, and this the Leekites seemed not to relish. I believe your players received rather shoddy treatment on the Leek streets, which I hardly thought the natives capable of.'

Above all, Marindin wanted to temper any sense of crisis, or association football being seen as dangerous. So Will Cropper's heavily publicised death only weeks later seriously undermined the Association: no 'football fatality had made a greater impression on the country'.

Instead, Marindin agreed betting 'is undoubtedly a great evil'. Without mentioning the League, in the North 'books are made on every great match, and a large amount of money, without question, changes hands'. Throughout the interview Marindin sought balance. He wanted to give an essentially positive message, to acknowledge evils but keep them in proportion. So he resisted when the interviewer homed on betting as football's chief attraction: 'is it for this reason that huge gates follow the great football matches?' 'Hardly. Football is rapidly becoming such a popular game that it is drawing even larger gates than cricket … [but] our clubs are not making as much money as the public think.'

Betting was an issue. In the far North, Sunderland began the season well with their expensive Scottish international centre Billy Dickson. They were naturally hot favourites visiting Darlington, where a local journalist bet odds of 10 to 1 against the home team. Perhaps others did too. Darlington won 2-1, occasioning both the 'giddiest heights of joy and jubilation' and scepticism: 'that Sunderland were beaten on their merits I refuse to believe. There are ugly rumours.' Billy Dickson and his 'shadow' Phemister, whose own goal lost the match, were both sent back to Dundee in disgrace. Dickson did not return to big-time football for a year, when he joined Aston Villa. A year later Sunderland suspended Rob

Brand, Accrington's old hero, after 'common rumour' said he 'sold' a Sheffield Wednesday game.

Whilst the press reacted and the authorities pondered, families had a think. Legendary England international Harry Cursham announced his retirement: 'the death of Cropper has frightened Mrs Cursham' and also his mother-in-law, so Cursham 'has sacrificed himself on the altar of domesticity'. Only weeks before, Notts announced Cursham as their League centre-forward. His selection was bad news, revealing County could get no one better, neither Scot nor anyone else, for this 'most onerous and thankless position'. Cursham's selection reflected less a fresh start than the club's 'all-round decadence'. He had been playing since 1876 and had eight international appearances, although none since 1884. Since then, County had struggled and Cursham frequently expressed a 'resolve to burn his boots and forswear football'. He had played intermittently during 1888's autumn: 'after oscillating between left wing and full back he springs up like a jack-in-the-box, full of dash and vigour ... How remarkable is this leap into the gulf.' Now, a month later, he was going again. It did not last of course: Cursham answered later emergencies too. Nevertheless, his retirement, however temporary, was striking: Harry Cursham 'was the ideal of every Englishman and Englishwoman for he looked "killing" in his football costume'.

The next month saw a succession of reported deaths. Dan Doyle once played with John Stewart at East Stirling. Stirlingshire's County right-winger was, at 23 and after ten years, the club's oldest and longest-serving playing member. After playing Montrose on Wednesday night he became ill and died on Saturday. Ashton-under-Lyme FC treasurer Knowlson, 25, fractured both bones in his right shin against Leek. They stuck a stick to the side of his leg, wrapped him in overcoats and carried him to hospital on a 'footboard'. Gangrene and tetanus set in and after two amputations, he died in 'terrible suffering' two weeks later.

A dying disposition by another broken leg victim, Butler, led Belfast police to arrest his assailant Doherty. In 1890 the Corinthian Brothers Walters retired when another brother died whilst playing. For some moralists these deaths revealed that the balance between the 'game' and the 'show' had become distinctly un-English: 'our game is little better than the displays in the Roman amphitheatre or Spanish bullring.'

Then, following the award of a disputed goal, Leyland's James Tattersall first knocked down Thomas Mawdsley, a consumptive umpire, then kicked him in the chest, after which he died. The coroner's jury determined 'death by natural causes, accelerated by the kick', but he was remanded in custody for trial on manslaughter charges. When this was initially reported as a 'referee murder', archetypal referee Fitzroy Norris appeared to anticipate 'martyrdom' at his next League match.

CAPTAIN DOYLE

On the first Saturday of the 1889-90 season, Tom Spittle was kneed in the stomach by Small Heath's Hall, and died next day. The coroner's jury found Accidental Death, then paused. 'But we think when people play football they ought to be very careful.' Within football, Dan Doyle had crossed a line that players recognised – there should no 'kneeing' an opponent. Two decades later, Sunderland and England forward Arthur Bridgett, an active Christian lay preacher, still had reason to fulminate: 'all footballers will agree, the real unpardonable sin in tackling an opponent is the horrible habit of going for a man with the knee up ... whenever one hears of an accidental death at football one involuntarily sees an opponent coming with his knee up ... we should do well to banish a man from the game forever who practises it.'

Dan Doyle became 'the best known footballer of his day' (the 1890s) but by the 1990s 'virtually represented all that had once been wrong with the professional football system' [Harding, 1991, pp.9-10]. This judgment had nothing to do with Will Cropper. Doyle was nearly in court several times after. His first match with Grimsby had been in October against Lincoln in the English Cup, and they drew the replay. Four hours without decision. Lincoln complained that Doyle was not eligible and issued a summons. The conflict was resolved out of court when Doyle was withdrawn from the team. Grimsby won the second replay, and Doyle returned for the 5-0 victory over Cleethorpes in the next round. Doyle soon established himself: his colleague Davie Riddoch, a former St Bernards forward, returned to Edinburgh for the New Year holidays and reported that 'most of the men who left are doing well, and the Englishmen are particularly pleased with Doyle'.

Dan Doyle went on to an illustrious career, and afterwards became a Glasgow city councillor [Lincoln, 1912 p.322], before coming 'to a predictably sorry end, dying in penury after drinking his way through at least three public houses' [Harding, 1991].

First, in April 1889, Jack Bentley recruited the 'amateur' to strengthen Wanderers against Preston a week after the Cup final. Bolton won 5-1 when North End 'could neither run, nor dodge, nor pass, nor shoot, nor exert themselves'. Doyle, sometimes watched out of 'morbid curiosity', quickly forged an 'especially fine' partnership with Jones the back and, when injured, acted as Bolton's umpire. In May, when Bentley persuaded the Association to ditch the rules on professionalism, he announced

Doyle as Wanderers' left-back. But in August 1889, Everton reported he was theirs. Bentley threatened 'a 'Doyle' case' in the County Court but was bought off. The new Everton were successful, finishing second in the 1889-90 League. Doyle's appetite was somewhat variable, and Anfield sometimes provided insufficient incentive to attend – 'Dan says Everton have not been giving away black puddings this last three weeks, so he has not troubled to go up there'. In 1890-91 Everton were champions, and Dan Doyle was poised to be their next captain.

But in 1891 Doyle resolved Scotland's 'epoch of doubt and difficulty' over 'the bogey of professionalism'. Throughout the 1880s their authorities indulged in wishful thinking about the 'omens of threatened evil ... if the skeleton be kept a little while longer in its cupboard it will fall to pieces'. Dan Doyle would not stay in his cupboard.

Doyle had a two-year agreement at £3 a week, two-thirds of which was paid upfront. But on July 31st 1891 he (and Everton forward Alec Brady) applied for the Scottish Association's amnesty for professionals returning from England. 108 took advantage of this 'clemency', although some soon 'crossed the border' again. Celtic needed Doyle, the 'big thundering player', having finished only third in the Scottish League's first season. Next day, Doyle was in Celtic Park's pavilion attending their sports event, but rejecting all inducements to strip for one of Celtic's ten five-a-side teams. The same day he scotched rumours in Liverpool by sending a telegram to a Lancashire paper: 'Kindly insert I intend play for Everton, certain – Doyle.'

Everton sent Tom Howarth, the agent who recruited Jack Ross, to Glasgow after the 'runaways'. Doyle said he would only return if Everton matched Celtic's offer, which was daunting: a first-class pub plus fixtures, fittings and stock yielding a guaranteed £5 a week, plus an 'additional allowance' per match. Alternatively, he wanted £100 for his past service, and an increase on his current deal to £4 a week. When Doyle returned to Liverpool, 'Evertonians breathe freely once more'. 'King John' Houlding said his demands were 'impossible' and 'absurd', then offered Doyle a 'premium as captain'. When negotiations reached 'breaking point', Doyle went off 'in a huff', only rescued from the Glasgow train five minutes before departure. A deal was agreed, but his 'mediated infidelity has given a rude shock to his old friends' and Doyle's former reputation – 'Daniel the Incorruptible' or 'Daniel the Man of Principle' – was no longer tenable. He went to Glasgow to participate in a 'quoiting handicap' (Doyle also once played bowls for Scotland against an England team including legendary cricketer WG Grace), giving a 'solemn promise' of his return.

On Saturday, August 8th, Doyle telegrammed his final decision. Celtic's fans were delighted: 'Mr O'Hara buttonholed me … "I was astonished to behold the Everton cracks, Doyle and Brady, in the Celtic ranks. I felt inclined to shout hurroo". O'Hara was so disconcerted he put a lighted cigarette into Mr McLaughlin's eye. 'Mr Curtis wrung my hand … too full of emotion to give utterance to the great joy he was experiencing … for a full hour and a half that party could do nothing but grin – and such a grinning.'

Evertonians were glum: 'have you heard the news?' Some of Dan Doyle's history was now remembered: he had left Everton 'shabbily', left Wanderers 'shabbily', and earlier left Grimsby 'shabbily'. In 1895 before the England v Scotland international at Goodison Park, his legend was reprised: how 'the biggest kicker in football was stolen by the Celtic, and although Everton offered him a brewery – more or less – he preferred to remain an amateur, and get a pub and £5 a week'.

The case rocked pro football. The Scotch façade of 'whitewashed amateurism' was exposed by Doyle's highly publicised commercial arrangement with Celtic FC. Doyle also had an existing professional contract, which he rightly judged was not 'legally enforcible', although Everton tried. Doyle also exposed the limits of the League's protective cocoon. Their clubs may have enforced consensual transfers of players between themselves, but they were only Twelve. The League proved no hindrance.

Celts were soon glum too, as Doyle's 'arrival at Celtic had sparked off a strike for higher wages' [Harding 1991]. He gained his first cap against England the following spring, when his 'quick and cunning' former Everton teammate Edgar Chadwick scored in 30 seconds. Then Celtic won three of the next four League titles and Doyle played in the 1894, 1895, 1897 and 1898 England internationals. Eight in all. He became a folk hero over again – 'That's Dan.' He foots the ball and answers 'I am'. The pinnacle of Dan Doyle's career was captaining Scotland against England on April 7th, 1894, before a record 50,000 at Celtic Park. The Thistle had not beaten the Saxons since 1889 but, with four minutes to go, Scotland were 'sailing home on the winged cherub of victory', 2-1. Then Billy Bassett and captain John Goodall set up England's equaliser: Scotland's 'joy – deserved if it ever was deserved – was just within our grasp, and surely it was the cruellest stroke dark fate ever administered to our country'.

In his 1894 pen-picture, Doyle's English travels were described as an education, in which he had 'picked up a wrinkle or two'. Will Cropper had become a wrinkle.

CHALLENGE

Cropper's death reverberated throughout the 1889 Challenge Cup competition. The Association immediately decided to appoint both referees and neutral umpires for the first round ties on February 2nd. No chances were taken with Dan Doyle: powerful Richard Gregson of the Lancashire Association refereed Grimsby's win over Sunderland Albion, and called it 'the greatest Cup-tie he had seen'. Grimsby thought Gregson's approval would get them into the Apostles: 'what price the League now! Evidently the Town have "caught the speaker's eye". Warm, ain't it?'

There were other ties with added value, and added risk. The Sheffield Wednesday v Notts County tie carried both a traditional inter-town rivalry, and an extra edge through its League significance. County would have to 'retire' from the League, and face re-election: Wednesday were favourites to replace them. County full-back John Clements had a reputation for lacking charity: in fact he was 'famed for having a fair share of the British lion or bull dog in his composition'.

When Clements' knee caught Wednesday's Tottles Woolhouse in the stomach, alarm bells rang. Referee Jack Bentley summoned doctors, who rushed him to the infirmary, fearing a ruptured stomach. The judgment was that Tottles would have suffered a fatal injury 'had he, like Cropper, eaten heartily before the match'. The crowd knew their recent history, and Clements needed protection. At the finish, he dropped back, 'a friend threw a coat' over him as he 'beat an unobserved retreat and was rapidly traveling in a four-wheeler to the Wharncliffe Hotel'.

Ominously, it was reported that North End's stars, unlike Will Cropper, only 'swallowed a bowl of soup' before they tackled Dan Doyle in the second round on February 16th. If Grimsby could win, surely they would join the Apostles.

Doyle was 'prodigious', being 'particularly rough with his charges', and 'made no scruple about bringing them down time after time'. Once he stood over Jack Gordon, 'with uplifted foot, with an expression which said, "If you stir you'll get it".'

Chapter Eleven

Each Match Meant Something

In the Premier League of the 21st century, every place is measured by prize money. Yet it is other prizes that provide the real incentive – winning the Premiership, getting into Europe, staying in the League. Through most of its history there was little prize money for places, no Europe, fewer relegation places, yet still the League structure itself created incentive. In the first season there was no prize money, no Europe, and no relegation, but there was 'withdrawal'. It all mattered just as much.

As football fragmented in early 1889 – cups took centre-stage and ordinary fixtures predominated – and the League as a competition meant less and less, magically each match meant something. North End had won the League after less than four months, and the season had almost four months to run. What sustained it was that every place mattered, and therefore every match mattered.

First, who would finish second? Of the four contestants, it was 'any odds' on Villa losing three of five after their bad show at Burnley, whilst Wolves had five 'considered easy wins'. Later there was the battle for fifth place, for the top half (i.e. sixth place), to avoid the ignominy of last place and, above all, to keep out of 'the last four'. Any club finishing there had to 'withdraw' from the League, and pray for resurrection.

JANUARY 12TH 1899 – ASTON VILLA 6, BOLTON 2 – (1,500)

Bolton's run of nine wins and two draws in all fixtures ended to the 'woeful tune' of 'weeping and wailing'. Villa's goalkeeper Jimmy Warner stopped twenty Wanderers shots, whereas Harrison had 'little to do'. Wanderers 'shot their bolt': they 'played a dashing game until some adverse decision of the referee disorganized them, when they seemed to fall to pieces, so to speak, and were quite listless in their movements'. The second especially was 'no goal at all'. All due to the 'Villan'ous decisions' of 'Mr Smith' from 'Nowhere [official information]'. Other commentators took a more philosophical approach: 'it is a well-known axiom that the looker-on sees most of the game, and in a hard fought encounter, the referee may possibly have got a trifle "mixed".'

The referee, whose real name was Chaplin, objected to the too-free criticism of 'Free Critic', because Jack Bentley was also Wanderers' umpire. Chaplin thought Bentley – Ace Reporter/League President-in-waiting/revolutionary Association councillor – was rapidly evolving from

The Kid into The Great Dictator: he 'cannot properly look after his duties as umpire when he has to keep thinking of a long report which he must write afterwards'.

What was Wanderers loss? Their hopes of 'an inch higher in the League results had been dashed'. More poetically, 'we have ventured like little idle boys that swim on bladders ... in a sea of glory.' Now, the 'rude world derides' us. Above all, 'to be out of the League practically means, in football, to be out of the world.'

DERBY 3, WOLVERHAMPTON 0 – (2,000)

Three Midland clubs contested second place, but the crowds only supported the big games. Wolverhampton didn't appreciate its Wanderers, and crowds were poor even before their January depression, when their 'go-ahead-play gave place to selfish gallery play'. A Wolves win was a 'moral certainty', but it was cold, windy and driving sleet. Alex Higgins was back and Lewis Cooper scored after five minutes. 'More hats! More excitement! More wet!' Derby goalkeeper Marshall only handled three times whilst Wolves backs Baugh and Mason had 'boots going like machines'. 'Towards the end the pace slackened somewhat, the players being wet through.' County have 'never played a better game since they have been a club'. True.

BLACKBURN 2, PRESTON 2 – (12,000)

This was the big game. 'Football fever' at its height. In fifteen games since February 1884, in other words before Rovers' trio of English Cup wins, North End had won thirteen, with a 56-18 goal difference. Rovers' only victory was Fergy Suter's benefit in February 1887, which Preston didn't think counted.

After their lucky one-goal win a fortnight earlier, the new League champions had 'not the ghost of a chance'. Bets on them were going begging. Wind-up rumours abounded. Rovers would be stronger this time. Maybe a couple of Cambuslang men, following their Christmas win at Deepdale, and Wilson in goal. Since the knee injury threatening King Arthur's career, Rovers were keener on James Wilson, who would get the prize Scottish caps against England in 1889, 1890 and 1891. The top Scottish goalkeeper over a four-year period had accompanied Jack Forbes during his negotiations and knew how Rovers set up Forbes in business. Wilson knew how much he had to lose – future international caps. A year later Blackburn Rovers, third in the League and about to face formidable Sunderland in the Cup, were again desperate for a goalkeeper. They offered Wilson £4 10 shillings per week and when that was not enough, secretary Tom Mitchell sent a telegram: 'come to Blackburn on your own terms.'

Rovers never closed the Wilson deal: instead they spent £100 anticipating the 'expected crush': improving the old stands and erecting a new one along the north side with a 4,000 capacity: raising the prices ('only' four shillings for a stand seat), they 'looked upon the gate to recoup their outlay'. A hundred cartloads of ashes were also spread around the ground. There was 'no vacant space anywhere'. So Rovers went with what they had on the playing front – teenage McOwen in goal, and fustian Dicky Whittaker, 'foeman worthy of his steel:' pure amateur and less expensive than a Scotch amateur.

North End recalled the crisis that split football in 1888 when they refused to play the Lancashire Cup final in 'unEnglish' Blackburn. They gave Rovers 'the snub' by wearing 'coats of many colours': four wore orange and black stripes; two were in dark blue; two red-and-white quartered; two all-in-white and one chocolate and blue. 'Universal surprise.'

Rovers had 'hard lines' when 'Fecitt shot hard against the upright'. Fecitt. Nice passing provided Sam Thomson with the 'offsidest cussedest score ever'. Rovers 'swarmed around the Preston posts, putting Trainer through along with the ball'. Sharp passing delivered Dewhurst's second. Blackburn 'peppered away' and Fecitt equalised. Fecitt. Rovers played their best; North End near their worst: 'Ross and Gordon were wrangling … as to a tendency to selfishness'. Both teams had hard-luck stories. North End said Forbes 'hooked the ball out when it was undoubtedly a yard through', and Fecitt was ruled to cross the touchline (wrongly, according to reporters) before 'Whittaker sent the ball flying through.' Fecitt.

Blackburn still intimidated: 'Mr Sudell was threatened in a very brutal language when waiting for a corner kick.' League, Cup, ordinary fixture, benefit, North End were what big football was about: 'the howling of the spectators and the jeering of the swelldom … as much as the Northerners are disliked in the smoky valley, they are the boys to draw a crowd.'

NOTTS COUNTY 2, WEST BROMWICH 1 – (1,500)

Who expected 'despised' County to beat England's Albion? Albion could offer 'little or no apology', although they fell behind playing into blinding sleet and snow. Bassett's reply only encouraged Notts' ruthlessness. One back was cautioned for intimidating Bassett, and another, not content with 'fisting out', actually 'dodged several opponents with the ball in his arms'. County were getting a 'very bad name'.

Jim Bayliss, back at centre, had 'never executed a run of such brilliance and he scored as true and grand a goal as ever was scored. But Mr McIntyre did not – I am told, could not see it … Bayliss absolutely refused to play on unless the point was allowed'. Albion were only stopped from leaving the field by spectators crowding upon the corner near their dressing room. After ten minutes Albion resumed, 'under protest', but thereafter did not exert themselves.

The win, 'like an oasis in the desert,' kept Notts off the bottom.

BURNLEY 2, ACCRINGTON 2 – (7,000)

Brand and Barbour 'made themselves scarce' Friday night, and on Saturday evening belatedly telegraphed from Sunderland. They 'were got out of the way somewhat mysteriously' by 'sporting gentlemen' i.e. bookies. No longer Accrington heroes, but 'deserters' in the face of the Burnley enemy. It was 'a mysterious freak' that radically 'changed the odds'.

Burnley's 'usual team' made 'special preparations … nightly trots to the Griffin's Head and back'. Burnley's usual crowd roughed up referee Roscoe and their President Massey was hit by a missile trying to spirit him away.

EVERTON 2, STOKE 1 – (6,000)

Stoke arrived with ten: Lawton came on a later train. Anfield was without a blade of grass, 'due to the authorities allowing the spectators to walk across after the matches.' At last, with their two future England internationals, Edgar Chadwick and Alf Milward, Everton's forwards played together: none 'particularly good but collectively they make a strong attack'. Later, when oblivion beckoned, Everton valued this win like manna from heaven.

JANUARY 19TH – EVERTON 0, PRESTON 2 – (15,000)

The biggest League gate, Anfield's 'huge circus, with its two immense galleries, rising tier after tier, and its covered stands stretching the length of the ground'. North End were stuck at the railway station until 'a dozen able-bodied with shoulders to the wheel gave them a generous start and amid cheers the geegees slowly proceeded on their journey'.

Everton had recruited Scotland's Bob Kelso to provide 'sterling defence', and the Ross brothers played on opposite sides to avoid direct confrontation. So Jamie Ross 'waltzed around Dobson and sent the ball past Joliffe in silence': later John Goodall's 'magnificent' dribbling effort was received 'in almost dead silence'. Everton's forwards were 'streets behind'. Their 'cash bags' began to think, with these gates [£215], we need 'cracks not crocks'.

ASTON VILLA 2, WEST BROMWICH 0 – (10,000)

The Villa-Albion matches were scheduled for successive weeks, and needed to show 'Midland football is not dead'. It was Perry Barr's biggest crowd since the epic North End Cup-tie a year earlier. Albion welcomed back Cup final hero Harry Green after three months, but he looked 'thin and very bad': 'what ravages rheumatism had made with this once stalwart figure.'

Albion's forwards were ravaged by irony: 'a wonderful amount of gallery play and selfishness we are treated to every week.' Bassett was 'particularly madheaded, and Woodhall seldom got the ball'.

Denny Hodgetts' 'rest' (that is, suspension) has done him 'incalculable harm' although his 'close, fast shot' gave Villa second place.

ACCRINGTON 0, BLACKBURN 2 – (5,000)

Accrington v Blackburn was always about local bragging rights. Accrington had suffered from Rovers' original Scots pros and teased King Arthur with his new vulnerability: 'Eh, yun no luck neaw. Yun lost 'owd Mac and Suter, them us used to knock 'em eawt wi' ther hands.'

Accrington's umpire went to Sunderland and 'bagged his prey', Billee Barbour. But not Brand, that 'peculiar customer': instead they brought their old favourite Bob Macbeth from Grimsby for this game. To referee Norris's frustration, Blackburn's umpire, Jesse Birtwhistle, 'on many occasions' 'accidentally' blocked Reds' passes with Rovers' defenders absent. Accrington's Scotch back McLennan's own goal 'took the starch out of the redcoats'.

Rovers' Scottish international back was so superior to Accrington's English international winger that it was 'most amusing to see Forbes laugh at Lofthouse'. Everyone was saving himself for the English Cup-tie between these rivals on 'the glorious 2nd [February]'.

NOTTS COUNTY 3, WOLVERHAMPTON 0 – (3,000)

Reviving Notts 'quite overplayed' Wolves: 'May beat Rose with a curly one.' Billy Rose, the restored amateur and former North End goalkeeper, was freelancing after Warwick County had 'gone to the bad', and 'did wonders in goal'.

BURNLEY 1, DERBY 0 – (3,000)

Both wore black, 'mourning for Cropper': Burnley jerseys, Derby arm-bands. Another ex-Staveley man, goalkeeper Joe Marshall, played 'champion' in his penultimate League game: the ball hardly left County's half. Like a 21st century goalkeeper, Burnley's 'Cox was playing at the centre line' and, as the 'patience of the spectators was well-nigh exhausted', their 'prominent supporter' urged him to go further forward. At the end Dannie Friel went to 'dispose of the custodian' and the ball went in off him.

STOKE 2, BOLTON 2 – (3,500)

Stoke were without star goalkeeper Billy Rowley and full-back Tom 'Ugly Rushes' Clare, who 'for some reason preferred to watch the game rather than play'. Stoke had a history of player strikes.

The League was planning its future. The other league was failing to persuade its members to keep their fixtures: every failure 'gave another kick to a dead horse called "combination".' The Combination should 'shut up shop', or be absorbed, creating 'two classes of League clubs' with 'first and second class championships'. Moreover, despite the unsurprising objections of the poorly supported Wolves and Albion, each club would keep its home receipts, giving the away club only £12. And they, and not the Association, defined which players were eligible. The League's power was growing.

It now seemed most likely that the four retiring clubs would be replaced by Notts Rangers, Small Heath, Newton Heath, and either Bootle or Darwen. All enticed equally good gates.

JANUARY 26TH – DERBY 2, STOKE 1 – (2,500)

It was the start of that old cliché: a draw was no good to either. Only one could escape 'withdrawal' and Derby got the late, late winner. Lol Plackett recovered from a nasty kick, then 'went for that goal like mad' and got it on the whistle.

BOLTON 3, BLACKBURN 2 – (6,000)

'A fair old crowd rolled up in the rain.' Rovers had not won at Bolton for six years and their defeat had ramifications. The Wolves overtook Rovers, Wanderers were fast overtaking Burnley out of 'the last four', and Davy Weir was overtaking Hodgetts and Townley into the England team.

ACCRINGTON 1, NOTTS COUNTY 2 ('WRETCHED WEATHER ... ATTENDANCE VERY POOR ... FOOTSTAND ENTIRELY DESERTED')

Accrington were 'Up like a rocket, down like a stick'. One wise-acre said County would 'go home with a double figure squash on the chest:

"he's in the asylum now" – or he orter be anyway.' The reporter put down a 'solitary dollar' and it went down the grid. County defended with ten backs: 'Notts didn't mean to throw too much energy away against wind and rain, and they were about right.' Accrington's goalkeeper was under-employed: 'Johnny Horne had little to do beyond squatting on the boards behind the goal, occasionally hopping down and taking a frisky kick amongst the backs.' But eventually Harry Daft 'dodged in and out of the mud and opposition, and got through with an equalising shot, when he ought to have been bundled over'. McLennan's second successive 'given goal' gave County a 'rather flukey victory' (and a miraculous third successive win), ending Accrington's hopes of a high finish.

WOLVERHAMPTON 5, EVERTON 0 – (5,000)

The world was against Everton: only the 'very intelligently-managed League clubs' might provide salvation from the 'original, aggressive and, worst of all, invertebrate referees fast becoming a nuisance'.

Everton were already planning next year's world. After two months of disarray, they thought they had made a major coup, obtaining Bob Kelso, the ex-Renton half-back 'who now bosses [Newcastle] West End'. 'Kelso was generally expected to remain' with a deal in 'apple-pie order', £3 a week, even £3 50s. But after playing against North End he visited Preston and signed for them instead: 'Here's toe ye, Bob.'

There was another moral to all this, albeit a rather less cheery one: 'Everton cannot hold out superior attractions to good players of every other club, and has shaken the faith of the believers in the rumours about the accession of a formidable string of players from all parts of the country.'

More fundamentally Everton had also lost their devil: 'it has leaked out' that Jack Ross was going home to North End, signing for two years. It had all gone wrong. 'What originally promised to be a more or less brilliant football season for the Everton club appears likely to end up in more or less disastrous fashion.' 'Who's to blame?'

It was the politics of football: 'it is an open secret ... Everton committee and Ross have been in some sort of antagonism.' Had Jack Ross been signed to run the team, or be one among equals: 'as a captain he should be as unfettered on the field as Grace or Hornby in the cricket field.' But instead of trusting their battle-hardened captain, the Everton committee had picked the players, and decided their placement against his advice. 'Too many cooks have spoiled the Everton broth and Ross has done quite right in showing his independence and his contempt for the childish mismanagement.'

West Bromwich 3, Aston Villa 3 – (10,000)

At last West Bromwich stirred – their English Cup was about to start. Albion's season had taken a 'false step' along a stony lane, because of 'foreigners – Scotchmen to wit – who have never done them a ha'porth of good'. They repented, and Jack Hendry was scapegoated. Since return from suspension, Hendry had fallen 'lamentably short': he had gone backwards, from centre to half-back to full-back, and was discarded for the cup-ties.

What to do? Get England's amateur centre, or reset their current jewel? 'They don't require any Tinsley Lindleys to put them right. Bassett is a gem badly set at present, but there is no reason why a little brushing up and toning of the other gems, might not put all in apple-pie order again.'

The whole town turned up: 'upwards of 10,000 present of all sorts and conditions, from the Lord Mayor and some of the town councillors to collier lads and downwards.' The players revived acquaintanceship: fragile Harry Green asked 'Cruel' Tommy Green to go easy: 'Don't bump me.' 'All right,' says Tommy 'but keep out of the road'. And Harry did.

Bassett scored with a 'capital shot' and Albion went 3-0 up. The turning point came when Denny Hodgetts left Albion's goalie Roberts 'lying in a heap, the Villa captain drove the ball all along the ground under the bar.' Archie Hunter headed a second and Green equalised with a marvellous 'back kick'.

From the exceptional gate, £10 went to the Children's Boot Fund, a philanthropic loan of marked boots in exchange for old ones: 'pawnbrokers notified in case kind parents want a loan on them. Good for the kids!'

And then it was February and March

'Good old League – goodbye. You've done a good turn to football in the dead season – the season when Cup-ties are unknown. I hope to meet you again.'

February 4th – Blackburn 4, Burnley 2 – 'only a moderate company'

Locality versus League versus Cups. A Monday League fixture, allowing Rovers to play their full strength in the Lancashire Cup the following Saturday, had now been overtaken by their replay with Accrington in the English Cup (see below p.237). Blackburn's crowd suspected 'Burnley had been squared by the Reds to kill off half the Rovers'. 'Heavy charging was the order of the day … Rovers played like demons throughout … and Burnley "skittled" their opponents whenever they had a chance.'

'A doctor was fetched' for Burnley's Jack Yates, but he recovered with 'astonishing zest ... coming the old soldier, for Jack is well-known to be of playful disposition'.

FEBRUARY 9TH – EVERTON 1, WOLVERHAMPTON 2 – (6,000)

The inter-association match between Lancashire and Staffordshire deprived the fixture of its three Jacks – Ross, Holt and Brodie. The Wolves intimidated: if they 'used their weight so unnecessarily on a strange ground what would they do on their own?' Everton's umpire rushed up to inform referee McIntyre that it was one minute after time, but whilst he was consulting his watch Wolves scored the winner.

ASTON VILLA 0, PRESTON 2 – (12,000)

Confident North End took four hours to travel to Birmingham with 'light hearts': they 'chatted and smoked around the card table'. After Wolverhampton they 'donned their football dress', drove in an open bus in bitterly cold weather, then 'coolly and relentlessly robbed' Villa. Reporters were kicked out of their stand seats, as 'Jack the Rambler' remembered years later: 'all was disorder, and I still have a vivid recollection of writing voluminous telegraphic messages on the back of a good Samaritan, and supported in the back by a gentleman for whom I shall always entertain the greatest respect, for he had to be content with the progress of the game by proxy.'

Villa wanted to end North End's unbeaten record and to avenge their controversial Cup defeat in January 1888, especially as they might meet again in the 1889 Cup. They never had a sniff. North End gave a definitive performance: 'time after time [they] worked the ball through the Villa backs with a magnificent combination; they dodged and passed and ran superbly.' It ended with trouble: 'Drummond expostulated, and the spectators took umbrage ... they made a demonstration against the Preston men and various missiles were thrown at them, including ginger beer bottles; two of which smashed on the iron railings ... the crowd would storm the Preston dressing room, but they were fortunately overawed by the police.'

Even at the end, newspapers would not toe the line about the points system, and reported that North End won the League with twenty points out of a possible 22.

But North End were done with the League, and coveted the Cup. The king was dead: long live the king. Yet there were still a dozen League fixtures to dribble out between February 9th and April 20th, Easter Saturday. Twelve matches in ten weeks. 70 days. Yet each mattered.

FEBRUARY 23RD – EVERTON 0, WEST BROMWICH 1 – (8/9,000)

It mattered most to Everton. In mid-January, after it seemed the League had accepted their captain's negotiated draw with Rovers as Everton's win, they had gained twenty points from eighteen games. Derby County were bottom, only five points from fourteen matches. Everton felt secure, and hopeful that Jack Ross would build a champion team. Now it was all different. Ross was undermined by the League's decree that a replay with Rovers would be their last game. Everton had lost four successive matches and had eighteen points from 21. Derby had won five out of six and had fifteen points from twenty. They could catch up, and make Everton 'retire'. Everton could even be replaced by Bootle.

In their efforts to recruit a new side, Everton had antagonised almost all the clubs – 'offering prominent players fabulous prices' – who would vote on the composition of the 1889-90 League. They made Bill Townley an offer he couldn't refuse, an hour after he finally turned pro with Rovers. They paid Jack Gordon £60 to sign from North End, and were after Jamie Ross, Davie Russell and John Goodall. They wanted Albion's jewel Billy Bassett, Wolves' back Richard Baugh, Villa's Hodgetts, Jack Southworth of the Rovers. But what's the good of gaining a team, and losing the League?

Apart from the grief, the end to sharing gate receipts meant there was no incentive to keeping Everton in the League. They were out on a limb, having lost form and getting nervy. Were their men letting down 'King John' Houlding's investment? Did Evertonians spend too much time in the Sandon Hotel, or take their 'two gallon jar' to too many away games? The joke was, Everton 'might be Houlding on better if there was less Sand-on the way to the ground'.

The Albion match was 'To be or not to be'. Only Jack Ross, required to see out his season's contract and to play centre-forward, could save them, or was he to blame? 'Generous supporters' including secretary William Barclay, offered Ross 'something substantial' if Everton 'could only draw', and 'must have felt intensely disgusted at the "fat-headed" fanatics who jeered and taunted Ross'. Ross was in 'bad boots' – they 'hound him at every opportunity'. Committeemen hurled insults and supporters 'journey down to their victim's private residence and smash all the windows in his house. This is rag-tag and bobtail footballism with a vengeance.'

Ross could not evade the best centre-half seen at Anfield: Albion's Charlie Perry demonstrated his 'marvellously clever trick of coolly walking behind his man, wrapping his leg around their bodies and dispossess'. Perry then turned down Everton's offer of £4 a week. Ironically the match was lost by the other Scotch folk hero, Alec Dick, when the own goal 'bobbled past Smalley off his cranium'. Maybe if he had not worn his cap.

WOLVERHAMPTON 2, NOTTS COUNTY 1 – (2,000 'WHICH GRADUALLY INCREASED AS PLAY WENT ON')

After County's revival in January, they faded away with four successive defeats. They needed more dedication. Their Shelton brothers were classy enough: Alf played six times for England between 1889 and 1892, and Charles was capped, with Notts Rangers, in 1888. But '[Charles] Shelton could not leave his office stool in time' to get to Wolverhampton for the League fixture, so he turned out again for Notts Rangers. Even at the death, County's tough-guy Clements had his nose broken by a Wolves' elbow in the scrimmage preceding their winner.

MARCH 2ND – DERBY 1, BURNLEY 0 – (3,000)

Everton breathed a sigh of relief when Burnley lost: surely they were now safe. Derby, without a League game for five weeks, started 'sluggish' but soon 'County were applying all the pressure'. The win saw Derby off the bottom.

MARCH 5TH – NOTTS COUNTY 0, BOLTON 4 – (3,000)

Shrove Tuesday. Bolton remembered their last visit to Nottingham. After losing to Forest, Wanderers found 'a load of laughing imps in possession of our saloon' for the 5.55 return. So it was an evening in the Maypole Inn, until six survivors, including Jack Bentley, returned to the station for the 11.45pm. There was no way back to Bolton from cold and snowy Manchester at 2.15am, so into the White Lion. There, the 'landlady used all sorts of arguments to get us to shunt, but it was no use … at 4am the female Boniface obtained the services of a couple of policemen, and we were turned out in the cold, morning air, with snow two inches deep and unwarmed by human beings. It was too bad, for we had another hour to wait.' They got home to Bolton at 5.30am.

This time Jack Bentley meant business. No withdrawal. At first Bolton's goalkeeper Harrison 'proved again and again it was his day out', but eventually County were overwhelmed: in one seven-minute spell Tom Widdowson handled five times.

MARCH 9TH – BOLTON 7, NOTTS COUNTY 3 – (3/5,000)

'Brilliant sunshine, a cool refreshing breeze' and Wanderers finally escape the 'quicksands of uncertainty'. The clubs were surprised to be playing one another again so quickly. When their secretaries arranged fixtures for Shrove Tuesday and March 9th, County's 'Nun' Browne thought Shrove Tuesday was February 5th, Jack Bentley thought February 12th, and the League's secretary February 11th.

Nottingham columnist 'Julius Caesar' feared the Ides of March. His ideal of football had been assassinated, first by the Scotch imports, now by the League. The 'game' had become a show, something for spectators not actors. 'Even in Nottingham', players were being routinely offered from 50 shillings to £3: 'wages have gone up considerably since the League was promoted'.

DERBY 5, ASTON VILLA 2 – (3,000)

Villa were leading until Dennis Hodgetts left with an eye injury: he 'bled like a cow, his face being covered with blood in an instant'. Derby were now gathering momentum. Alex Higgins' finest match, his four goals swamped Villa (he scored 25 goals in only 42 games in 1888-90 for a struggling side, remaining 'one of the finest goalscorers of the Victorian era' [Gibbons, 2002]). County had 'increased confidence, and they may get still higher in the League ladder'.

MARCH 16TH – NOTTS COUNTY 3, DERBY 5 – (5,000)

Fixture problems. At last the League got tough with Notts. This was the match the clubs had postponed four months before, so Notts could play their strongest in the Cup's qualifying competition. Notts arranged a traditional fixture with Queen's Park for this Saturday, but the League insisted theirs took precedence. Queen's Park were annoyed – if they had known earlier they could have played the Corinthians.

The League match kicked off late because a Church Cup semi-final had booked the Castle Ground first. You knew the season was coming to an end when cricketers watched, including Australia's 'demon bowler' Fred Spofforth. A Melton Mowbray 'youth' became Notts' thirteenth League centre. George Bakewell, Derby's hero in their first League match, had a foot in most of their goals.

Derby were now full steam in pursuit of Everton to get out of 'the last four', whereas Notts feared the 'wooden spoon'.

MARCH 23RD – ACCRINGTON 2, BOLTON 3 – (3,000, 'TEN THOUSAND' IN ALL, MOST ON THE 'FREE STAND, KINDLY PROVIDED ON THE TOWN SIDE').

The Reds had sworn 'they would lose every match before they would condescend to bring Brand' back, and Barbour had recently 'vamoosed' again. But this match was important, for fifth place, so both prodigals were in 'scarlet'. Wanderers won it two minutes over-time, and Jack Bentley celebrated by 'wildly waving his Sunday white pocket handkerchief'. He had turned things around. After their traumatic 1887-88 and their inauspicious start to the League, Wanderers finished fifth, and overall won 32 of 53 fixtures.

EVERTON 3, BLACKBURN 1 – (7,000)

Everton's Cup final. Would they remain Apostles? Jack Ross went to the real Cup final, to support North End, his past and future love.

Everton feared a plot: there was a 'very ugly rumour in the air'. Everton's pursuit of as many as five Rovers created 'intense feelings of hostility' in Blackburn. Would Rovers beat Everton, then let Derby win and kick the Merseysiders out of the League?

King Arthur inadvertently put Everton ahead: his 'fist out' hit a prone Davey Waugh and bounced into the goal. Waugh was rewarded for this vital goal by being appointed trainer to the 1889-90 side. Rovers back Jim Southworth left the match early to catch a train back to his other work. His replacement for 1889-90, top Scot Tom Brandon, was soon 'living on the fat of the land'.

The Judas club continued to mock the Apostles. Rovers half-back Bill Almond had re-signed for 1889-90 after a fine season, but he was tempted by Everton's 'great inducements' to 'come over and help'.

APRIL 6TH – STOKE 1, DERBY 1 – (4,000)

A beautifully fine day. Cheap tickets by the North Staffordshire Railway Company persuaded many supporters to travel with their team on the 2pm. Their original match ended with County's last-gasp winner, and when Stoke equalised, Derby 'protested on the ground of over time, but the objection was disallowed'. Derby had turned their season around: only four wins in eighteen to January 1st, only four defeats in sixteen since.

MONDAY, APRIL 15TH – BLACKBURN 3, DERBY 0 – (4,000)

The one exception to the principle that each match meant something, displaying 'apathy ... so comically nonchalant'. Rovers could get no higher and Derby no lower. Well after the advertised start, County was seen 'ascending the hill on the tortoise-paced tram ... Indignation was too deep for words'. Derby's speed merchant George Bakewell responded 'Why, we are not late, are we?' 'A 'Mondayish' air pervaded the whole performance, very unlike a conflict when there is anything of serious importance at stake'. This was where the League came in ...

APRIL 20TH – ACCRINGTON 2, STOKE 0 – (2,000)

The last of the inaugural League fixtures for 1888-89. It had originally failed the fixity test, being called off in March with a foot of snow on the Cemetery Ground. Unfortunately the overnight telegram informing Stoke 'fell asleep during the night on the wires', so they made the journey anyway.

'Under ordinary circumstances' Accrington would have forfeited the fixture, but the League required it was played. Stoke got their own back: they 'wouldn't play for want of coming'. After losing to Bootle on Good Friday, they had a night out in Southport, and took some rounding up. Pat Gallocher (having moved from Burnley) and Bill Barbour scored the last of the League's 586 goals.

JUDGMENT DAY

'The League's Work Done. At last …' It began with Jack the Ripper's crimes, and ended on the day Adolf Hitler was born. It was a puzzle to the end. When its aggregated records were publicised, what a 'singular point' it was that the number of wins equalled the losses.

The League was an amazing success, and the paradigm for future football competition: within days five new Leagues were formed, and many more followed. But initially, it did not make much material difference. Third-placed Wolves made just £300 (losing £130) on their 22 League fixtures, less than one match made in itself (Rovers versus North End, £335) and less than Bootle and Everton each made from their 'ordinary' matches. Wolves changed grounds, to Molineux. Stoke had 8,000 fewer spectators than in 1887-88, and Burnley spent nearly 20 per cent less on wages for their 'lazy Scotchmen'.

The League increased its pressure on the Association to free up more Saturdays: by playing the Welsh and Irish internationals on the same day; and switching North v South to Monday. There was one stat everyone understood. The League's income had been £25 4s and it had lost £5. No problem: increase subscriptions to £5 per club.

The League's stats were a small part of the 1888-89 story. Most of each club's matches were ordinary fixtures. The pattern varied. North End and Albion mostly played away, whereas in Liverpool, Bootle played 37 of 51 games at home and Everton 41 of 61.

In later League tables Accrington are listed seventh with twenty points, both scoring and conceding 48 goals, beating Everton (also twenty points, and a 35-46 goal difference) into eighth place, one above 'the last four'. At the time Everton was seventh … because they won the toss. Each place mattered. Unlucky Accrington.

ONWARD TO 1889-90

Initially, betting for re-election to the League was against the retirees. Sheffield Wednesday and Newton Heath (later Manchester United) were evens, Darwen were 6 to 4 against, 2 to 1 was offered against Stoke, and Notts were the outsiders (3 to 1). There was just a hint of the potential for bribery: 'how much would some club give for a place in League No. 1?'

Newspapers got into the act, persuading four thousand people to vote for the League's last four. Sheffield Wednesday won this 'competition', with 942 votes, along with Bootle, Newton Heath and Burnley (Stoke only got 88). Wednesday strengthened their case by twice defeating Burnley in April. Bootle made a late run, beating Everton to prove – 'no question' – Liverpool's 'premier club'. They had beaten five League clubs, including Stoke (3-0) in a triumphant 13-0 Easter haul. Stoke was thought unwise – 'taking the bull by the horns' – making the fixture, especially as afterwards England goalkeeper Billy Rowley acknowledged Bootle's superiority: 'ah, we expected that from the champions.'

Stoke were complacent on strange grounds. Harry Lockett 'was the only hope they had' – it would be a 'grave injustice' for the League to ditch its secretary. Otherwise, there was no other local first-class club, certainly not sad Port Vale. The League now increased its missionary edge, reaching the parts other football could not.

Punters would have lost their money. Sunderland and Grimsby offered to subsidise the other Apostles, but Lockett knew there were no rules. The 1889-90 membership was not decided until the League's AGM on May 3rd at the Douglas Hotel, Manchester, where the 'four last clubs' pulled a stroke. When did they retire? North End and Rovers thought it was before the vote on next year's membership, but the retirees fancied voting for themselves. There was nothing in the League's meagre 'bye-laws' to prevent this, and of course they could also vote on the question itself, which they won 7-4. This 'unholy alliance' gained 'tremendous power': as each Apostle had four votes, they could practice mutual back scratching. Thus six clubs voted for the same membership *en masse*. Two clubs voted back only one retiree.

Bottom-club (in some tables) Stoke gained ten votes; Burnley nine; Derby eight and Notts County seven. Birmingham St George's received the most votes of the outsiders, five; Sheffield Wednesday four; Bootle and Sunderland two; and Newton Heath just one. Could this have been from Bolton's Jack Bentley, who enjoyed his visit on the Saturday before the League started, and later was chairman of Manchester United during their first golden age [Taw, 2004]. Four other would-be disciples received no votes at all.

Sunderland immediately led the rejected and other prominent clubs in forming a second League, soon called the Alliance. Grimsby's representative was schoolmaster Patmore, who had spent a night with a dying footballer three months before.

Stoke carried their complacency into 1889-90. Their Potteries public thought they needed three good forwards and 'a Committee who knew how to manage a football club': then voted off its most knowledgeable member. They continued to sign cheap Scots, including ones (Mudie and Coupar) who had not impressed (with Burnley and Bolton respectively) during 1888-89. Stoke had a terrible season, after which they were the first of the Apostles to lose League status.

Derby County prepared for 1889-90 by securing the Goodalls: John for £4 per week, Archie £3, plus The Plough, on London Street, 'a nice public house is to be taken for the brothers by some gentleman.' They would repay weekly an advance of £800.

Notts wanted to buy a 'ready-made team for next season', so wisely invested in shopkeepers. For centre-half they thought they had obtained Davie Russell, but when he stayed with North End, they secured Davey Calderhead after he won his Scottish cap this spring. Calderhead was once given £10 by Queen of the South Wanderers to set himself up as a coal agent, but the business failed. Similarly, at forward Notts initially boasted North End's Sam Thomson's signing, and when he did not join, County made the biggest coup of the summer. They signed centre Jimmy Oswald (scorer in Scotland's win over England, and Third Lanark's Scottish Cup win) at enormous cost: a tobacconist's shop with £500 of stock and two guaranteed seasons for £160 each.

It did not all go well. Mr Harrison, Notts' agent, caught 'redhanded' attempting to 'tamper' with Falkirk players, was 'rather severely mauled'.

North End seemed in danger of losing too many Invincibles, and William Sudell had to dig deep to persuade the likes of Russell, Thomson and Gordon not to leave. Getting replacements was becoming harder. Sudell offered young forward David Baird of Hearts £50 down and £2 a week in the reserves. Baird wanted more: an apprenticeship and 30 shillings a week for a chaperoning relative. Sudell sent him home: 'By Jove! You are a cool 'un. Thirty bob to your brother for doing nix, and £2 to you for playing funny, and all that cash down – well that lifts the League championship, and no mistake. Come, there's a train for Edinboro' at 12.30, better get off at once – you and I won't make a bargain.' Baird played for Scotland in 1890, 1891 and 1892.

Accrington, the League's Poor Boy, read the runes. Joe Hartley still felt that to find footballers a job and keep them at it was the way to avoid them becoming a 'sucked orange' after their football time. But the summer of 1889 saw a different way forward. Everton and Notts were giving men money as if 'Rothschild must surely be at the head of affairs, and might as well aspire to keeping a small racing stable as to run a team of professional football players ... Failure, certain, nothing less, will result'.

Everton, boasting a turnover of £4,328, signed Scotland's other Most Wanted Forward, Celtic's Willie Groves, fresh from scoring a hat-trick for his country. He then 'repented' the signing. Celtic lined up behind Groves, accusing Everton of 'slave trading'. Initially Everton stood their ground, saying Groves had 'already received wages', but eventually relented. It was said he turned down £200. Two years earlier, Groves was an apprentice boot finisher earning eight shillings a week.

In and out of court, Everton won two, lost two. They took Sunderland Albion to Liverpool County Court for £35, forcing them to pay up. When Jack Gordon welched on his deal, Everton threatened breach of contract but North End saw them off by demonstrating he signed for his £60 in Scotland, a separate jurisdiction. Bolton's threatened court case over Dan Doyle disappeared, perhaps because Everton paid compensation. Wanderers quickly gave John McNee £100 to leave Renton.

Similarly, when goalkeeper Ted Doig took Blackburn's £30 and returned to Arbroath, Rovers issued a criminal summons, so Doig, or Arbroath, paid back £26.

Nevertheless, Everton built a strong team, produced by such hit-and-miss methods as advertising in the Scotch press. Andrew Hannah was captain, reportedly on £6 a week. Hannah would have done so much for Albion's first League season, had he not been driven away the previous September. The Scots claimed he was 'about done' but Hannah was only 24, and three years later became Liverpool's first captain too. Hannah recruited teenage forward Alec Brady who in the last year had gone from Renton to Sunderland, onto Gainsborough Trinity, then Burnley and back to Sunderland. Scotland's winger Alex Latta initially refused Hannah: 'I was the mainstay of my mother', but eventually accepted £30 down, £3 a week plus a shipbuilding job. He sent a letter home every week.

But no big-name centre would join. Notts Rangers' Fred Geary said no, 'fearing the High Rip Gang,' but weakened when Everton's secretary 'fluttered a couple of fivers and said they would give me these for signing ... the £5 note was a great temptation. 'Flimsies' of that sort were not common among young players of that day'. Cut-price Geary became 'the Dixie Dean of his day' [Ross and Smailes, 1988, p.75]. With Latta, Brady and Geary, and Chadwick and Milward becoming the best left-wing in Liverpool, Lancashire, England, Britain, the world, Everton could challenge the best.

Jack Ross went back to the best. He became North End's decisive League Championship centre-forward – three hat-tricks in his first five matches. The 1889-90 League was tougher to win as the competitive pressures increased. North End beat Stoke 10-0 in their first fixture but lost their second at Villa. North End won the League from Everton by winning their last match. The Ross brothers scored 40 goals in a combined 40 games.

In 1890-91 Preston were second to Everton and in 1891-92 and 1892-93 to newcomers Sunderland. Jack Ross contracted tuberculosis and died in August 1894. In his penultimate match North End beat Reading 18-0 in the Cup. It recalled the 26-0 win in 1887, when the jokes against Hyde's goalkeeper developed the theme of the Victorian Age's favourite quasi-religious tract, *Pilgrim's Progress*. Jack Ross had led the pilgrim's life, from Scotland to Preston, to create a shrine of scientific football.

Chapter Twelve

'Shift the stand or a row of houses'

THE ENGLISH CUP: QUALIFYING ROUNDS

The 1888-89 Cup was a funny competition. Cups had always derived their power from simplicity. Two teams play, the winners go on, the last two standing contest a final. Simple. But the English Cup had been undone by detail: eligibilities, regulations, timescales, protests. And also class. North End should not have to beat the likes of Hyde 26-0. The class imagery was unmistakable: clubs 'entitled to rank in the first-class were saved the toil and inconvenience of knocking out a lot of inferior rivals'. So it was restructured.

The new structure yielded simplicity to the League. The League already had symmetry, twelve competing clubs playing home and away. It also had a pleasing way with time and vision. Moving pictures were an important Victorian motif. Chinese lanterns, kaleidoscope, photography, and a few years later, cinematography. So the League's 'weekly picture of kaleidoscopic change' seemed set to dim the Cup's 'lustre'.

The English Cup had turned into two ill-fitting competitions. Before Christmas ten divisions delivered, after four rounds, ten clubs for the final 32. Their 'real struggle' would start February 2nd and end on March 30th. Read carefully now. The ten divisional survivors would join the four semi-finalists from 1888 and eighteen others selected by the Association as of sufficient class. Only a Victorian committee could have devised it.

Some selections seemed overtly provocative to the League: Bootle, not Everton; Halliwell rather than Bolton Wanderers; even Burslem Port Vale over Stoke. Several were public school; others, like little Witton, had had plucky moments and powerful patrons. As well as the unselected League members, other big clubs fell during the qualifying competition.

Especially in the North East, where only one club could reach the last 32 from – Sunderland and Sunderland Albion; Newcastle West End, Newcastle East End and Middlesbrough – almost all comprised imported Scots. It was a series of battle royals, with a divisional decider between Sunderland and Sunderland Albion. 'There will be a lot of shouting, swearing, drinking, and betting over the result.' And the largest ever local attendance. Except that Sunderland scratched. All these clubs risked Association inquiry into eligibility, and therefore disqualification.

Instead, they played an ordinary fixture, with a large force of 'blue-coated custodians of the peace' present, and Sunderland beat previously unbeaten Sunderland Albion 2-0. The gate was an impressive £154. But win and gate did not help: '[Sunderland] ... the very word bears the stamp of cowardice! Beware. It is by such treatment that you lose the confidence of the public and the respect of the football community.'

FEBRUARY 2ND 1889 – FIRST ROUND

Weather was awful, sometimes too bad for extra time. Sunderland Albion lost 1-3 at another home of ex-pat Scots, Grimsby. Derby County at last won a Derby derby, against Junction Street – in a snowstorm. They also took the biggest chance of a protest – Scotch 'amateur' Alex Higgins scored, weeks after the Scottish Association had declared him professional. Burnley also took a chance after their original selection, shorn of its ineligibles, lost 2-11 in a practice with the rest of the club. Albion, the holders, played before a real Brummie crowd, 7,000, and beat Small Heath 1-0. Little Witton held Aston Villa into the second half, until Tom Green's 3-2 winner. League clubs Wolves, Notts and Burnley overwhelmed Old Carthusians (4-3), Old Brightonians (2-0) and Old Westminsterians (4-3). The public school old boys complained of a 'poor game on a filthy ground', all for 5s 7d. The only clash between Apostles was local, and real needle: Accrington versus Rovers. It was bitterly cold, a perfect hurricane blew and rain and sleet fell with great fury. One half was puddles – 1-1.

FEBRUARY 9TH – FIRST ROUND REPLAYS

The intense interest had shown that the Cup had survived 'to disabuse the public mind of the idea that cup competition was doomed, and the associations were discredited failures'. Even North End returned to the nest of the Lancashire Association after the previous spring's spat. The replays, headed by Blackburn's 5-0 defeat of Accrington, competed for pre-eminence with North End's last League game, against Villa.

The most eventful replay showed that the world of protests and feigned protests was not dead. Nottingham was lucky to have three in the Cup's last 32. One list of the 36 'chief Association clubs' saw Notts Rangers seventeenth with a 1.87 goal average, Forest 32nd with 0.93, and County last but one, 0.75. Nottingham needed someone to come through: 'everybody knows ... today is big.'

Against Linfield Athletics, Forest did not bother to import their occasional Scottish international playing members William McLeod and Tom Robertson. 'So sure were the Notts of winning the tie that they were offering 20 to 1 on themselves'. The Ulstermen had a rough passage across the Irish Sea, setting off Thursday morning, arriving Friday afternoon, at a cost of over £40. The reporters had a rough time writing: 'blinding snow in our eyes and the wet soaking the paper through' – 2-2.

Forest's committee spared no expense for the replay in Belfast, securing William McLeod to keep goal; arranging that, as the storms had already caused fatal collisions, the players should make the shortest crossing, from Stranraer at a cost of £2 a head, with 'rugs provided by the committee'. Forest spent £50 and lost 1-3 to Linfield, yet they went through.

Why had Linfield scratched? Was it because they could not afford travel to Chatham in the next round? No, it was because they were blackmailed. At the 'sumptuous tea' after the original match, an Athletic gave a Forester his card, which unfortunately bore a different name from that on the team sheet. Once in Belfast, Forest committeeman Sam Weller Widdowson unearthed the fact that this 'Johnson' had no qualification for Athletics. Widdowson wired goalkeeper McLeod and referee Gregson not to cross the Irish Sea. Linfield were advised to retire gracefully rather than be 'chucked out' but, just in case, Forest threatened not to play … with a 7,000 crowd outside.

Five minutes before kick-off, Linfield scratched. Forest refused to allow the crowd and the Athletics to be informed of the 'sham cup-tie'. Afterwards, having apparently won, Linfield 'were cheered and chaired over the ground', whilst 'anyone watching [Forest] coming up the steps of the pavilion would have guessed from the expressions of their countenance that their defeat was not troubling them to any great degree'. Forest had to return via Barrow, and to change trains seven or eight times before arriving back in Nottingham at 7.30 Sunday evening.

FEBRUARY 16TH – SECOND ROUND

Halliwell 2, St George's 3 was a colourful affair: Halliwell 'arrayed in all the gorgeousness of jerseys of a brilliant scarlet'; St George's wore 'white, trimmed with black, and trousers of black and amber. Quite a gay set out, thought the onlookers'. They soon looked 'ludicrous' in the mud, the Dragons 'terribly bedaubed with slutch and mire'.

Eight of the Apostles were through to the Cup's last sixteen, and several clashed. At last Albion showed Cup-holder form. Burnley's discipline as usual proved fragile: Bayliss's first goal was 'palpably offside … Burnley, much chagrined, hotly but uselessly, contested the point, demurring for some moments to continue'. They responded 'hot and rough' until four down, then subsided 'dispiritedly' – 5-1. Barely a thousand supported the Albion. Only twice that number saw Villa swap goals with

Derby County until 3-3, then they pulled away – 5-3. The three main Midland contenders were getting into their stride – sixteen goals.

One tie had League significance: Wednesday versus Notts County. Nottingham feared inferiority. Sheffield Wednesday had knocked out of the Cup both Nottingham Forest and Notts Rangers in the last year and seemed the strongest of the challengers for a League place in 1889-90. Notts County by contrast were the favourites to lose League status. Two thousand of a 7/8,000 crowd came from Nottingham and saw Tom Widdowson make a 'juvenile' error: he 'stepped out and struck at the ball. It came about knee-high and he missed it'. Wednesday won 3-2 whilst playing with only ten men. Nottingham had to admit Sheffield 'are a cut above us', and feared the worst. If Notts are not re-elected to the League, 'I tremble for the prospects of football in the town.'

When they were re-elected, County bought a 'ready-made team' and squashed Rangers: 'competition is the soul of trade, within certain limits.'

The amateurs caused the only frisson – London Swifts, with several Corinthians, refused to come to Blackburn: 'many of our men know your ground very well, and do not care to face after this week's sun.' Rovers replied that two Association councillors (probably including Jack Bentley) said the pitch was dry; and that the match was advertised all over the county. In vain. 'The Swifts ought to be made to pay.' They were. £16.

The other amateurs, Chatham (an unbeaten team of Royal Engineers) failed the hospitality test when they neither welcomed nor lunched with their opponents. In the first round South Shore had complained of the expense of coming at all without recompense. Chatham's ground was open. No admission charge, although they sent 'round the hat'. Forest (for whom Tinsley Lindley played, rather than for England) made enough for a crust by taking Chatham back to Nottingham. The referee wanted to play the replay to a finish after extra-time, but Chatham's 'boss' drove his men to their hotel. Chatham won the second replay at the Oval before a big, paying (at least a shilling each) crowd.

MARCH 2ND – THE QUARTER-FINALS

CHATHAM 1, WEST BROMWICH 10 – (17/20,000)

Chatham's win caused an 'earthquake down West Bromwich way when they discovered they had to go and play on an open ground today, and that when funds are low. Och!' So the Albion entertained their highest crowd ever. No one knew for sure, as 'unluckily there was no gate'. A demonstration of how popular football could be when you did not have to pay (Albion expected nothing from the 'poor box' collection). Chatham's defence was unfortunately named: full-back Conquer had been in bed since the quarter-final, and was well-and-truly conquered, and goalkeeper Soppitt needed an early 't' to his name. Chatham's humiliation reflected badly on Forest. The English Cup 1888-89 had done nothing for Nottingham's reputation.

PRESTON 3, BIRMINGHAM ST GEORGE'S 0 – (8,000)
WOLVERHAMPTON 3, SHEFFIELD WEDNESDAY 0 – (8,000)
BLACKBURN 8, ASTON VILLA 1 – (10,000)

Blackburn had achieved one of the most shocking victories in Cup history. Rovers against Villa seemed a clash of resilient Cup champions. It 'aroused untold interest', especially as Villa constantly threatened to protest that Jack Forbes was ineligible as a professional. Rovers had suffered a different humiliation the previous week. Quickly 3-0 up, a near-full-strength eleven went out of the Lancashire Cup to little Higher Walton 4-5.

King Arthur, back in Rovers' goal, was superfluous, whilst Villa's Jimmy Warner made four early saves, but three goals came within twenty minutes. Warner 'performed marvelously, saving shot after shot'. Rovers' Bob Haresnape and Jack Southworth scored seven between them.

That injury-hit Villa had a 'maimed and shattered team' was kept secret. One supporter took odds of 6 to 4 after the first goal, 2 to 1 after the second, and 3 to 1 after the third. Saner observers wrote the poems

You took them in front, you took them in the rear,
You treated the Brums like very small beer

Alternatively, Villa 'were as stale, flat and unprofitable as last season's cucumber steeped in flabby vinegar'.

THE SEMI-FINALISTS

The semi-finals vindicated the Cup's new system. Unlike the David and Goliath encounters of 1888, these were 'real struggles' between 'real champions' watched by massive crowds.

Lancashire again hoped for the ultimate final, North End against Rovers. It was on. Should Haresnape & Co play as well again 'not much doubt need exist in the minds of anyone' that Blackburn would win their semi-final. Any doubters were reassured that, 'by the way [Rovers] are taking care of themselves' – code for not drinking too much.

But their opponents were not intimidated. The formidable Wolves regained strength through their Cup run, which they entered to a sad tune: 'the pine tree waved its branches in mournful dirges.' After competing strongly for second place in the League before Christmas, in January they were forced to 'lick the dust', 0-3, against bottom clubs Derby and Notts County. The Cup's first round was the following week, against the Old Carthusians, with Major Marindin as referee. Rain and morning snow made the Dudley Road pitch very heavy and slippery, and the exposed 5,000 observers suffered a raging snowstorm towards half-time with the southern amateurs winning 2-0. Afterwards a Walters brother agreed that captain Jack Brodie's tactics won the game 4-3. He gave 'express instructions ... whenever Brodie shouted to any of his leading division to shoot, he and the rest of the forwards dashed in to rush the ball through'.

During the fortnight, 'very large quantities of ashes [were] banked up around field'. Snow and rain again. When Walsall Town Swifts (featuring Albion's Cup-winning Albert Aldridge) scored first, their forward star 'Shiner' Shaw became a marked man. Wolves' Baugh knocked him out of the first half for twenty minutes and then, short of the hour, out of the game – Shaw did not entirely regain consciousness until 9pm. After that Wolves scored five goals – 6-1. Swifts protested Wolves' roughness. A theme emerged.

Sheffield Wednesday, prime candidates to join the League, had grown in confidence since they beat North End before Christmas but were undone in the quarter-final by Wolves' 'peculiar ground', their 'short passing being utterly useless amongst the ridges'. Wolves passed from wing to wing, 'whilst the three inside men went in for knocking their opponents' defenders down'. Three late goals persuaded Wolverhampton's Reverend Jones to propose a new holy day: 'St. Paul was such an admirer of physical games that, he had no doubt, were he alive now, he would exercise his diligence to complete his week's work by midday in order to witness a football match' [Young, 1964, p.58].

The other semi was like old times. Everyone remembered North End's unexpected defeats by Albion in the 1887 semi and the 1888 final, which meant North End had never beaten Albion on neutral ground. The Throstles, not the Throstles of old, strengthened their defence with Bolton's 'amateur' back Bethel Robinson. In effect Robinson was playing the Cup for Albion, and the League for Wanderers (with whom, as a result, he was at 'daggers drawn'). 'Bethel has an eye to business ... Quite amateur, you know.'

Everyone expected North End to win the Cup: otherwise it would be a 'disgrace' to players, club and town. North End's progress to the semi had been nothing like the epic encounters of 1886-87 or the triumphal march of 1887-88. But, having dominated the League, the Cup provided the opportunity to extend their invincibility to the League's rival, the Combination, beating their best. Three solid performances against genuinely challenging opposition, and all outside the League.

Bootle were found at a disadvantage when their pitch was discovered to be short of minimum dimensions. It was a case of 'shift the stand or a row of houses'. Instead any Preston protest was bought off by a half-share of the stand receipts. North End won 3-0. Bootle's uncovered ground gave no comfort on a raw winter's day. Dr Mills-Roberts left home in Stroud at 5am and after the match examined North End half-back Sandy Robertson to find his collar-bone broken. Robertson came back, to be the unlucky twelfth man for the final.

North End's 'toilsome' six-hour journey in the second round began before dawn when they were collected by horse-drawn cabs from their homes. Grimsby had erected new stands, unfortunately little protection against a cold, bitter wind and flurries of snow. Grimsby had only lost twice all season, with a North End-type goal average – 90 for, only 29 against. Like all North End opponents, Town's 6/7,000 spectators 'constantly showered bitter taunts and cruel jeers upon Mr Sudell', and afterwards, non-gambling referee Charles Clegg was 'grossly blackguarded and wantonly accused of wagering on the result'. Grimsby's Scotch-dominated team was competitive, and scored – 'cheer after cheer rent the air' – but offside – 'sorrowful wail from the whole multitude'. Men like Lundie and Macbeth had famously beaten North End with other clubs. Grimsby's goalkeeper had a 'fist like a frying pan', and exceptionally, 'could pick up the football with one hand and throw it a tremendous distance' [Lincoln, 1912, p.327]. Lundie impressed as a man with a 'very unruly tongue and a churlish manner', and Dan Doyle, a month after causing Cropper's death, simply played 'heavy'. In response North End constructed a 'picture and poem of football motion' until they realised that if there was extra-time they would not get home before Monday morning. Goodall and Gordon scored 'very nice goals' in the last fifteen minutes. As it was, they returned at 2.15am, amid rumours of surviving a railway collision overnight.

Birmingham St George's provided Deepdale's first important English Cup-tie since Upton Park in 1884 (after which North End's disqualification ushered in open professionalism). A 'safe thing' maybe, but 8,000 watched St George's provide a tough quarter-final. John Devey, Villa's 1897 double-winning captain, later recalled his early match with the 'finest team in existence … no finer since'. St George's leader, Harry Mitchell, inspired the Dragons with the maxim 'the greater the struggle, the greater the hope for glory', then took away their fire: 'the trainer's chief idea was to make the men what he termed "tough", and he had any amount of fun out of it. When he got the men into the stables, ordinarily used for horses, he would turn the hose pipe on and fire away until they almost thought their last hour had come! Then, with the remark "I think that will do" he would cease, and you would scuttle away, wondering whether you would ever breathe properly again.' Again, it was anybody's game until the last ten minutes. St George's cold water preparation evaporated when North End proved 'pretty determined during a hot scrimmage' – 2-0.

They did not stop there. An international Saturday enabled North End to challenge the last top Combination side, Newton Heath. Whilst North End were missing six first-teamers (several playing for England against Wales) the Heathens refused to allow Doughty and Owen to play for Wales. It was the bigger game. The gate was £100 more. The ground was on one level so 12,000 Mancunians ('what magnets these Preston players are') inevitably encroached three or four yards over each goal-line. Seven or eight minutes from time the game was abandoned.

North End had not conceded a Cup goal but had only scored seven, and their forwards were criticised for their declining potency: '[North End's] combination is perfection itself, and their passing as accurate as the workings of a machine, but that sort of thing, though all very well in bringing the leather down, is of no use unless when they get it there they shoot with accuracy.' Critics fancied a lost *esprit de corps* in the League champions – their forwards were 'too slow, or too lazy, or too timid, or too uncombined, or too self-confident'.

MARCH 16TH AND 23RD – THE SEMI-FINALS

Rovers were in rare 'nick' and favourites to reach the final. Before 'thrashing' Villa they had beaten Accrington 5-0 in a Cup replay and warmed up by mauling old rivals Darwen 6-1. In Blackburn, odds of 3 to 1 on Rovers were accepted. Their season's record did not just include League matches: 41 games; 24 wins and nine losses. The Wolves took confidence that both their League meetings were drawn. They needed something to hold on to, as charismatic captain Jack Brodie was missing because of his father's death.

Wolverhampton's pessimism was conveyed by their local reporter when he chatted with Wolves' stand-in captain Charlie Mason, round and open-faced with a 'sprinkling of flaxen hair', in the waiting room of High Level Station.

'What do you think of the match, Mason?'

'Oh, I don't see why we shouldn't win. Anyhow, we're going to try.'

'You've got a hard fight before you.'

'Yes, we all see that, but we are going into the field with the intention of struggling to the finish, and fancy we can pull it off.'

'You have no cause to be dispirited?'

'Not in the least. The Rovers couldn't beat us in the league matches, and so we don't see why they should conquer now …'

The interview was possible because their train was late, so Rovers had been on the field fifteen minutes before the Wolves appeared at Crewe. Between twelve and fifteen thousand watched in-form Haresnape put Rovers ahead late in the first half, but Wolves were in the mood to 'strike terror'. Half-back Fletcher was particularly good at charging the new England cap Bill Townley. Rovers' general, Jack Forbes, chose not to charge David Wykes and his splendid shot equalised.

Like North End's epic ties with Renton in 1887 and Villa in 1888, an overwhelming crowd broke onto Bramall Lane for their semi with Albion. Once again, 'on the cards no cup tie.' The difference with the earlier incidents was that this was the Association's responsibility, and they had no one else to blame. Three groups of excursioners left Preston. The team itself took a roundabout route from 9.15am on the West Lancashire line; others travelled on the London/North-West; and the cheapest excursion cost 2s 9d on the Lancashire & Yorkshire. There were three more from West Bromwich (which arrived late anyway). But the crowd was a Sheffield one. And enormous. 22,688 paid, and many more got in free, at least 25,000. The sixpenny gate alone was £558. Famously the local response persuaded influential local football men like Charles Clegg to exploit Sheffield's potential, and so that summer formed a new rival to Wednesday, provocatively called Sheffield United.

On one side an immense covered stand, on the other 'the sloping embankment provided a rare vantage ground', despite being 40-50 deep, as did the roofs of adjoining houses and the stand (causing a spout and slates to fall). The beleaguered press table was quickly overrun, as the unanimous cry 'Hats off' rang out at kick-off.

The decisive moment followed a long argument yards from Albion's goal. Whose free-kick? On the field Albion's Bayliss, North End's Scots, two umpires and a referee debated. On the touchline Bill Paddock 'vociferously' claimed for Albion: standing behind, Major Sudell 'forcibly' told him to shut up. Next to both was North End trainer Concannon, who quietly informed Sudell that Paddock (who had scored for Albion against North End in the 1887 semi-final) was West Bromwich's trainer. Sudell in turn took Paddock aside, begged his pardon and placed a 'half-a-sovereign' in his hand with which to drink his health. Meanwhile, referee Clegg enforced the six-yard wall on the free-kick, which produced a 'rare melee' and Russell's only goal.

Earlier both captains protested when crowd incursions caused play to be suspended for twenty minutes but were ordered to resume. It was a day for municipal action. The mayor of Sheffield (who was the referee's father) acted special constable, 'seizing intruders by their coat collar and unceremoniously placed them on their own side of the touch-line.' And at Albion's post-match dinner, their mayor and town clerk announced a protest: 'as mayor of West Bromwich he felt it his duty to look after the sport of the town as well as other matters.'

The Association had learnt that delay was deadly for their reputation, enabling the press and all the parties to rehearse the pros and cons of the options. So they met Monday, and voted down Albion's protest (naturally North End forgot theirs) that the crowd hampered throw-ins and corners (and threatened to 'land him one' on Darkie Timmins). Albion punished the Association by publishing their evidence in a Press Manifesto: and punished North End by claiming, like Villa a year earlier, they never lost their Cup 'on the field'. North End punished Albion by refusing further home and away ordinary fixtures. The two semis had made over £1,000.

Nine Wolves had again repaired to the Yew Tree Hotel, Wall Heath for four days' training before their replay. A journalist left the city's 'smoke, dirt and close atmosphere' to visit the location, between Kinver Edge and the ruins of Dudley Castle. He heard the team's walks included one of sixteen miles, plus a bit of 'ratting' with a 'not very prepossessing terrier'. Observers saw them as 'ratting terriers' against Rovers, whilst Wolves thought 'we ran them off their legs'. True, Hunter and Harry Wood 'were a bit off their hinges' but Hunter suffered a split lip and two loose teeth even before the referee cautioned him. Wolves' international half-back Albert Fletcher had attracted particular notice as Rovers forwards were 'knocked about like shuttlecocks'. 'Which was him?' asked a lady spectator. 'Him wi' t' red face.' 'Oh him that knocked the others down.'

Rovers' triple-winning cup captain Jimmy Brown had reduced his odds for the replay. With 'fresh officials' (Marindin was refereeing) to keep Wolves' roughness in check, he had many takers, so many Blackburnians 'dropped' a lot of money in a reprise of that awful 1888 defeat by little Derby Junction Street.

Wolves' pack leader was coming back: 'if Brodie were to play, I should think it is a "dead snip".' Wolves' confidence was justified. When the local newspaper listed their semi-final team, the centre-forward was, simply,

'Captain J.B.' He was not quite himself, having lost two stone since his father's death three weeks before.

March 23rd was an 'exceedingly fine day' in Crewe: the turf was 'as level as a bowling green, as verdant as a well-kept lawn'. Another 12,000 crowd saw Wolves, in reddish-brown jerseys, defend the Cattle Market end. Herby Fecitt had a second-minute goal for Rovers disallowed and Wolves took the lead. It was to be an old story. Hunter, set up by Brodie, would not have scored 'had the Rovers not stopped to plead offside'. Captain Jack Southworth equalised, but afterwards Rovers 'scarcely got a look in'. They got disheartened, went behind when twenty-year-old Harry Wood headed in a corner, and were 'quite out of gear' as Captain JB scored a 'beauty amid cheers' – 3-1. Captain Jack said 'if' he and Almond had not been injured … 'It will not do, Jack'. Rovers were fairly beaten. Jimmy Brown was as 'blue as a harebell'. After Rovers had beaten famous Aston Villa 8-1 in the quarter-final, how could they lose the semi-final to unheralded Wolves? ''Tis wondrous strange.'

The Association made £500 from the three semi-final matches: the four clubs shared a 'rather big haul', another £500. Yet Wolves and Albion both posted seasonal financial losses: ''Tis wondrous strange.'

MARCH 30TH – THE FINAL

The road to the final was against type. North End, famous for its forward combination, had played steady, not conceding a goal and scoring but seven goals. Wolves, renowned for its all-England defence, had scored seventeen goals (and conceded six). Both had outlasted their opponents, and been stronger at the end – fifteen of Wolves' goals came in the second half: they had broken a 'quartette that take some knocking under'.

Their origins again presented a fundamental contrast. The only Wolf not born within six miles of Wanderers' Dudley Road ground was brought to Wolverhampton as a 'mere babby' of two. Just like Albion in 1888, the Wolves were the English.

Yet Wolves were not receiving their proper reward. Identity and success went hand in hand – their 'principal players have stuck together – which is the great point – and they are now an organisation of which any town might be proud.' And yet the acclaim accorded Preston's cosmopolitan team was absent: Wolverhampton's slowness in 'supporting its chief football club … [is] altogether unexplainable', especially as they 'bring much money into the town'. Its 472 pubs certainly benefited.

This contrast was harder to take because North End owned Wolves. In five seasons the Wanderers had lost all nine times. North End had an aggregate advantage of 36-6, and won both League games 4-0 and 5-2.

These encounters left some feeling. The Wolves had played tough in Wolverhampton, but were under-strength and North End rubbed it in at the end. It gave Wolves reason to believe. They were interviewed during training:

'Can you win?' 'We haven't much doubt about it.' 'You all look in splendid condition.' 'Yes, we were never so thoroughly well in our lives. Every one of us is in perfect health and spirit.'

'You have never beaten North End.'

'No, but we have never met them with our full strength ... There will be no lying down and laughing at us as some of the North End did when we fought them with half a team ... They have certainly the cleverer forwards, ... especially Jimmy Ross, being very tricky, but we are a match for them in defence.'

'They play a more scientific game than your's?'

'That, we admit, but to-morrow there'll be no time for them to play in the "don't-careish" manner in which they do very often ... if it's a hot day, we think we shall have a better chance, for our men are trained like thoroughbreds, while theirs carry too much flesh.'

'What has been your practice this week?'

'The ball we have not seen ...'

A sixteen-mile walk on Wednesday, a two-mile run Thursday, Friday sprinting. Both clubs said they were careful not to overwork: North End 'resolved to avoid all training' and just practised each day at Deepdale.

The statistics were reviewed. At the end of 1888 Wolves had won 21 of 34 matches, with a goal difference of 125-37 and a 3.37 goal average; in 1889 they had won twenty of 33, 95-55, an average 1.72. The League was leveling out top football. Except North End, that is. They had played 49 matches, winning 39, drawing and losing five, scoring 152, conceding 42.

North End travelled Friday. The team's express gave Preston's excursionists an hour's start and overtook them before Bletchley. By changing their plans North End missed a treat: a supporter, Mr Green, had provided 300 delicious oysters for their original train. They also missed a crash: 30-year-old James Barnes, the only passenger not destined for the Oval, was killed. Apart from his excursion ticket, all Mr Barnes possessed was a copy of *Tit-bits* and a penny insurance entitling his widow to £100, and his 'four or five' children to £200.

That evening North End watched 'Faust' at the Gaiety. There were some who thought William Sudell had made a pact with the devil in creating his Invincibles. North End brought their own devil, as Jack Ross moonlighted from Everton's last League fixture.

To match North End's devilry, on Friday evening Wolves were inspired by the magical entertainment of Professor Evansion, the 'Royal Conjuror.' Like Albion in 1888, Wolves travelled Saturday morning. Wouldn't it be better to stay overnight in London? 'Our trainer thinks not, then we shall have to sleep in strange beds.' They rose at 7 and took an open conveyance to McGregor's Café for breakfast. The crowds cheered them from Queen's Square to Low Level Station and the 8.40am: 'a sturdy bystander, in his work-a-day toggery, who just came down to see them off, an' if good wishes have owt to do wi' it yow'm bound to bring the cup wi' ye.' 'The bell rang for "Take your seats"... "Play up Wanderers." "Right ahead," said the guard. The whistle blew, and off went the team amidst deafening cheers.'

Londoners responded to the latest Lancashire/Midlands final: 'the densely packed stands ... the sea of faces from surrounding housetops.' 'Soldiers in uniform, as usual, formed a goodly proportion of the crowd.' Over 25,000: the biggest crowd in London's sporting history – 'even Derby Day pales' before this spectacle. The pitch was moved 40 yards nearer the pavilion for better views.

Wolves had early moments. Albert Fletcher sent Sam Thomson flying, 'spinning like a top', and Hunter's shot was 'a moment of breathless anxiety, a huge sigh of relief'. But North End would not be knocked aside like the Rovers. They were a little heavier than Wolves and, despite six years at the top, only averaged 26 years. Both sides shared a profile of stocky young men: only Wolves goalkeeper Jack Baynton was over 6ft and only John Graham was over 30. There were two twenty-year-olds and one teenager, David Wykes.

North End were 'like high-mettled racehorses' and their short passing over-matched Wolves' long passing. Ross hit the bar; Knight the post. Baynton took the blame for Wolves' defeat when the second goal slipped between his legs – 'a schoolboy could have saved'. But 'no one could have stopped' Fred Dewhurst's opener after fourteen minutes, which 'travels through the air with ... a baseball pitcher's curve ... just under the bar on the extreme left'. Pressurised Wolves conceded many free-kicks for hand-ball. In the second half Brodie and Fletcher inspired recovery, but near goal Wolves were very 'loblolly'. This time North End's shooting was brilliant and after 67 minutes splendid combination set up another Thomson goal – 3-0 was the biggest winning margin in Cup final history. The Lancastrians celebrated: 'men rushed about wildly ... they leapt about them. They seemed in danger of becoming a mob.'

The Wolves had 'done honour to Wolverhampton'. Jack Brodie said it was their 'proudest match' and he went on to play for England against

Scotland. On Monday evening Councillor Holling hosted a celebratory affair at Mrs Wood's New Inn. There the motto 'Nil Desperandum' was 'written with flourish in soap on the face of the large mirror above the fireplace', and players gave party-pieces: 'it was something about killing a pig that Mr Wykes gave us, and the poor pig appeared to be getting the worst of it.'

Wolverhampton's press paid tribute. For four, maybe six years North End's 'picked men of the country' had seen the Cup won by 'teams in every way inferior to themselves.' They 'can play as if part of one machine, subject to one motive force' yet also as driven individuals, secure that the result was safely 'solely placed in their keeping'.

Major Marindin handed out the gold medals (Geordie Drummond had snaffled the ball) and presented the Cup to Fred Dewhurst, acknowledging the trophy was 'very small … rather old … a great many pots are bigger and more handsome but …' Dewhurst handed 'the mother of all cups' to William Sudell as 'the father of the team'. Dewhurst particularly praised Sudell for keeping the team together: that is, paying some not to migrate to other clubs. Major Marindin had made some digs: noting the Wolves 'all hail from one town', and hailing North End as Champions of the League Combination. Sudell hit back: winning the League had been 'more creditable' than the Association's Cup, because North End not only won 'on the field', but 'it has occasionally been our lot to fight the battle over again in the Council'.

After their dinner in London's best, the team and its supporters 'spread themselves over the town'. After all the wins, the goals, and all his 1887 Prince of Wales-acclaimed celebrity, Jamie Ross thought this was it: 'I'm somebody the noo.'

North End's 19s train fare included a Monday seaside trip to Brighton, where 5,000 saw them beat Sussex and some Corinthians 5-1. Then they were 'holding high holiday'. At home on Tuesday, 7,000 squeezed into Preston's Hall after the team was escorted from the station by Preston Rifles and pulled in wagonettes by 'hero-worshippers' who detached the horses. Saturday, it all started again. Taking the Cup wherever they went, North End played twice a week during April and May, with only one game at home: twice to Scotland, the North East (they made £102 at Sunderland and £112 in Glasgow in three days), even Belfast, where 10,000 saw Jack Ross play his first game back with North End. Then another 10,000 against Everton, who stoned Ross afterwards. Sudell preached to the end, saying charging 6d and 9d was 'a wrong policy': North End never charge more than threepence and 'two boys can get in for one ticket'.

Jack Bentley got the plum, persuading them to defend their new status as Cup and League champions in Bolton. Pike's Lane displayed an honorific banner: 'Welcome to Mr Sudell and the Champions'. An amazing 16,000 paid £260 to see Wanderers win 5-1. Were North End playing games again? No, they had 'religiously obeyed' the Bacchanalian injunction of winners, 'pour out the Rhine wine.' They enjoyed too much the 'pleasures of the world'.

Wanderers promptly agreed another match on May 18th, risking their retributions of 1886 and 1887. That is what the League built upon. One match led to another.

If Sudell made a pact with the devil to outclass the other Apostles he suffered in the end. At 5.20pm on March 20th, 1895, he was lifted from the street 'quietly and unostentatiously' by Detective Inspector Gardner. His arrest, trial and sentence for fraud and embezzlement was 'quite a sensation'. Since 1886, William Sudell had been paid £500 a year for running John Goodair and Co, cotton spinners and manufacturers, a £60,000 business. In 1888 or 1889 he started cashing the firm's cheques into his account, eventually using them for North End's benefit: £5,000 between 1890/93. The local magistrates felt Sudell had not 'shown enough remorse'. Sentence: three years. Jack Bentley, President of the League, appealed for football's support for his family. When released in 1898, Sudell became a Rambler: he emigrated to South Africa as a football reporter. One of his last assignments, before he died in 1911, was to report a tour by England [Taw, 2004, pp.132-42]. At the heart of the team were League professionals from Lancashire. Apostles.

Bibliography

Bentley, JJ 'The Growth of Modern Football,' 1905, pp.11-14, in Leatherdale, C *The Book of Football: a Complete History and Record of the Association and Rugby Games, 1905-06*, Desert Island Books, Westcliff-on-Sea, Essex, 1997.

Blakemore, M 'The Lancashire and Yorkshire Railway', Ian Allen, London, 1984.

Cockbill, WW 'Annals of Stoke Football Club', 1905, pp.87-88, in Leatherdale, C *The Book of Football: a Complete History and Record of the Association and Rugby Games, 1905-06*, Desert Island Books, Westcliff-on-Sea, Essex, 1997.

Curtis, L Perry Jr *Jack the Ripper and the London Press*, Yale Press, London, 2001.

Football League, The *The Story of The Football League 1888-1938*, The Football League, Preston, 1938.

Gibbons, P *Association Football in Victorian England – A History of the Game from 1863 to 1900*, Upfront Publishing, UK, 2002.

Goldstein, W *Playing for Keeps: A History of Early Baseball*, Cornell Press, London, 1989.

Green, G *Soccer: the World Game: a Popular History*, Phoenix House, London, 1953.

Harding, J *For the Good of the Game: the Official History of the Professional Footballers' Association*, Robson Books, 1991.

Hunt, D *The History of Preston North End Football Club: the Power, the Politics and the People*, PNE Publications, Preston, 2000.

Jones, G Stedman *Outcast London: A Study of the Relationship between Classes in Victorian England*, Penguin, London, 1976.

Levine, P *A. G. Spalding and the Rise of Baseball: The Promise of American Sport*, Oxford University Press, Oxford, 1985.

Lincoln, B *Reminiscences of Sport in Grimsby*, Grimsby News Co, Grimsby, 1912.

McBrearty, R 'Andrew Watson – The World's First Black Football Internationalist,' in *Soccer History*, 2, Summer, 2002.

McGregor, W 'The Romance of Aston Villa,' 1905, pp.6-10, in Leatherdale, C *The Book of Football: a Complete History and Record of the Association and Rugby Games, 1905-06*, Desert Island Books, Westcliff-on-Sea, Essex, 1997.

McGregor, W 'Football Fiascos,' 1905, pp.37-40, in Leatherdale, C *The Book of Football: a Complete History and Record of the Association and Rugby Games, 1905-06*, Desert Island Books, Westcliff-on-Sea, Essex, 1997.

McGregor, W 'The £. s. d. of Football,' 1905, pp.60-62, in Leatherdale, C *The Book of Football: a Complete History and Record of the Association and Rugby Games, 1905-06*, Desert Island Books, Westcliff-on-Sea, Essex, 1997.

McGregor, W 'The League and the League System,' 1906, pp.170-74, in Leatherdale, C *The Book of Football: a Complete History and Record of the Association and Rugby Games, 1905-06*, Desert Island Books, Westcliff-on-Sea, Essex, 1997.

Nannestad, I 'The Survival of the Fittest: The rise and fall of Sunderland Albion', in *Soccer History*, 3, Autumn, 2002.

Ross, I and Smailes, G *Everton: a complete record, 1878-1988*, Breedon, Derby, 1988.

Schama, S *A History of Britain: the Fate of Empire 1776-2000*, BBC Worldwide, London, 2002.

Taw, T *Manchester United's Golden Age 1903-1914: The Life and Times of Dick Duckworth*, Desert Island Books, Westcliff-on-Sea, Essex, 2004

Vasili, P *The First Black Footballer: Arthur Wharton 1865-1930, An Absence of Memory*, Frank Cass, London, 1998.

Williams, G *The Code War*, Yore, Harefield, 1994.

Willmore, G *West Bromwich Albion: The First Hundred Years*, Readers Union, Newton Abbot, 1980.

Football Club Official Programmes
The Albion News and Official Programme; Villa News and Record.

Newspapers
Accrington Observer; Accrington Times; Athletic Journal, Manchester; Athletic News, Manchester; Athletic Star, Stoke; Blackburn Times; Blackpool Football Telegraph; Blackpool Times; Bolton Chronicle; Bolton Evening Guardian; Burnley Express; Burnley Gazette; The Cricket and Football Field, Bolton; Birmingham Daily Post, Birmingham Daily Mail; Cricketers' Herald, Athletic and Football Times; Derby Evening Telegraph; Derbyshire Times and Chesterfield Herald; Evening Express and Star, Wolverhampton; Evening Star Daily Times, Sheffield; The Free Press, West Bromwich; Glasgow Evening News; The Globe, London; Gorton, Openshaw and Bradford Reporter; Grimsby News; Illustrated London News; Illustrated Sporting and Dramatic News, London; Lancashire Lad and Athletic Gossip, Blackburn; Lancashire Daily Post; Lancashire Evening Post, Preston; Liverpool Athletic Times; Liverpool Daily Post; Liverpool Mercury; Liverpool Review; Manchester Guardian; Midland Evening News, Wolverhampton; Newcastle Daily Chronicle; Northern Daily Telegraph, Blackburn; Northern Magpie; Nottingham Daily Guardian; Nottingham Daily Telegraph; Nottingham Daily Express; Nottingham Daily Guardian; Nottingham Evening Post; Potteries Sporting News , Stoke; Preston Herald; St. James Gazette, London; Saturday Night, Birmingham; Scarborough Mercury; Scottish Athletic Journal; Scottish Referee, Glasgow; Scottish Sport, Glasgow; Scottish Umpire, Glasgow; Sheffield Daily Telegraph; Sport and Play, Birmingham; Sporting Mail, Birmingham; Sporting Buff, Birmingham; Sporting Chronicle; The Times; Ulster Cyclist and Football News, Belfast; The Umpire, Manchester; Weekly Sentinel, Stoke; Wolverhampton Chronicle.

Index & Glossary of Personalities Featured in the Text

Printed in Great Britain
by Amazon

59651044R00154